Women of Discovery

Women of Discovery

A CELEBRATION OF INTREPID WOMEN
WHO EXPLORED THE WORLD

MILBRY POLK & MARY TIEGREEN

CLARKSON POTTER/PUBLISHERS
NEW YORK

Published by Clarkson Potter/Publishers, New York, New York. Member of the Crown
Publishing Group.

Random House, Inc. New York, Toronto, London, Sydney, Auckland
www.randomhouse.com

CLARKSON N. POTTER, POTTER, and colophon are registered trademarks of
Random House, Inc.

Printed in Hong Kong

Design by Mary Tiegreen with Maggie Hinders and Jan Derevjanik

Library of Congress Cataloging-in-Publication Data
Polk, Milbry.
    Women of discovery : a celebration of intrepid women who explored the world
        p.   cm.
    1. Women—Biography.   2. Women explorers—Biography.
3. Women travelers—Biography.   4. Women adventurers—
Biography.   5. Women scientists—Biography.   6. Women artists—Biography.   I.
Tiegreen, Mary.   II. Title.
HQ1123.P65 2001

920.72—dc21   99-089063

ISBN 0-609-60480-5

10 9 8 7 6 5 4 3 2 1

First Edition

TITLE PAGE: ARRIVAL AT THE MONASTERIES OF WADI NATRUN, EGYPT, IN A FIERCE
SANDSTORM, 1980. PHOTOGRAPH BY MILBRY POLK.

OPPOSITE: WILLIAM R. POLK IN THE NAFUD DESERT DURING HIS 1971 1,200-MILE
CAMEL EXPEDITION FROM RIYADH, SAUDI ARABIA, TO AMMAN, JORDAN.

To William R. Polk
the best of guides on the greatest journey

"When you start on your journey to Ithaca
then pray that the road is long,
full of adventure, full of knowledge…"

—CAVAFY

...when you see, however distant, the goal of your wanderings...

Contents

Reflections in a Distant Mirror: The Stories of Early Voyagers

The few stories that have survived of early women voyagers tell of explorers who traveled as pilgrims, colonists, guides, captives, and disguised as men.

Forever New Horizons: Intrepid Explorers

These women were inspired by the blank spaces on the maps.

To Catch a Falling Star: In the Field with Scientific Explorers

Explorers who were driven by an insatiable thirst for scientific discovery.

Transcending Time and Place: The Visions of Artist Explorers

*Painters, photographers, filmmakers, and writers who evocatively
captured the essence of exploration.*

The Lure of the Unknown: Explorers on the Edge

These are the remarkable explorers who test the limits of endurance.

my Journey to Lhasa

West with the Night

I MARRIED ADVENTURE

GORILLAS IN THE MIST

Foreword

Christiane Amanpour
Kabul, Afghanistan

I SHALL NEVER FORGET the first explorer's book I ever read. It was Freya Stark's *Valley of the Assassins,* and it fired my young imagination, not least because it recounted a dangerous journey through the northern Persian mountains. Persia, of course, is modern-day Iran, and that is my homeland. I was fascinated to read about this woman who dressed up as a man to explore some of the most remote areas of the country I lived in. Later, additional reading about Freya Stark taught me much more about her: a woman of frail health, but towering inner strength, a woman of some emotional insecurity, but also of overpowering ambition. She contained many contradictions, but the constants in her life were her lust for discovery, her passion for wandering, and her courage in adversity.

Beryl Markham, the intrepid woman in a flying machine, was another favorite of mine, and I read her book, *West With the Night,* enraptured. I also remember reading about Jane Goodall's work with chimpanzees, and how she brought up her baby son with the primates. I remember lying in bed, wishing I could be transported to Goodall-land, where everything was surely perfect. The thought of a brave world waiting out there and of fearless women setting forth into it was enormously appealing, as were their own skillful descriptions of their adventures.

Much has changed since these great explorers opened up the world to me. There are virtually no more "blank spots on the map," as Freya Stark called them. But the work these women did and the stories they told continue to motivate me. I, too, feel that I am an adventurer; although as a journalist, I am exploring the human condition rather than physical space. I don't expect to discover someplace idyllic, but I may add something new to the store of human knowledge. When I report on an important event, I can serve as the eyes and ears for millions, and maybe, just maybe, what I show and tell may help to make the world a better place.

Like the explorer Alexandra David-Néel, many of us have "craved to go beyond the garden gate . . . and set out for the Unknown." History has lionized the world's great male explorers: Lawrence of Arabia, Dr. David Livingstone, Samuel Johnson, Richard Burton and Wilfred Thesiger are legends. But this wonderful book, *Women of Discovery,* shows us the other side of adventure. It introduces us to the great female explorers, whose take on the world is every bit as exhilarating as that of their male colleagues. These are women who in many cases had to overcome profound cultural, sexual, and economic prejudices to make their dreams come true, to pursue their visions. Many of them set off with little support from their families or communities, but all of them were motivated by a passion for life and the possibilities it holds. Surely the names on these pages will also become legends. They then can inspire new generations of young women—and men—to go beyond their own boundaries and set out for the Unknown.

CHRISTIANE AMANPOUR

Introduction

WAVE AFTER SCORCHING WAVE of haze boiled off the bleached dunes beyond the tent flaps. Almost in a trance from the heat and exhausted from my long ride on camelback, I gazed outward toward the thin line of the horizon. Then, shifting my eyes under the burnoose that had guarded my face from the wind and sun, I caught the astonished stare of the Bedouin men. To them, I was an apparition as bizarre and provocative as a woman in the shower of a football team. They were not impolite, but could not resist stealing glances when they thought me unaware. The effect on me was oddly disconcerting. Though my head was wrapped against the desert sun in a multilayered scarf and I was completely hidden by a long black dress, I felt naked under this furtive scrutiny.

ABOVE: MILBRY POLK WITH THE MAYOR OF QARA, A SMALL OASIS PERCHED ON A MASSIVE ROCK OUTCROP IN THE WESTERN DESERT OF EGYPT.

OPPOSITE: THE ALEXANDER THE GREAT EXPEDITION CROSSING THE QATTARA DEPRESSION IN WESTERN EGYPT, 1979.

Within shouting distance, another tent, set in the jagged shade of a few palms, held the Bedouin women. The young, the nubile, and the child-encumbered remained within. One ancient crone, her face etched with blue tattoos, silently approached "our" tent, clutching a pot. Seeing her, a young man jumped up and took her pot to serve us small glasses of hot sugared tea.

Watching the woman retreat across the sands, her long gown erasing her footsteps, I longed to follow her. In her tent, I knew I would find women gossiping about me. One might be weaving a colorful rug on a loom stretched from the tent pole and anchored around her waist. The others would be cooking or tending to small children. But I was stuck. Since I was engaged in the "manly" business of hiring a guide and buying camels to go deep into the desert, to these people I wasn't quite a woman.

As an anthropologist might say, in that group I was "structurally" a man, doing a man's work. Custom and circumstance narrowly defined my role. However, my position there was ambiguous: I was also not a man. Although I was surrounded by people, I felt utterly alone. The truth, my truth, was that I was at the beginning of what would be an arduous camel trek across the bleak Qattara Depression of Egypt. I was twenty-three years old.

My journey to the Qattara had begun years earlier, although I did not realize it at the time. My earliest dreams and strongest desires all had to do with travel and discovery. The more remote the journey, the more it appealed to me. Even as a

TOP: CROSSING THE QATTARA DEPRESSION, 1979.

ABOVE: SHADOWS ON THE SAND.

child I wanted to go beyond the impassable wastes, to the "back of beyond." I didn't know what I was looking for, but I knew it meant following in the footsteps of people like Sir Richard Francis Burton, the great nineteenth-century Orientalist, soldier, and explorer. Most people just paid lip service to adventure, but Burton had really lived it. I would later add to my personal pantheon other heroes of exploration such as Sir Henry Stanley, Dr. David Livingstone, Charles Doughty, Wilfred Thesiger, and Thor Heyerdahl.

But, I wondered, were all the explorers men? Was there some barrier or boundary that kept women from setting forth on voyages of discovery? My lone heroine was Amelia Earhart. I wanted to be like her and to follow my own destiny, whether it was riding a camel, sailing a boat, or piloting a plane. I was damned if I was going to sit the rest of my life on the wrong side of some invisible line.

What I didn't know then was that there were many other women who felt as I did. It took me years of reading and researching and talking to people to learn about women explorers and what they had done. Until I began to hunt for these women in books, in archives, in different corners of the globe, I didn't realize that women even had a history of exploration. Uncovering this history wasn't easy, since virtually all books about discovery focused exclusively on the feats of men. Women, apparently, weren't explorers. I now know that this is untrue—the world is out there for all of us to explore.

But before I could truly appreciate what other explorers had done, I had to serve my own apprenticeship in discovery. This is why I was in that desert tent. My goal was to follow the track of Alexander the Great from the oasis of Siwa, across the Qattara, to the monasteries of Wadi Natrun near the Nile.

Making this expedition happen took me two years, and that only brought me to the starting line. Ahead lay weeks of exhausting loading, unloading, riding, walk-

ing, searching for water, and avoiding *subqa* (salt bogs) and leftover minefields from Rommel's Afrikakorps and Montgomery's Eighth Army.

I paid my dues as I experienced the desert's searing sandstorms and the indescribable beauty of its clear night sky, the exquisite taste of a mouthful of water from an abandoned well, and the warmth of the fire in the cold evening air.

At the end of this trip the first lesson I drew was that exploration is not just a trip; it is a *process* that can—and I believe should—go on throughout one's life. The second lesson I learned is that a voyage of exploration and discovery can happen anywhere—in a desert or jungle, or in a library or laboratory—because, whatever the goal may be, the process is about discovering one's self. In my expedition, I confronted my fears, tested my strengths, plumbed my capacities, and expanded my dreams.

ABOVE: BEDOUIN GUIDES BELHAQ AND MESHAYT BY THE EVENING FIRE IN THE QATTARA DEPRESSION.

Exploration is a process from within and without. At least, this is what exploration has come to mean to me. What has it meant to others?

In school I first learned about explorers when studying a period of European history called the Age of Exploration. History books tell us that the great adventurers were those men—Columbus, da Gama, Magellan, Hudson, Cook—who sailed across the seas to find new worlds. Without in any way belittling their achievements or the great dangers they faced, I find it sad to think that they (and we) evaluated what they did in terms of the vast treasures of gold, spices, slaves, and rich land they seized from less powerful civilizations. Exploration has too often been synonymous with exploitation, theft, and rape.

That exploration was not the kind I wanted to engage in; nor was it the way I defined exploration.

For me, exploration is about the expansion of knowledge and experience. And this is why one can explore in a laboratory or a library. Of course it is more excit-

ing to put oneself into harm's way as I did in the desert and as many of the women about whom I am writing have done, but exploration is not necessarily an Indiana Jones–style adventure.

We all know about the explorers whose discoveries were dramatic: Columbus's landing in the Americas, Pizarro's conquest of the Incas, Speke and Burton's search for the source of the Nile, and Scott's race to the North Pole. But what do we know about the exploits of countless others, many of whom were women? Why aren't Mary Kingsley's travels up the Congo's tributaries with Fang cannibals, Lady Mary Wortley Montagu's "discovery" of the smallpox vaccine in eighteenth-century Turkey, Alexandra David-Néel's journey to Tibet to study Buddhism and become the first Western lama, or the South American mountaineering of Annie Smith Peck just as familiar to us? These women and numerous others made comprehensible a part of our world that we didn't know, understand, or appreciate until they revealed it to us. Thanks to their dedication, courage, and scholarship all of us can share in more of the world's wonders.

Why is so little known about women's exploration? Perhaps it is because women explored differently from men. Ignored by the institutions that often subsidized the travels of male explorers, women did not need to satisfy the interests of wealthy patrons. Thus, while men tended to travel in straight lines to find their destinations as quickly as possible, women had the luxury of meandering. Not being in the race for first place, they often noticed what others missed.

The story of women explorers is as old as time, as old as myth, and as real as memory. But, as in other areas of women's endeavors and contributions to human culture, it is a story obscured. Even when women of achievement and accomplishment were recognized and hailed during their lifetimes, they were often buried by later historians. Women explorers also had to use a variety of foils, such as publishing under the title "anonymous" or with a man's name. Most often, though, the records they left were simply forgotten or attributed to others.

The story of explorers, both men and women, is also one of class and race. Individuals who became explorers were most often those fortunate enough to have secured an education, to have acquired the means to finance their expeditions, and, eventually, to have published their findings. This has never been an easy task. And though I have endeavored to include non-European women explorers, their stories are especially hard to uncover. Over the past centuries the lives of many non-Europeans have been hidden by colonialism and oppression.

This book relates the stories of eighty-four women explorers. There are many more to be told—more than even the most well-informed travel buffs know about and far too many to include in this book. I have therefore selected a few whom I admire. This is just the beginning of a voyage of rediscovery.

It is my fervent hope that this book will encourage others to search for and celebrate the many women who were, are, and will be notable explorers. And that the stories here will inspire the reader to set forth on his or her own voyage of discovery.

MILBRY POLK
Palisades, New York
September 2001

LEFT: THE WOMEN'S TENT OF A BEDOUIN FAMILY
CAMPED NEAR SIDI KREIR, EGYPT, 1977.

Reflections in a Distant Mirror

The Stories of Early Voyagers

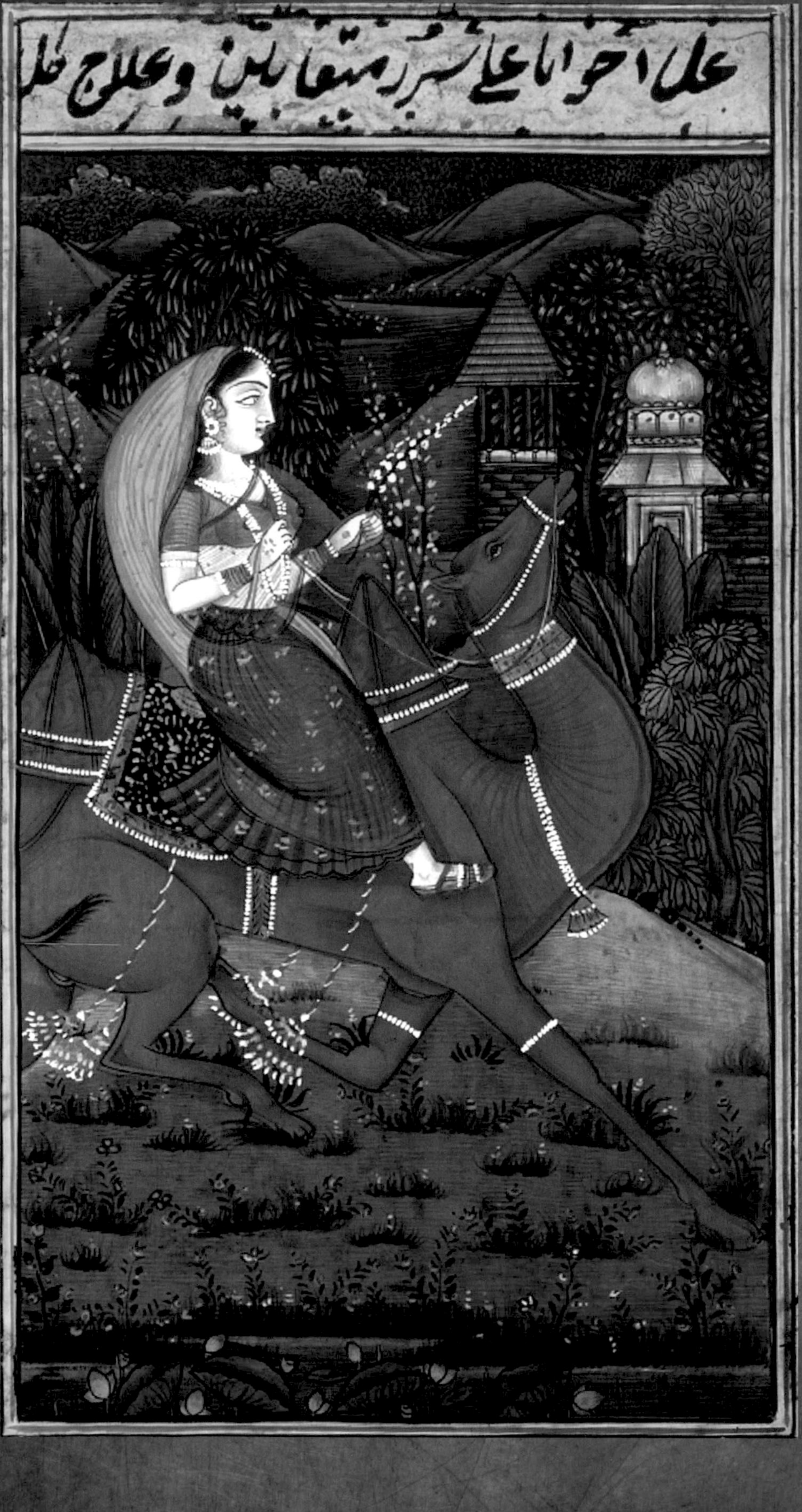

THROUGHOUT HISTORY, women yearned to travel and explore the world even though they were almost everywhere forbidden to wander far from their homes. To go beyond the narrow perimeters set by their culture was usually to become an outlaw, literally to be cast out by society to die. But in spite of these limitations some intrepid women persevered and found ways to explore their worlds. Some of these routes to the unknown were involuntary: women as well as men were cast by accident into places of danger and excitement, while others were carried off as the prize of raiders or were pressed into service as guides or translators. Some of these routes were voluntary, as when women ventured far on pilgrimage or voyaged as colonists. And, finally, there were the wilder spirits who, to escape the restraints imposed upon their sex, traveled incognito as men.

Most women who acted upon their wanderlust did so as pilgrims. Pilgrimage remains to this day one of the few accepted means for non-Western women to travel away from their culture, country, and even family. All the major world religions—Islam, Buddhism, Hinduism, Christianity, and Judaism—and many of the more localized religions incorporate pilgrimage into their tenets. While pilgrimage is considered a journey for the soul—those undertaking it are assumed to be seeking spiritual awakening, redemption, and salvation—it is by definition a physical act. Safely circumscribed by the spiritual goal, the pilgrim can widen his or her horizons. At least some medieval women were acutely aware of the multiple functions of

ABOVE: IN MANY CULTURES, CUSTOM DICTATED THAT WOMEN TRAVEL HIDDEN FROM VIEW AND VARIOUS MEANS OF TRANSPORT WERE DEVISED FOR THEM.

OPPOSITE: THE INDIAN MUSLIM LADY TRAVELED BY CAMEL ON HER PILGRIMAGE.

PRECEDING PAGES: EARLY VOYAGERS OFTEN TRAVELED GREAT DISTANCES ON FOOT THROUGH RUGGED TERRAIN. THIS ETCHING, "JERUSALEM FROM THE SOUTH," BY DAVID ROBERTS, DATED JULY 2, 1855, DEPICTS THE CHALLENGING LANDSCAPE THEY WOULD HAVE TO FACE.

Voyages of Faith

EARLY CHRISTIAN PILGRIMS

THE FOURTH-CENTURY BYZANTINE EMPRESS HELENA IN THE
HOLY LAND ESTABLISHING THE ROUTE CHRISTIAN PILGRIMS HAVE
FOLLOWED EVER SINCE. FROM VELDENER'S *THE LEGENDARY HISTORY
OF THE CROSS*.

I N T H E F I R S T millennium of the Christian era a
number of women ventured far beyond their homelands on pilgrimage. Although pilgrimage was thought of
as a spiritual quest rather than a worldly excursion, it was
expensive and required great organizational skills. To
avoid robbery, rape, or enslavement, all of which were
clear dangers on land and sea, pilgrims needed armed
escorts. No sure source of food existed in areas where
even the local population was barely able to feed itself;
clothing, equipment, and pack animals were similarly
unavailable in most areas; and since inns and other forms
of sanctuary were few and far between, each party had to
be a sort of mobile village. Traveling in large groups could
solve some of these problems, but doing so also created
the difficulty of outrunning whatever local resources
might be available.

We do know that wealthy and titled European ladies
traveled extensively in North Africa and the Holy Land,
founding religious centers wherever they stayed. That this
practice was far more common than the sparse remaining
records would indicate is revealed by comments made by

pilgrimage: spiritual uplift, intellectual illumination, and
social liberation.

While pilgrimage was historically the most acceptable
reason and form of travel for women, it was not the only
one. Some women had secular motives for their voyages,
such as trade, colonization, and exploration. These were
common, for example, among Viking women, although
because the sagas, the Viking version of history, were written
by men, their stories were rarely mentioned.

In fact, we know little about the motivations of the earlier women who traveled because there were so few records
left by or about them. While some must have simply acted on
the urge to travel, others undoubtedly sought to escape grim
lives at home. Since most ways of escape by land were either
blocked or led nowhere safe, some women went to sea, even
though superstitions were widely held that a woman aboard
ship could cause storms. For instance, in 1379 the ships of
the English captain Sir John Arundel were struck by a sudden
storm during a short voyage across the English Channel. On
board was a mixed lot of sixty women—prostitutes, married women, widows, young ladies of rank—who had just
been ransomed from pirates. In a panic, Arundel ordered all
the women thrown overboard. It did him no good: all
twenty-five ships in his fleet were wrecked, and Arundel lost
his life. Those who did brave the omens often included the
wives or mistresses of ships' officers. The frequency of
women on board ship is attested to by the phrase "son of a
gun," which originally referred to boys born at sea on a table
suspended between two guns.

Some women overcame the obstacles to female adventure by masquerading as men. Such a daring choice not only
freed a woman from the prejudice directed at her sex, but
had the added benefit of freeing her from cumbersome,
restrictive female clothing. The American Ann Johnson, for
example, served on the whaler *Christopher Mitchell* in 1848 as
"George Johnson," and Georgiana Leonard served as
"George Welden" on the whaler *America* in 1863. We know
about these two women because Johnson later wrote up her
account and Leonard was "unmasked" when she was stripped
to be flogged.

Some women even became pirates. One, a fifth-century Danish woman known to us only as Alfhild (who was said to have been born a princess), apparently led a whole crew of cross-dressing women pirates. According to legend, she later married a Danish king. Whether it was her verve or her loot that captivated him, we are not told. More documented was the Swedish woman known as Sigrid the Superb. She certainly was married to a king. But, apparently having been betrayed by him, she gathered a band of his dissatisfied subjects and, in a move many abandoned wives could only dream of, harried his kingdom.

If some women were adventurers by choice or revenge, others were driven by happenstance. Shipwreck was one obvious cause. Another was captivity. A few captives transcended their experience, even becoming prototype explorers by writing about their experiences or serving as a liaison between hostile groups.

Finally, there were the indigenous women who simply stood in harm's way. Some were pressed into service as guides and interpreters and thus played a crucial, but often little-known role enabling male explorers to make their famous discoveries and conquests. Native women have often been interpreters, guides, and bridges between cultures. Their actions had profound effects on their people and on the people they aided. Some, by our standards, played tragic or destructive roles similar to those of the men with whom they associated, but however we judge their participation, we can only marvel at their courage. Above and beyond their acts of physical courage, they faced the challenge of encountering an alien culture and attempting to not only understand it but make it comprehensible to their own people.

The few stories gathered here will have to suffice as examples for the many dozens more that are known to us and the untold thousands that have been forever lost to history. Yet we know now that even in the earliest days of explorations, women were there.

an irate Egyptian ascetic, Abba Arsenius, to a rich Roman matron who had invaded his privacy. He decried her and her kind, who threatened to "turn the sea into a thoroughfare with women coming to see me."

But come they did. In fact it was a woman, Byzantine Empress Helena (died c. 328) who set the standard for all later Christian pilgrims. Together with her son, the Emperor Constantine (d. 337), she voyaged numerous times to Palestine, visiting Bethlehem, Jerusalem, and Sinai, where she founded many churches, including the Church of the Holy Sepulcher.

And, regardless of what the grumpy Abba Arsenius may have thought, the Catholic Church declared many of these early travelers saints. One of the best known was the very wealthy highborn Roman matron and widow Paula (d. 404), who traveled extensively in the Middle East with her daughter Eustochium. While in Jerusalem they wrote a letter to a friend in Rome, a woman we know only as Marcella (published as Jerome's *Epistola XLVI/46*), in which they described their journey to North Africa in 385. Making their way along the Libyan and Egyptian coasts, they finally reached Jerusalem, where they spent the rest of their lives financially supporting and assisting the monk Jerome, who was then translating the Bible from Hebrew and Greek into Latin.

Some women returned to their former homes, but many were so captivated by the East or by their religious mission, or so wanted to avoid what awaited them should they return to the cold and dreary north, that they decided to stay abroad. One who settled down in Jerusalem was Bridget (c. 1303–1373), who upon the death of her husband in 1344 had set off to the Holy Land with her daughter. Ultimately she became Saint Bridget of Sweden.

Christians were not alone in setting forth on voyages of faith. Thousands of Muslims from the Middle East, central and south Asia, and Africa made the pilgrimage across deserts, mountains, and seas to Mecca. Like the Christians in Jerusalem, so many stayed that they founded little colonies in Mecca of Berbers, Tuareg, Sudanese, Turkomans, Chinese, Indians, and others.

To the Ends of the Earth

LADY WEN-CHI

CHINESE CAPTIVE/POET • C. A.D. 178

F EW OF THE STORIES OF INVOLUNTARY travel are more poignant than that of Lady Wen-chi. Kidnapped by Mongols from a life of luxury and privilege, she became a part of their society and lived a nomadic life for years as the captive bride of a Mongol chief.

Wen-chi was the high-born daughter of a scholar-statesman of the Han Dynasty. During this period, Mongol tribes ranged along the lands north of the Great Wall, attacking Chinese settlements. The Chinese sought to forestall these attacks by making marriage alliances with the nomads. Occasionally, when brides were not offered, Mongol warriors raided Chinese villages and took women by force. Thus it was that Lady Wen-chi was abducted around A.D. 190 at the age of twelve from her home in Honan. Her captors were southern Hsiung-nu or Huns, wild nomads of the steppes, who carried her off to Inner Mongolia. "I was taken on horseback to the ends of the earth," she wrote at the beginning of her journey. "Alas, a helpless woman carried away into the aliens' dust."

Upon her arrival, she was forced to wed one of the senior commanders of the tribe and adopt the life and customs of the nomads. She traveled with the Huns, lived in tents, searched for food, and suffered hardship and loneliness. Lady Wen-chi bore two children with the Mongolian chief. Of her family, she later wrote, "When I became pregnant with a barbarian child, I wanted to kill myself, yet once I bore it, I found the love of mother and child."

Fifteen years or so after her capture she was ransomed by Chinese officials and had to make a heartbreaking choice: return to the civilization she once knew in China or remain in the wilderness with her husband and children. She chose to return to her original home, but not without sadness: "Now I must abandon my children in order to return home. Across ten thousand miles of mountains and rivers, I shall arrive at our border stations. . . . I was grieved then by coming away, and now I hate returning. . . . Long before the end of the journey no more horse tracks can be seen. No other humans are in sight, only the yellow grass of the steppes. . . . I return home and see my kin."

Upon her eventual return to the Chinese court, she immortalized her journey in *Eighteen Songs of a Nomad Flute*, a series of poignant poems about her nomadic experience, so foreign to cultured life in Chinese society. Lady Wen-chi's story opened a window to life beyond the Great Wall, a life viewed as strange and frightening by her contemporaries.

LADY WEN-CHI'S POETRY REVEALS HER PAIN:

"EACH TIME AFTER I AWOKE MY
SORROW WAS DEEPER STILL.
NOW THAT I AM FACED WITH
WHAT I DREAMT,
GRIEF COMES AFTER JOY; MY
EMOTIONS BECOME UNBEARABLE

MY CHILDREN PULL AT MY CLOTHES,
ONE ON EITHER SIDE;
I CANNOT TAKE THEM WITH ME.
WITH TEAR-STAINED FACE I TURN
TOWARD THE SETTING SUN
I WAS GRIEVED THEN BY COMING AWAY,
AND NOW I HATE RETURNING;
I NO LONGER UNDERSTAND SUCH
EMOTIONS OF WORRY AND SORROW,
AND I FEEL ONLY A SHARP
KNIFE STABBING AT MY HEART.

I REALIZED WE WOULD BE SEPARATED
WITHOUT HOPE OF REUNION;
IN LIFE AND DEATH WE WOULD
FOREVER BE PARTED . . ."

A Journey to the Holy Land

EGERIA

SPANISH PILGRIM • FOURTH CENTURY A.D.

ONE OF THE EARLIEST AND MOST articulate eyewitness accounts of a pilgrimage was discovered by chance in an Italian monastery in 1884. While only a fragment of this remarkable document remains, enough survives to indicate that when intact it must have had a profound effect on those who read it. It is actually a series of letters, preserved as a diary, chronicling a three-year journey to Egypt, Byzantium, and the Holy Land. It was written by a woman from the "farthest shores of the ocean to the West," identified as Galicia, Spain. She was a pilgrim, probably a nun, named Egeria who undertook her journey toward the end of the fourth century. Her purpose was to see the lands of the Bible for herself, in order to tell her "sisters" what she saw and experienced.

Egeria's diary is unusual in that unlike most other travel accounts of her day, which were usually mere lists of place names, her record reveals more personality. She describes her surroundings and the people she encounters. Of her visit to Mount Sinai she writes, "Early on a Sunday morning, accompanied by that priest and the monks who lived there, we began climbing the mountains one by one. The mountains are climbed with very great difficulty, since you do not ascend them slowly going round and round, in a spiral path as we say, but you go straight up all the way as if scaling a wall."

From the fragments of her diary, scholars were able to determine that Egeria journeyed to Mount Sinai to retrace the route of Exodus, to Mount Nebo where Moses died, to Carneas to visit Job's tomb, and to Edessa to see the tomb of Saint Thomas the Apostle. She mentions previous journeys to Upper Egypt and Alexandria as well as to Syria and Constantinople. She includes an amusing tale of her search for Lot's wife, who had been turned into a pillar of salt. Sounding like tour leaders of our day, her guides assured her that the pillar had been there until just recently.

LEFT: MANY EARLY EXPLORERS WERE TANTALIZED BY MAPS SUCH AS THIS ONE OF PALESTINE, WHERE NEARLY ALL OF THE INTERIOR LAND MASS WAS UNKNOWN AND INSTEAD POPULATED BY FANCIFUL ANIMALS AND IMAGINARY GEOGRAPHICAL FEATURES.

RIGHT: A DEPICTION OF AN EARLY CHRISTIAN CROSS, FOURTH CENTURY A.D.

OPPOSITE: TRAVELERS IN PALESTINE.

We were also shown the place, and this place is even mentioned in Scripture, where the pillar of Lot's wife stood. Believe me, reverend ladies, the pillar itself is not visible now, although its location is shown; but the pillar is said to have been covered by the Dead Sea. Indeed we saw the place, but we did not see any pillar and on this matter I cannot deceive you. The bishop of that place, of Segor, that is, told us that for some years now the pillar has not been visible. The spot where the pillar stood, and which is now totally covered with water, is about six miles from Segor.

Along with details of the places she visits, Egeria includes interesting asides like this one describing how the tribesmen navigate in the desert.

There is no road at all only the sands of the desert all around. The Pharanites, who are accustomed to move about there with their camels, place markers for themselves here and there. It is by aiming for these markers that they travel by day. At night, however, the camels follow the markers. To be brief, from force of habit, the Pharanites move more skillfully and securely about this place at night than it is possible for other men to travel in places where there is an open road.

Descriptions of the desert are followed by her detailed discussion of the rituals of Lent and Easter in Jerusalem. Sadly Egeria's diary ends abruptly and nothing more is known of this traveled lady. By the time of such later pilgrims as Bridget of Sweden, one thousand years later, all memory of Egeria was lost.

IN HER DIARY, EGERIA WROTE: "ON THE NEXT DAY, CROSSING THE SEA, I ARRIVED AT CONSTANTINOPLE, GIVING THANKS TO CHRIST OUR GOD WHO DEIGNED TO GIVE ME SUCH GRACE, UNWORTHY AND UNDESERVING AS I AM, FOR HE HAD DEIGNED TO GIVE ME NOT ONLY THE WILL TO GO, BUT ALSO THE POWER OF WALKING THROUGH THE PLACES THAT I DESIRED, AND OF RETURNING AT LAST TO CONSTANTINOPLE."

Crossing the Bridge of Dreams

LADY SARASHINA

JAPANESE PILGRIM/POET • 1008–?

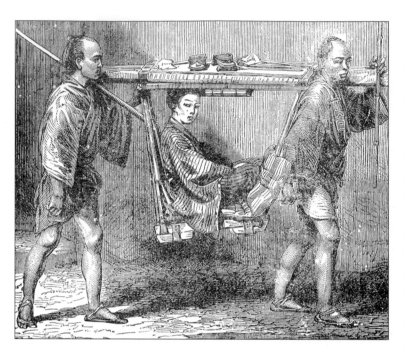

ABOVE AND OPPOSITE: LADIES OFTEN WENT ON PILGRIMAGES TO BUDDHIST AND SHINTO TEMPLES IN MEDIEVAL JAPAN.

T HE HEIAN PERIOD (C. A.D. 950–1050) of Japanese history is known today for the novels, poems, and diaries written by exceptionally talented, literate, and cultivated upper-class women. Among them, the best known today is Lady Murasaki's *The Tale of Genji* and Sei Shōnagon's *The Pillow-Book.* Also written in the Heian period was the diary of a woman whose real name is unknown. While the diary was private, a copy of the manuscript was deposited in the imperial archives a century later under the title *Sarashina nikki,* or the "day-record" of Sarashina, a mountainous region in central Japan. The writer is commonly referred to as Sarashina, and her diary is a personal record of journeys and pilgrimages she made throughout Japan.

What is known about the writer is that her father, husband, and son all served as provincial governors. To be a provincial governor was often a lucrative appointment but, because it necessitated long periods of time away from the court at Kyoto, such postings were unpopular among the highborn. That attitude is clear in the opening pages of *Sarashina nikki.* "I was brought up," Sarashina wrote, "in a part of the country so remote that it lies beyond the end of the Great East Road. What an uncouth creature I must have been in those days! Yet even shut away in the provinces I somehow came to hear that the world contained things known as Tales, and from that moment my greatest desire was to read them for myself."

In this single line, she reveals much about the Japan of her time: that life in the imperial court at Kyoto was most desirable; that even short distances were often long and arduous to travel, and that it was not unusual for women to be not only literate but also well read in the refined and complex literature of the times.

At the age of twelve, Sarashina begins her diary with a description of a journey to Kyoto from the province where her father had been posted. While the distance was not great, the trip took her party three months of marching, fording rivers, and, because there were no inns or hotels, camping. Of one camp she wrote, "That evening we stayed in Kuroto Beach, where the white dunes stretched out far in the distance. A bright moon hung over the dense pine groves, and the wind sighed forlornly in the branches." Traveling past Mount Fuji, she wrote that its "thick cover of unmelting snow gives the impression that the mountain is wearing a white jacket over a dress of deep violet."

Throughout her diary, Sarashina, like other Heian-period authors, blends poetic descriptions of the dramatic vistas of the Japanese countryside with indications of her romantic emotions and sentimental contemplation. In translation, of course, much of the power of her writing is lost. But like the nineteenth-century romantic writers of western Europe, it is her inner reaction to the stimulus of nature that concerns her; hardly ever does she even hint at the various political, familial, or social events that must have touched her life.

The theme of partings, whether due to loss and death, or distance, runs throughout her diary. "As I was whiling away my time in gloomy musings, it occurred to me that I might go on some pilgrimages. . . . 'How terrifying!' said Mother, who was a very old-fashioned woman. 'If we go to Hase [a pilgrimage site], we may be attacked by brigands on Nara Slope and what will become of us then? Ishiyama is also very dangerous because one has to cross a barrier mountain.

And Mount Kurama—oh, how that would scare me!'" But Sarashina went anyway. "We crossed Mount Ashigara at dawn. If even the bottom of the mountain could scare me, how much more terrifying it became as we made our way into the depths of the forest, going higher and higher until we were stepping on the very clouds!"

Returning from a pilgrimage to Izumi she was caught in a storm in the Bay of Otsu. "On our first night the rain came down violently, and the gale was fierce enough to dislodge the very rocks. The roar of the waves as they beat against the shore and the wild howling of the wind put me in such a state of terror that I thought my last day had come. The men pulled our boat into the dunes, and there we spent the night."

Except for her pilgrimages, Sarashina remained at home with her father until she went to the imperial court to serve as a lady-in-waiting. At what was then considered the advanced age of thirty-six, she finally married. After having three children, her marriage fell apart and she wrote, "Now that I was able to do exactly as I wished, I went on one distant pilgrimage after another. Some were delightful, some difficult, but I found great solace in them all, being confident that they would bring me future benefit."

Future benefit apart, Sarashina appears to have had sad and lonely later years. The diary ends with these words:

Wildly the sagebrush grows outside this house where no one comes to call, and my tears well up like the drops of dew upon the leaves.

*Even as I wander
    on my journey
It is always above
    me in the sky,
This moon at dawn,
This moon I gazed
    on in the capital.*

Adventure Has Its Costs

ELIZABETH VAN DER WOUDE

DUTCH VOYAGER • 1657–1694

We were well furnished with linen and woolen goods, pewter and copper wares, all manner of tools for husbandry, and carried one whole year's provision for all our people and for our beasts.

WHEN FIRST DISCOVERED in the sixteenth century, Guiana was thought to be the site of El Dorado, the fabled city of gold. For decades Holland, Portugal, and France struggled with one another for dominion over the South American colony, and in 1676 the Dutch government decided to make its claim concrete by planting a colony there. A campaign was mounted to recruit colonists and encourage investment in what was hoped would become a thriving settlement on the Oyapock River.

One of the colonists was a well-established citizen of the little town of Nieudorp. There, Harman van der Woude was the town bailiff and the official in charge of supervising the town's vital dikes. He determined to give up these positions and to embark with his whole family for the New World in search of riches. During the trip, his twenty-year-old daughter, Elizabeth, an educated and observant woman, kept a diary in which she recorded her experiences. The diary lay undiscovered for more than two hundred years, but it reads with the urgency of a contemporary experience.

"We started from Colhorn," she begins on December 5, 1676, "aboard two or three lighters, to gain our ship. Our strength was as follows: my father, I, my brother and my sister; with five maids, and forty-five serving men. Further, three horses, two cows, a few sheep, and a number of chickens and pigeons."

Sailing the Atlantic was, of course, a dangerous undertaking. There were no accurate charts, no means of determining longitude, no lighthouses; running aground on reefs or shoals was a constant threat. Ships were still hard to steer and their only means of propulsion was the capricious wind; they were apt to be struck by sudden storms or stalled by doldrums. With no means of refrigeration, food rotted. Without fresh vegetables and fruits, passengers were afflicted with scurvy, and cooped together in unsanitary conditions, they were assaulted by a variety of diseases. Beyond all these "normal" dangers lurked the ultimate terror of piracy.

Elizabeth's diary gives us evidence of all these threats. Ships in the convoy collided with one another; some were damaged by ice storms; they barely escaped French privateers as they rounded the Bay of Biscay. So dispirited were the sailors that the ships carrying the supplies and armed escorts turned back to Holland. This defection was a devastating blow but an understandable one, since off Madeira Island they had narrowly missed capture by pirates during a devastating storm.

On January 8, 1677, van der Woude recorded the death of her father. "This day, Friday, my dear Father Harman van der Woude, did go to rest in the Lord, after that he had been ill from 12 to 14 days; leaving me, my brother and sister in great tribulation, journeying to a strange land and bereft of our best friend." A month later, still out of sight of land, her sister also died.

A few days later, two months after leaving Holland, the convoy sighted land,

and soon after found a site where they would establish the colony. Elizabeth's relief is clear from her diary entry:

> *Certain Indians came to us in their canoes and gave tokens of friendship. We landed with the Indians, and these to show us a very proper place for our settlement; this being . . . a natural stronghold. It was a cliff at the bend of the river, and good clay on the top, though very many young trees did grow there. . . . We set up tents for our people and for our goods so as not to remain in the open, for it was the season of rain; then did decide which trees to cut down and which to burn, and then we to bring the beasts and our chattels ashore and to set to work to build our houses. The land was covered with trees and thick brushwood, and a rich clay soil, somewhat marshy in places. There were many ants, which covered whole tracts of land with their nests and did much damage. . . . There was an abundance of wild beast such as deer, pigs, tigers, leopards, baboons, apes, sloths, saguwyne [monkey], crocodiles, sea cows and tortoises; also many feathered creatures, wild fowl, turkeys, peacocks, parrots, red falcons, Indian ravens, cockatoos, and many other birds and beasts beyond number. Much fruit grew there too, like bananias, pisang, pineapples, acasjou, apples, cocoanuts, sugar cane, cassava, potatoes, fennel and all manner of fruit unknown to me. There were also flying dragons [flying lizards], serpents, ant eaters, scorpions and other reptiles. . . . In the middle of the river were a number of islands covered with trees growing right in the water. We saw oysters hanging in their branches at low water.*

Despite the exotic appeal of her surroundings, van der Woude quickly became disenchanted. In addition to the loneliness she felt after the death of her father and sister, constant rain kept her almost as cooped up as she had been by storms at sea. All around her, people were falling sick from unknown but insidious tropical diseases. As her despair increased, she petitioned to leave on the returning ship. When she was refused permission, she went aboard anyway.

The return voyage was every bit as uncomfortable as the voyage out, but was made even more traumatic when the Dutch ship was captured by French pirates. As Elizabeth wrote in her diary on June 1:

> *About two o'clock in the morning we saw three ships bearing down on us. Seeing no chance of escape, we made everything ready for battle. The crew swore to stand by each other to the death. All then fell to prayer and did sing a penitential psalm, and so awaited the enemy. Our captain, who was afeared of the enemy,*

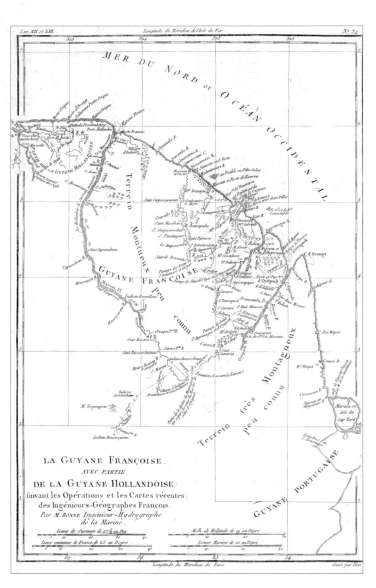

ABOVE: EIGHTEENTH-CENTURY MAP OF FRENCH AND DUTCH GUIANA BY M. BONNE.

There was an abundance of wild beast such as deer, pigs, tigers, leopards, baboons, apes, sloths, saguwyne [monkey], crocodiles, sea cows and tortoises; also many feathered creatures, wild fowl, turkeys, peacocks, parrots, red falcons, Indian ravens, cockatoos, and many other birds and beasts beyond number.

jumped into a boat with 6 men, thinking to leave the ship and escape the fighting; for we had but 20 fighting men and there came three privateers against us that had had at least 100 men aboard. Captain Jean Bart who did command the greatest privateersman, seeing that our captain was taking flight, set a straight course for the boat, meaning to drive it under his keel. Our hero, marking this, turned back in all haste. . . . The French did shout, "Attack! Attack!" and fell upon our ship with hangers in hand, and pistols and hatchets in their belts; but seeing the flag lowered they did no harm to anybody.

The French commander of the pirates, known as "Black Bart," decided to keep van der Woude alive. For this she might have been grateful, although for three weeks, she was his prisoner while he rampaged up the western coast of Europe. Finally, when he reached Norway, he put her on a regular merchant ship bound for Holland. Her great adventure was nearly over, but its full sadness comes clear in her diary entry for June 23: "I did return alone to Nieudorp, from where I had started last December with father, sister, brother, and so many servants and possessions. All can imagine how full my heart was." Soon she would hear that the French had overrun the Dutch colony in Guiana. Her brother managed to escape with his life but everything they had was lost.

The detailed account Elizabeth kept in her diary reveals the dangers colonists faced when traveling to little-known lands. It paints a picture of a young woman of courage and resilience who faced loss and tragedy, eventually returning to a quiet life in the Netherlands.

Sagas of Courage

VIKING VOYAGERS

ABOVE: EIGHTEENTH-CENTURY DUTCH ENGRAVING DEPICTING SEA MONSTERS AND ICE FLOES OF THE LAND OF FIRE AND ICE, OR ICELAND.

FOR CENTURIES THE the word *Viking* conjured fearsome images of dragon-crested ships sailing from rough northern homelands bearing warriors bent on looting monasteries and towns along the coasts of Europe. In their heyday, between A.D. 800 and 1100, they were supreme explorers. To expand their trading empire they established colonies throughout a vast area stretching from the Volga in Russia, to Constantinople in the East and the New World in the West. Viking women often traveled alongside their men. On occasion they even led their own expeditions. The stories of the first Viking colonists to set sail in their small boats for the New World were recounted from generation to generation until they were finally written down. In these sagas, two women stand out as bold adventurers, as daring as any of their menfolk.

TO THE NEW WORLD
Freydis Eiríksdottir
Norse/Icelandic Explorer • a.d. 1000

AMONG THE HEROES of Norse sagas, Erik the Red occupies a towering position. Less known was his redoubtable daughter, Freydis Eiríksdottir, who performed feats of valor, daring, and ferocity matching his own. Her legendary exploits in open boats are partially described in two twelfth-century sagas, the *Groenlendinga* and *Eiríks saga*. In them, she is credited with commanding an expedition across the vast, ice-covered seas to Greenland and on to "Vinland," which was probably a part of North America. This was, of course, centuries before Columbus "discovered" the New World, and it stands out as one of the most remarkable feats of exploration of all time. Freydis probably would have regarded that feat as being of lesser importance than two others. In the first, when she was in need of a better boat, she is credited with the treacherous and bloody massacre of her brothers and their followers. In the second, she is portrayed as saving her people by leading a counterattack on the *skraelingar*, or native peoples. In these actions, she established a claim to the role that really mattered to her people: being a warrior.

ACROSS THE ICY SEAS
Unn the Deep Minded
Norse/Icelandic Colonist • a.d. 900

THE COLONIZATION of Iceland was one of the great Viking adventures, and the stories of the people who braved the Arctic waters in this journey were told and retold around campfires while warriors feasted on roasted wild boar and drank their mead. Like most Norse tales, the thirteenth-century *Laxdaela saga* recounts Icelandic history through the actions of heroes and heroines.

The story begins with Unn the Deep Minded, the daughter of a Viking chieftain, Ketill Flatnose, and the grandmother of Thorstein the Red, who then ruled over part of Scotland. The Vikings were engaged in constant warfare; Thorstein's hold over his Scottish territories did not last long—he was involved in a feud in which he was murdered—and his wise grandmother, Unn, realized that there was no safety in Scotland for her or her family. She had to flee—and quickly. She secretly had a boat made to carry her children, grandchildren, servants, and followers across the northern ocean to a safe haven in the Faeroe Islands. But finding no refuge there, the small party sailed on to distant Iceland.

Largely uninhabited, Iceland was a world away from even the rough-hewn civilization of the Vikings. Before landing, Unn's party sailed around the coast to explore the territory and establish a claim. Sailing up a fjord, Unn found what appeared to be a suitable place to settle. A short time later, she died, and in a legendary Viking ceremony, she was placed in a ship that was then buried under a mound. Unn thus became the matriarch of the first colony in Iceland and a heroine of the *Laxdaela saga*.

Between Two Worlds

MALINCHE/MALINTZIN/DOÑA MARINA

MEXICAN GUIDE • C. 1508–C. 1528

LAGUNE DE MEXICO lors du Siège par F. CORTÉS. d'après l'édition mexicain DE CLAVIJERO

WHEN THE SPANISH conquistador Hernán Cortés landed on the coast of Tabasco, Mexico, in March 1519, the terrified local people sought to placate him, and send him on his way, with marvelous gifts. One of those gifts was a beautiful slave woman, whose original name was Malintzin. Cortés latinized the name and ennobled her to Doña Marina, but the Aztec Indians knew her as Malinche.

Malinche served Cortés, first as his mistress and then as his interpreter, negotiator, and diplomat. He desperately needed her help: the odds he faced seemed so impossible that he was forced to burn his ships in order to prevent the mutiny of his soldiers. Thanks in part to Malinche's advice and shrewd diplomacy, Cortés managed to win over more than two hundred thousand Indian allies in his assault on the mighty Aztec empire. Malinche stayed with him loyally for ten years, bearing him a son and sharing his trials and triumphs.

Malinche, like the better-known Pocahontas, has another story that, at this distance, is hard to untangle from myth. What we know is that she was born into a noble family in the Nahua Indian society of central Mexico. For unknown reasons, perhaps to cement diplomatic ties, she was given to the Chontal Maya in Yucatán. Then along with some twenty other women, she was given to Cortés. It is clear she was from a noble family because she knew how to speak to the Aztec chief Moteuccoma (Montezuma) in the "lordly speech" of the high court, a language not spoken by common people.

Malinche was to demonstrate remarkable linguistic abilities. With dozens of separate cultures, Mexico was divided not only by its languages but even further

by the numerous dialects of these major languages. Malinche was able to understand and translate these and could even translate the speech of ambassadors from places as far off as Honduras. Within a short time of meeting the conquistadores, she was also speaking fluent Spanish.

These very skills account for a large part of the hatred many Indians would later feel toward her. During her lifetime, she was seen by her own people as a feared communicator with Cortés while the Spaniards viewed her as a shrewd diplomat and interpreter, virtually a conquistadora. But among those who fought Spain for Mexican independence in 1821, Malinche came to be seen as a traitor and sexual slave. Today we can see her as a gifted woman living in difficult circumstances, surviving as best she could. Alas for her, she did not survive long and apparently died at the age of twenty.

ABOVE: THIS PAGE FROM A MID-SIXTEENTH-CENTURY MANUSCRIPT ILLUSTRATES MALINCHE ACTING AS INTERPRETER FOR HERNÁN CORTÉS IN THE PALACE OF TLAXCALAN LORD XICOTENCATL. OPPOSITE: AN EARLY MAP OF THE LAGUNE OF MEXICO DURING THE SIEGE OF CORTÉS.

The Air of a Soldier

CATALINA DE ERAUSO

SPANISH VOYAGER • 1585–1650

ORN INTO A HIGH-RANKING Basque family, Catalina de Erauso, like many young women of her time, was promised to the Church by her family. The thought of leading the cloistered life of a nun made her bitterly unhappy, and she determined to run away. But the convent was closely guarded, and she had been so confined during her youth that she knew almost nothing about the outside world.

Her opportunity to escape came by chance. The night before she was to take her vows, she saw that the keys to the gate were hanging nearby on a nail. Frightened but desperate, de Erauso stole scissors, thread, and a little money and, taking down the big iron key ring, let herself out onto the street. Her later account reveals the terror of her situation.

I went out onto the highway without ever having seen it before or knowing which way to turn. At random I went . . . I took cover and spent three days planning, fitting and cutting out [men's] clothes [for she had only her nun's habit]. My hair I cut off and threw away and on the third night I started off I knew not whither, hurrying along the roads and skirting villages so as to put a distance behind me.

As we learn from Spanish government edicts issued in 1600, 1608, 1615, and 1641, her escape disguised as a man was not unique. The edicts made cross-dressing punishable by death. But, if she knew of the danger, it did not stop Catalina. Disguised as a boy, she supported herself by doing odd jobs and working in stables. In 1605 she joined a ship bound for South America as a cabin boy, determined to put an ocean between herself and the nunnery.

Because the port where she landed in South America seemed too exposed, she jumped ship and joined travelers bound overland for Peru. Older by then and no longer able to pose as a boy, she got herself trained as a swordsman and enlisted as a soldier in the Spanish army. It was in this guise that for the next thirteen years she was stationed in a garrison on the Chilean border, fighting the Araucanian Indians.

This remote and harsh life would seem to be little improvement over the convent she had escaped, and eventually she departed to become a miner. Northern Chile was not promising for mining, however, so again she set forth. With a few companions, she decided to cross the mountains to Argentina. But there was no road from Chile, and the trails over the mountains were dangerous. Her companions died of the cold.

Argentina proved disappointing and in 1620, de Erauso again signed up as a soldier. During a sword battle, she entered a church for refuge and there confessed her story. Ironically, and for her probably almost unbelievably, she was not punished but was instead granted a pension by the Spanish army.

As curious as we may find her life of journeying, her contemporaries found it

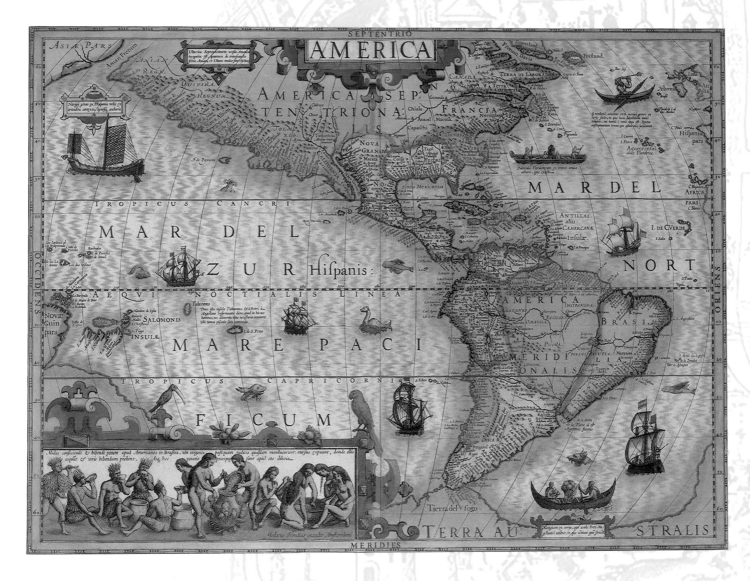

utterly baffling. They could hardly accept her own banal explanation—"I had a mind to travel and see a bit of the world."

Having become something of a heroine among the soldiers, Catalina decided to return to Spain. Once there she was again restless; she could neither fit into the conventions of her sex nor escape as a man. So she took the only other way out and became a pilgrim.

It was as a pilgrim that she left Spain for Rome. Her route took her across France where, apparently, the story of her wild escapades had preceded her. The French were not amused by her odd story and arrested her as a spy. Once freed, she was then robbed. Bedraggled and worn, she finally reached Rome where she had an audience with the pope.

What happened in that audience we do not know, but de Erauso seems to have found no comfort. She determined to make her way back to the New World. There, no longer fit to be a soldier and certainly not accepted as a lady, she found a curious niche for herself as a mule caravan driver, herding her stock between Mexico and South America until her own trail vanishes.

ABOVE: SOUTH AMERICA WAS AN UNEXPLORED TERRITORY AT THE TIME THAT CATALINA WAS SEARCHING FOR RICHES AND LEADING THE LIFE OF A VAGABOND.

ABOVE: JEANNE BARET, DISGUISED AS A MAN.
SHE WAS DESCRIBED BY A CONTEMPORARY:
"WE HAD SEEN HIM [BARÉ] ACCOMPANYING
HIS MASTER ON ALL HIS EXPEDITIONS AMIDST
THE SNOWS AND ICEY HILLS OF THE STRAITS
OF MAGELLAN, CARRYING, EVEN ON THOSE
LABORIOUS EXCURSIONS, PROVISIONS, ARMS
AND PORTFOLIOS OF PLANTS WITH A COURAGE
AND STRENGTH WHICH GAINED FOR HIM THE
NICKNAME OF COMMERSON'S 'BEAST OF BUR-
DEN' . . . HOW WAS IT POSSIBLE TO DISCOVER
THE WOMAN IN THAT INDEFATIGABLE BARÉ,
WHO WAS ALREADY AN EXPERT BOTANIST."

Pacific Naturalist

JEANNE BARET/JEAN BARÉ

FRENCH NATURALIST

1740?–1803?

I F THERE WAS A PLACE on Earth that eighteenth- and nineteenth-century sailors regarded as heaven, it was surely Tahiti, where they could get off their lurching, noisy, stinking ships; escape the privations of hunger, thirst, and scurvy; sleep on soft sand; breathe scented air; drink fresh water; and eat unsalted meat and fruits. There, the dream of all sailors awaited them: sloe-eyed, bare-breasted, uninhibited maidens. Tahiti, after its discovery by the expedition of French admiral Louis-Antoine de Bougainville in 1768, became the magnet that drew many sailors back to sea.

Bougainville had set out to discover the riches of the South Pacific, where islands, a cape, straits, reefs, and even flowers now bear his name. But Bougainville was no mere adventurer: his ships carried a number of scientists, including botanists and astronomers, whose studies set an example for voyages to follow. Indeed, the ship's botanist, Philibert Commerson, had serious scientific pursuits in mind when he first rowed ashore with his assistant, Jean Baré.

No sooner had Baré reached the beach than Tahitian men rushed up and began to whisper the word *aiene*. After milling around, one of them seized the assistant and started to run toward the forest so that Jean, as Bougainville wrote, could "receive the honors of the island."

Astonished, a French sailor whipped out his sword and chased the pair. It was one thing for the sailors to sport with native girls but quite another for the native men to rape one of the crew. What the sailor did not know was the meaning of the word *aiene*. It soon became evident that the Tahitian men had discovered in moments what the French had not learned during the long sea voyage: *aiene* meant "girl"!

Jean Baré had shared meals, living quarters, and toilet facilities with the officers of the ship and, together with the eminent scientist Commerson, had collected, preserved, and cataloged a vast collection of plants. So closely did Commerson keep his eyes on his scientific endeavor—a collection that would eventually include five thousand species, three thousand of them new to

science—that he was, or appeared to be, oblivious to the sex of his assistant.

After the incident on the beach, Bougainville was summoned. Confronted by the admiral, "Jean Baré" tearfully confessed that in truth she was Jeanne Baret. Astonished but gallant, Bougainville made the best of this discovery, writing with a touch of foreboding: "She will be the first of her sex who has circumnavigated the globe."

Commerson's will, drawn up before the voyage, showed that Baret was already an accomplished naturalist and revealed he did in fact know the truth about her. The will directed that the contents and use of Commerson's home be given for one year to "Jeanne Baret, my housekeeper [to give] her the time to put in order the natural history collection which is to be taken to the royal Cabinet des Estampes."

Commerson and Jeanne now asked leave of Bougainville to stay on Mauritius. The admiral, probably with a sigh of relief, gave his consent, and the two botanists remained there for nearly five years, exploring both that island and Madagascar. Commerson died on Mauritius at the age of forty-four. As he had hoped she would, Baret organized their collection, had it packed, and shipped it back to France, where it was soon recognized as one of the most significant contributions to botany in that great age of exploration. Jeanne, too, returned to France, where she lived out the rest of her life in obscurity.

Into Green Hell

I N THE EARLY DECADES of the eighteenth century there was an ongoing academic debate regarding the shape of the earth. The English scientist Sir Isaac Newton proposed that it was flattened at the poles and slightly bulging at the equator. The French astronomer royal Jacques Cassini thought it was slightly elongated at the poles and thus more constricted at the equator. To end the debate, and hopefully uphold French honor, several expeditions were sent out to determine the actual shape of the earth. One, under the command of Charles-Marie de la Condamine, went to Peru from 1735 to 1743, to measure along the equator. Among the impressive group of scientists, mathematicians, and technicians in this expedition was a young chainbearer by the name of Jean Godin des Odanais; his not very grand job was to hold the lines used in making the measurements. But he was well treated by his hosts. While in Peru he stayed in the house of General Grandmaison, the governor of Guayaquil province, and to pass the time took lessons in the indigenous language, Quechua, with one of the general's young daughters. After five years with the family, in 1742, he won permission to marry the then-thirteen-year-old Isabel Grandmaison y Bruno.

In 1749, hearing of the death of his father, Godin decided to return to France with Isabel to check on his inheritance. At that time, most people who traveled to Europe sailed from Peru to Panama, crossed the isthmus, and then continued on across the Atlantic. Traveling east across the continent by way of the Amazon River was a perilous, indeed often fatal, undertaking. Vast and unmapped, the territory was laced through with meandering and treacherous rivers. In the jungle the perils were many: hostile indigenous Indians, poisonous snakes and frogs, piranha fish, clouds of mosquitoes, and armies of fire ants. There was the constant threat of deadly tropical diseases. The greatest difficulty, however, was the impenetrable jungle. But for a young scientist and his adventurous wife, traversing South America via the Amazon seemed to be a worthy goal.

Godin was cautious: he decided to first travel the river alone to make sure that the route was safe before he took his wife and young family. It took him more than a year to reach the mouth of the Amazon and sail around to Cayenne in Guiana. He immediately applied for permission from the Portuguese and Spanish authorities, through whose territory he had to again pass, to ascend the river to return for his wife. Thinking he was crazy or perhaps a spy, they denied his requests. Incredibly, he remained at one end of the Amazon and Isabel at the other for twenty years.

They did write to one another, but most of the letters went astray, since the postal service was composed of occasional travelers. One letter reached Isabel several years after it was written, just as her only remaining child died; it inspired Isabel to wait no longer to rejoin her husband. She gathered ten people, including her brothers, a young nephew, and three maids, to make the trek downriver. After two years of preparation, she left on October 1, 1769. With thirty-one Indian porters carrying their possessions, the group traversed the mountains and descended to the river village of Canelos. But when they arrived they found the inhabitants dead or gone. Smallpox had decimated the town. The survivors had fled, taking all the canoes that Isabel had intended to use to continue the journey downriver. Worse, Isabel's own porters disappeared, fearful of catching smallpox. She managed to find two native men hiding in the forest whom she coaxed into making a canoe by hollowing out a log as well as a rough raft to carry their supplies. Though she had to abandon much of her baggage, Isabel did manage to find room on the raft for her silver plates and bowls, dresses of velvet and taffeta, and her box of jewelry.

After leaving Canelos, one disaster after another befell the party. Their supplies were lost when the raft split apart after hitting a submerged tree trunk. One Indian guide drowned and the surviving Indians ran away. Abandoning the canoe, which they could not steer without the guides, the party hacked their way through the dense undergrowth along the riverbank. But in trying to take a shortcut across the jungle, they became lost. For days the group wandered in the forest, succumbing one by one to madness brought on by starvation, thirst, and despair. One horrible day Isabel awoke to find the rest of her companions dead, their bodies already decomposing in the fierce tropical heat.

To replace her own lost shoes she had to "cut the shoes off her brother's feet, and fastened the soles to her own." Wandering alone in the forest for days, she chanced upon some Indians who took her downriver to the mission of Andoas, in present-day Peru. There an Indian woman made her a skirt of rough cotton to replace her own clothes, which were in shreds. Isabel was so grateful to the Indians who had rescued her that she gave them her gold necklace, her last possession of any value. She continued downriver and eventually reached the hamlet of Loreto in Brazil, where her father, who had sailed upriver to greet his family, awaited her. Together they sailed down the Amazon and around the continent to Oyapock in Guiana, and on July 22, 1770, after twenty years, she was reunited with her husband. Three years later they set sail for France, where Isabel lived out the rest of her days.

The remembrance of the shocking spectacle she witnessed, the horror incident on her solitude and the darkness of night . . . the perpetual apprehension of death . . . had such effect on her spirits as to cause her hair to turn gray.

JEAN GODIN

Forever New Horizons

Intrepid Explorers

By the early nineteenth century, travel had become slightly more comfortable. Canals, privately financed roadways, and later the railroad made it much easier, cheaper, and faster to move between cities. Probably the single greatest boon to women travelers, however, was the advent of steamships in the 1800s. These ships were not only faster but larger, and for the first time private cabins became available. That women could now journey in some privacy undoubtedly was attractive to them and made their husbands and fathers more willing to let them go.

The greatest inspiration for travel in the nineteenth century was the notion of empire. It gave women, English women in particular, reason and unparalleled freedom to leave home. Travel they did, as missionaries, teachers, writers, pioneers, colonizers, wives, painters, and botanists. Women began moving around the globe as never before, and often alone. They kept journals, wrote streams of letters, published books and articles, collected specimens. More significant, they joined in the founding of new sciences such as geology, paleontology, botany, and biology. Some of these women even earned an income from their experiences by going on the lecture circuit or by becoming journalists.

Despite the greater ease of travel, to be a woman explorer was still difficult. Without the support given to men by colleges, exploring associations, or governments, and rarely able to tag along on official expeditions,

ABOVE: *ARCTIC IN WINTER QUARTERS, FULLERTON HARBOR, 1904–1905*. GERALDINE MOODIE PHOTOGRAPHED THE *ARCTIC*, A BOAT SHE SAILED IN ON HER EXPEDITION TO FULLERTON BAY, CANADA.

OPPOSITE: OSA JOHNSON POSED ASTRIDE A DEAD CROCODILE.

PRECEDING PAGES: A CARAVAN IN THE WADI DU'AN HADHRAMANT, ARABIA, C. 1935.

ROAMING THE NORTH LANDS

Geraldine Fitzgibbon Moodie
Canadian photographer • 1854–1945

GERALDINE MOODIE was the first woman photographer to work above the Arctic Circle and the first professional photographer to make a record of the Inuit peoples. She sailed to the Arctic in 1904 to join her husband, who was then the superintendent of Canada's Northwest Mounted Police in the Hudson Bay and eastern Arctic areas.

Moodie had the advantage of being raised in a family of successful women. Her grandmother, Susanna, wrote a book entitled *Roughing It in the Bush* about her frontier experiences, and her grandmother's sister, Catherine Parr Traill, was well known in Canada for her books on flowers. In 1878 Geraldine married her cousin, John Moodie, and went on to give birth to six children. As they moved from one frontier post to another, Geraldine collected and painted flowers and taught herself photography. In 1895, on the Saskatchewan prairies, Moodie began a series of portraits of the native Cree Indians and their ceremonies.

When Geraldine's husband was posted to the Arctic in 1904, they moved first to Fullerton on Southampton Island and later to Fort Churchill on Hudson Bay. Once again she set up her studio and began to photograph the local Inuit and the wildflowers. She later said, "I put in three very lonely years climbing over rocks and hills to procure plants, and then to photograph them." Loving the frontier life, the Moodies requested postings even farther north. In 1912 they moved to Dawson in the Yukon for several years. After her adventurous life Geraldine retired to a small farm in Maple Creek in western Canada. Her work was forgotten after she died, and only now is she being celebrated as a pioneering photographer of the Plains and of the Arctic who captured on film the twilight moments of the traditional Cree and Inuit peoples.

women had to make their own way. Many of them learned to live with indigenous peoples, upon whom they depended for their survival. Eschewing the usual trappings of colonial-era expeditions—tents, tin baths, and silver dishes—some chose instead the simple clothing and rough shelters of their hosts. Sleeping on the sand under rough goat-hair tents, poling through rapids in hollowed-out tree trunks, or sheltering in caves from blizzards, these explorers learned essential truths that male-only expeditions sometimes missed.

"A sense of wonder": that is how many women explorers described what they felt. Swiss photographer Trudi Blom spoke for many of her colleagues when she reflected on the beginning of her treks into the jungles of Mexico: "I was held spellbound by the incredible musical sounds of the insects. . . . I listened in amazement to the peculiar cry of the howler monkey. . . . This jungle has filled me with a sense of wonder that has never left me."

Although exploration would seem to require youthful physical energy and strength, the records make clear that many women did not begin their journeys until they were past middle age. This was because as daughters, wives, and mothers they were not free of familial duties. Only in their mid-forties and fifties could they take up such "youthful" and "masculine" activities as climbing virgin peaks or walking through dense jungles. Once they had begun, many refused to be sidelined by age. Indeed, many pursued their dreams and ambitions even in the most severe circumstances, and pursued their explorations until the very end of their lives, often well into their eighth and ninth decades.

Of course, exploration was not only about mastering high mountains and dense jungles. But the physical demands of these journeys had an unintended side effect for which women today can be grateful: a change of dress style. Some early explorers remained in their heavy Victorian dress even

ABOVE LEFT: WHILE WORKING IN THE ARCTIC, MOODIE PHOTO-GRAPHED TWO INUIT WOMEN ON THE BEACH NEAR CHURCHILL, MANITOBA. ONE IS CARRYING A CHILD AND THE OTHER, A SEAL.
INSET: PORTRAIT OF GERALDINE MOODIE, 1910, TAKEN IN OTTAWA.

in hot and humid climates, but most forswore "ladylike" fashions. Climbing in long skirts, riding sidesaddle, and marching through deserts in whalebone corsets was simply too impractical and uncomfortable. Climbers were some of the first women to wear trousers; split skirts were designed so women could ride astride; and women explorers in the Middle East sensibly dressed for the desert in loose robes.

Since women have been traditionally restricted to a narrow life, those who sought to break free found it easier to do so when they were far from home, where they could either adopt new habits or float between the norms of their own societies and those of the people among whom they traveled. Thus, they became, in a special sense, outlaws; that is, they put themselves beyond the conventions of their own societies without really becoming a part of their host society. For most people, male and female, the horizon represents danger. But for an adventurous few the horizon speaks of possibility and adventure and knowledge. The explorers in this chapter were looking beyond the margins of their world to embrace the unknown. They were seekers of new visions and ideas. They carved out an area uniquely theirs and left an indelible mark on the fabric of knowledge.

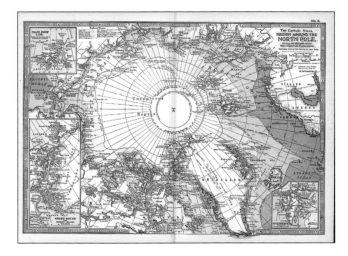

TOP RIGHT: PORTRAIT OF MINA BENSON HUBBARD.

CENTER RIGHT: HUBBARD IN CAMP DURING HER EXPLORATION OF THE NASCAUPEE AND GEORGE RIVERS IN LABRADOR.

BOTTOM RIGHT: HUBBARD BRAVING THE ELEMENTS ON HER CANADIAN EXPEDITION.

ACROSS LABRADOR
MINA BENSON HUBBARD
CANADIAN EXPLORER • 1870–1956

MINA HUBBARD aided, supported, and listened as her husband Leonidas, an editor of the popular *Outing Magazine,* planned his 1903 dream expedition to survey and map the last unexplored region of America, the interior of Labrador from the Northwest River Region up to Ungava Bay. She sailed north with him in what turned out to be his final voyage: he died of starvation beside a small river, far from his goal.

Spurred partly by the desire to finish Leonidas's work and partly to refute an account of the expedition given by one of its other members that ignored her husband's con-

tributions, Mina began to plan her own expedition. She trained for two years, learning navigation, surveying, and canoeing. Leaving for Labrador in 1905, Hubbard made the 576-mile journey in less than two months, thus becoming the first white woman to cross Labrador. She was also the first person to chart the Nascaupee and George River systems; the first to record local flora and fauna; the first to witness the great caribou migrations; and the first to make a record of the local Inuit. She wrote, "My expedition demonstrated that geographers were mistaken in supposing the Northwest River, draining Lake Michikamau, and the Nascaupee River, draining Seal Lake, to be two distinct rivers. They are one and the same, the outlet of Lake Michikamau carrying its waters northeast to Seal Lake and thence southward to Hamilton Inlet."

Ladies Traveling Without Any Gentleman

ALEXANDRINE PETRONELLA FRANCINA TINNÉ

DUTCH EXPLORER • 1835–1869

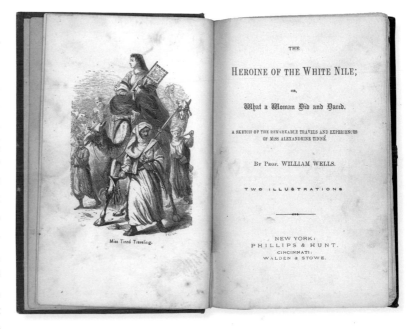

Miss Tinné Traveling.

THE

HEROINE OF THE WHITE NILE;

OR,

What a Woman Did and Dared.

A SKETCH OF THE REMARKABLE TRAVELS AND EXPERIENCES OF MISS ALEXANDRINE TINNÉ.

BY PROF. WILLIAM WELLS.

TWO ILLUSTRATIONS

NEW YORK:
PHILLIPS & HUNT.
CINCINNATI:
WALDEN & STOWE.

In the 1850s and 1860s Europeans and Americans were mesmerized by the reports of explorers in Africa. People like Sir Richard Francis Burton, Dr. David Livingstone, Sir Henry Stanley, John Speke, and Florence and Samuel Baker were lionized for their daring exploits. Alexandrine Tinné was so inspired by these heroes that she decided to embark upon the greatest quest of her time: the search for the source of the Nile River. Only nineteen when she began this adventure, she spent the next fifteen years becoming a skilled photographer, botanical illustrator, and naturalist before she was murdered in the Sahara Desert.

Alexine, as she was called, was born in The Hague in 1835 into a wealthy and influential family. From a young age she traveled with her mother, Baroness Harriet von Capellen Tinné. Their first expedition, when Alexine was just sixteen, was across Scandinavia on horseback. Inspired by the success of this trip, they eagerly sought another voyage.

Adventure came their way three years later. To help Alexine recover from the heartbreak of a broken engagement, her mother took her to Venice, where the two learned they could sail to Alexandria, Egypt, from nearby Trieste. Despite pleas from family and friends to return home, including one from the queen of the Netherlands, they decided to set sail. Tinné was enthralled with Egypt. She began learning Arabic while sailing up the Nile to Luxor and when she and her mother arrived in Luxor they decided to ride camels across the desert to the Red Sea. Alexine was so captivated by the desert that she decided not to return to The Hague but to spend the remainder of the year in the Holy Land and then return to Egypt with her mother to make a second voyage up the Nile. The goal of the second voyage was to reach the Sudan. But the infamous Nile cataracts, the roiling rapids above Aswan, stopped them, as they did all travelers. Realizing they needed more equipment and better boats, the two women returned to The Hague to outfit themselves for a lengthy expedition to the Sudan, where they were to search for the source of the Nile.

There are Dutch ladies travelling without any gentleman. . . . They are very rich and have hired the only steamer here for a 1000 pounds. They must be demented! A young lady alone with the Dinka tribe . . . they must really be mad. All the natives are as naked as the day they were born.

EXPLORER SAMUEL BAKER

Tinné and her mother, along with Alexine's aunt and their servants, returned to Cairo in 1861. They lavishly outfitted several boats with porcelain, silver, a library of books, a photographic studio, and plant-collecting paraphernalia, in preparation for a long journey. On their last night in Cairo, Harriet wrote, "This is our last night and Alexine played some tunes we may perhaps never hear again. Everything is sad for the last, but it is a good time to leave the country without regret: so many lifeless trees, all the oranges picked, and the morning and evening really cold."

The little group had only a vague idea, derived from sketchy travelers' accounts and colored by their romantic notions, of what faced them. The reality was forbidding—rugged and dangerous terrain, scarcity of food and water, unsanitary conditions, and, ominously, slavers and tribesmen who were hostile to Europeans. But Alexine was determined to go places no one else had been. After their boats were pulled over the cataracts the women sailed south to the village of Lorosko. There they reloaded their belongings from the boats onto 102 camels for the seven-week trek over the desert to Khartoum.

In Khartoum Tinné bought her first slave, a girl she named Rosa, whom she immediately freed. She would eventually purchase many slaves in order to free them. To sail from Khartoum to the next stage, Jebel Dinka, the women hired several boats. Jebel Dinka, they found, was not just a river port but also a slaving outpost. There the piteous condition of the terrified, starved, and chained Africans so horrified the women that Alexine lost no opportunity to denounce the slavers to Sudanese officials.

Leaving Jebel Dinka, the women sailed up the White Nile until they encountered the Sudd, a vast swamp so choked with vegetation that large animals could walk across parts of it. From there Tinné sent reports back to her brother John in London, which he submitted to the Royal Geographical Society. Among them, she wrote that "this part of the voyage was exceedingly tedious, the river resembling a narrow canal, full of curves and windings, walled in by impenetrable thickets of reeds or else mud banks. Huge herds of elephants were passed, with hippopotami, buffalo, and other wild animals but hunting is impossible due to the nature of the soil." It took them five months to reach Gondokoro, where the boat became mired in mud and could go no farther.

Disappointed, they sailed back to Khartoum, where Alexine began to restock their boats for another attempt. This time the Tinnés had a flotilla of six boats carrying guards, servants, maids, a botanist, an ornithologist, and enough supplies for a year. They decided to turn westward in the direction of Bahr al-Ghazal. From there they planned to trek overland to the unexplored territory of the Nyam-Nyam or "great-eaters" who lived in the northern Congo and were widely thought to be cannibals.

"I write at present from one of the most singular spots on the globe," Alexine

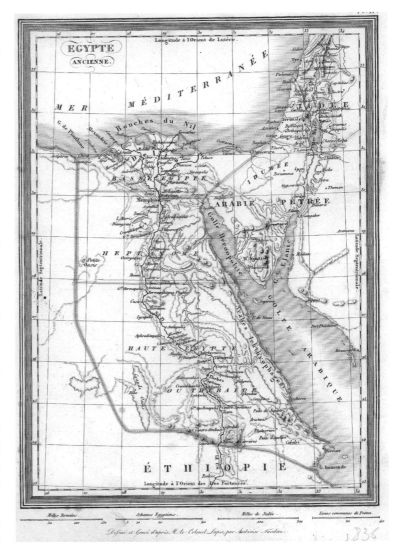

Crinum Tinneanum Schady et Zeyherl

She was a zealous collector of plants and had a number of camels loaded solely with blotting paper and immense collections of plants. The labor promised to be very valuable, for the flora of Soudan is almost unknown, and of previous African travelers only Dr. Vogel was a botanist, and all his papers were lost.

NEW YORK TIMES, AUG. 30, 1869

reported, "which can only be reached by a route as singular. We pushed along up the Ghazal for three or four days, the river in front always appearing to have come to an end in a sea of herbage." Tinné hired porters when the boats became mired, and continued overland. "Once more en route," Harriet wrote, "we shall I trust, arrive safe and sound at the mountain Casinka, where we are to remain until the weather is fine and the earth dry . . . no Europeans have been there. We have already sent off three companies of porters, about 400 men in all. They carry but little, say 40lbs each, and all on their heads."

In London a dispute arose at the Royal Geographical Society when John Tinné read an expedition report from his sister. Nile explorers John Speke and James Grant belittled her account of her overland trek beyond Bahr al-Ghazal, but the president of the society supported their efforts, saying, "The ladies were really on the right road to obtain this knowledge; for their great object was to reach the mountainous region whence the Bahr-el-Ghazal flowed . . . notwithstanding the discussions of Captains Speke and Grant—should they discover that its waters are thrown off to the Nile on the one side and to Lake Tchad and the other great lakes to westward on the other, it would be a most important geographical result."

Back in the Sudan the Tinnés continued toward their goal, crossing the Jur and Kosango Rivers toward the territory of the Nyam-Nyam. Needing more porters and provisions, they stopped at the only place of supply—a slaving outpost. Tinné left with a small party in order to scout the route, and discovered their way was blocked by the yearly floodwaters. While she was gone, sixty-five-year-old Harriet became ill with fever, and after a few wretched days, died. Soon after, the two Dutch maids also died.

So it was to a sad camp that Alexine returned. The loss of her mother devastated her and crushed her dream to map unknown territory. The expedition turned back to Khartoum, bearing the caskets of the three women. They were unable to get food from local tribesmen, who, fearing they were slavers, fled at their approach. The porters, worried they would be sold into slavery at the end of the expedition, were sullen. After months of difficult and sorrowful travel Tinné reached Khartoum only to discover that her aunt, who had stayed behind, had also died. Heartbroken, Alexine wrote to her brother, "I was so sick with sorrow that I lay for days in my bed, trying not to think."

For a time after her Sudanese expeditions, Alexine settled in Cairo. Tiring of Cairo, Tinné purchased a yacht in 1864 and sailed to Algiers with her Sudanese servants. A newspaper later recorded the stir her arrival caused:

Visitors to Algiers some years ago will remember the air of mystery hanging about a certain yacht lying off the harbor. Rumor spread all kinds of glowing reports about the mistress of its motley crew—Europeans, Negroes and stately Nubians. Some said it was an Oriental princess; one invented a love affair, to account for the lonely wanderings of this female Odysseus . . . the yacht, indeed, belonged to a lady, young, beautiful and possessed of a queenly fortune, whose existence, almost from childhood, had been spent in the East; who had already accomplished several voyages of discovery in Central Africa; and who, undaunted by the mishaps of former pioneers in the same direction, now projected an undertaking, which, if carried out successfully, must place her in the foremost rank of African discoverers.

Alexine's new plan was to cross the Sahara from the north to the southwest, from Tripoli to Timbuktu, traveling with the little-known desert nomads, the Tuareg; to prepare, she learned Tamachek, their language. In 1869 she left from Tripoli, heading south across the desert toward Lake Chad, and after a month she reached the oasis village of Murzuch. This she described as "a queer little place, built of mud, or rather of salt. It looks as if some dreadful earthquake had taken place, so crooked and tumble down look the houses." Outside of Murzuch she met the Tuareg leader Ichnuchen, who greatly impressed her. She wrote:

I cannot tell you the impression Ichnuchen in his strange stately dress, and all of his followers made on me, old traveller as I am. I may say, with that stern valley . . . for scenery, I never saw a grander and handsomer sight, those variegated colors, martial appearance, singular trappings, and elegant dromedaries with long snake necks. One cannot describe it! But it was a blood stirring scene.

Blood-stirring it literally was: unwittingly, Tinné became a pawn in a Tuareg feud between Ichnuchen and his nephew. The feud climaxed when, to spite Ichnuchen, his nephew killed Alexine during a raid on her camp.

Young, beautiful, intelligent, and rich, Tinné sacrificed much in her quest of the unknown. With her collections destroyed in later wars, and her life cut short before she had a chance to document her discoveries, the only existing monument to her is an obelisk in Juba, Sudan, which lists her among the explorers who searched for the source of the Nile.

TOP: PANORAMA OF THE NILE VALLEY WITH PYRAMIDS.

OPPOSITE AND ABOVE: AFTER TINNÉ RETURNED TO CAIRO FROM HER SUDANESE EXPEDITIONS, SHE PACKED AND SHIPPED OFF HER BOTANICAL SPECIMENS AND DRAWINGS TO THE BOTANIST THEODORE KOTSCHY IN VIENNA, WHO WOULD LATER PUBLISH HER DISCOVERIES AND PAINTINGS IN AN OVERSIZED VOLUME ENTITLED *PLANTAE TINNEANAE*. HER HUGE ETHNOLOGICAL COLLECTION WAS SENT TO HER BROTHER JOHN IN LIVERPOOL, ENGLAND. HOUSED IN THE LIVERPOOL MUSEUM, IT WAS TRAGICALLY DESTROYED BY AN AIR RAID DURING THE SECOND WORLD WAR.

Arabian Nights

LADY ANNE BLUNT

ENGLISH EXPLORER OF ARABIA • 1837–1917

We are starting, rather like babes in the wood, on an adventure whose importance we are unable to rate . . . we shall slip away into the desert, and trust to Providence.

L ADY ANNE ISABELLA NOEL, Baroness Wentworth, was the first Western woman to travel with the Shammar tribes in what was then called Mesopotamia, and the Anazeh tribes of the Syrian desert. Lady Anne, as she was called, was the only daughter of William, earl of Lovelace and the Honorable Ada Byron, a daughter of the great poet Lord Byron. In 1869, Anne married Wilfrid Scawen Blunt, an eccentric poet, diplomat, and diarist. Together they shared a love of horses and desert exploration, and in 1875, "tiring of too inadventurous life at home, a sudden impulse started [them] on a series of romantic horseback journeys in Spain, Algeria and Asia Minor, and eventually in that still wilder wandering in Mesopotamia, Persia and the as yet quite unvisited regions of Central Arabia."

Anne Blunt wrote two volumes documenting her travels with her husband by horse and camel on two long expeditions through the Arabian deserts from 1877 to 1880, searching for elusive Bedouin tribes. Her books are packed with informative detail about the tribes and with detailed geographical descriptions of the lands she traversed. On their first journey, the Blunts joined the Anazeh tribe on their annual migration toward central Arabia in order to purchase breeding horses for their renowned Crabbet Arabian Stud in England. Anne wrote that she wanted to go because "the Bedouins, when on the march, go quite slowly—ten or twelve miles a day—and we should have an opportunity of seeing, what has always interested me, the original home of our Arabian horses." In addition, she wrote, "The fact is, the Euphrates is more of a mystery to the general public than any river. It has never been popularly described, and, since the days of Xenophon, has hardly been described at all."

Travel in Arabia at that time was dangerous, since the desert tribes were engaged in almost constant warfare. The Blunts therefore adopted unorthodox travel methods: they dressed like the Bedouin; they learned to speak Arabic; they slept on the ground; and they ate Bedouin-style whatever was locally available—roasted grasshoppers and wild hyena were part of their diet. On occasion the couple was even mistaken for Arabs. They traveled without escort, without interpreters, and even, on occasion, without guides, throwing themselves on the mercy of tribal hospitality.

On their first expedition the Blunts crossed the desert to Baghdad, where they were put up at the official British residence. But the sumptuous surroundings there held little appeal for the two. "Our first thought

Bedouin.

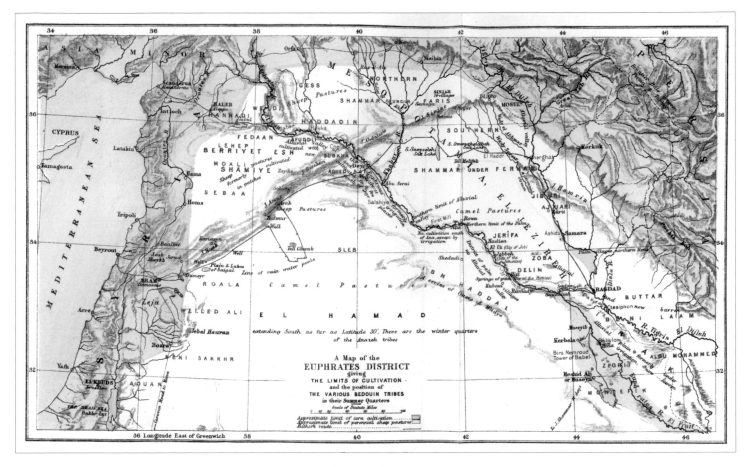

on arriving in Bagdad, was how to get out of it." Instead of waiting for official permission, they slipped quietly out of the city "toward an unknown country where there were no towns, no markets, no guard houses."

Lady Anne wrote of her joy in leaving a little desert oasis: "We have left Deyr, and are once more in the desert—our own desert . . . for indeed we are more at home in it than in the towns." They were arrested a day later because the local chieftain, unable to comprehend why foreigners would search for desert tribes, assumed they were spies. "Full of gloomy forebodings, the least of which was an immediate return under escort to Deyr, and the worst a summary execution as Russian spies, we passed a miserable night, sometimes dreaming wildly of flight on our mares." After a long wrangle, they were able to convince the chief to let them continue on their way.

Their Spartan existence in the desert made the Blunts increasingly uncomfortable with European society. Lady Anne speaks for many explorers when she relates an encounter with their countrymen.

> We were not prepared for the vast change a winter spent among the Arabs
> would make in our tastes, our prejudices, and our opinions. . . . As we were sitting
> on a divan at the end of the dining-room, drinking our coffee in all the solemnity
> of Asiatic repose, a sudden noise of voices and loud laughter resounded through the
> house . . . a tumultuous throng of men and women clad in trousers and coats or in
> scanty skirts and jackets . . . all with heads uncovered and looking strangely

ABOVE: MAP OF EUPHRATES DISTRICT USED BY LADY ANNE BLUNT DURING HER EXPLORATION OF THE ARABIAN DESERTS.

OPPOSITE, TOP: LADY ANNE BLUNT.

OPPOSITE, BOTTOM: A BEDOUIN OF THE PERIOD.

naked, rushed across the floor . . . they passed in front of us without pause or salute. . . . The dresses, voices, gestures, and attitudes of these men and women struck us as not only the most grotesque, but the most indecorous we had ever seen . . . these travellers are English milords of distinction.

Their second expedition was to the Nejd in central Arabia, a thousand-mile journey during which they had to cross the Great Nafud Desert. The purpose of this trip was to visit the ruler of the oasis of Hail, Prince Ibn Rashid; they hoped to purchase some of his famous horses for their breeding farm in England. As they got closer to Hail, the Blunts started to worry about how they would be received by these most isolated of desert Arabs, who had had little contact with Christians and certainly none with a relatively liberated Western woman. In fact, Lady Anne was the first Western woman to visit Hail, and a century later the local Arabs were still talking about the vivid impression she made.

The Blunts did come under attack during their second expedition while camped in the sands just beyond Wadi. As they rested beside their camels, the quiet was suddenly rent by the shrieks of mounted horsemen bearing down on them. As they crashed into the little party, one Bedouin knocked Wilfrid senseless and another hit Lady Anne with a spear. She raised her arms to protect herself and cried in Arabic, "We seek your protection." Astonished to hear a woman's voice, the attacking Bedouin pulled up short. They were even more astonished when they realized it was a foreign woman addressing them in Arabic. After examining the couple closely, the Bedouin rode away and the Blunts, nursing their wounds, resumed their journey across the desert to Hail and Jebel Shammar. There they met with the Arab prince, Ibn Rashid, and joined a band of pilgrims on the road back to Damascus.

After these journeys the Blunts divided their time between Cairo and England, where Lady Anne translated ancient Arabic poems that evoked the desert she had so loved. The rest of her life seems somewhat anticlimactic; she separated from Wilfrid in 1906 and died in Cairo in 1917.

ABOVE: BLUNT ILLUSTRATED HER BOOKS WITH HER OWN SKETCHES, SUCH AS THIS ONE OF HER TENT. IN PREPARATION FOR THEIR FIRST EXPEDITION ANNE DESIGNED AND MADE A LIGHTWEIGHT DURABLE TENT. UNLIKE OTHER TENTS THEN USED, WHICH REQUIRED AT LEAST SIX PEOPLE TO ASSEMBLE THEM, THE BLUNTS' TENT WAS "LOW, BUT COVERS FOR ITS SIZE A GREAT DEAL OF GROUND, AND CAN, IN WET AND WINDY WEATHER, BE MADE ALMOST AIR TIGHT, WHILE UNDER A HOT SUN IT IS TRANSFORMABLE INTO A GIGANTIC UMBRELLA." SHE SAGELY NOTED THAT "ONE ADVANTAGE OF SLEEPING OUT OF DOORS IS, THAT EVERYBODY IS READY TO GET UP IN THE MORNING."

OPPOSITE: LADY ANNE BLUNT ON AN ARABIAN MARE.

The Blessings of a Good Thick Skirt

MARY HENRIETTA KINGSLEY

ENGLISH EXPLORER • 1862–1900

ABOVE: FANG WARRIORS IN THE CONGO, PHO-
TOGRAPHED BY MARY KINGSLEY IN THE LATE
NINETEENTH CENTURY.

OPPOSITE: A STUDIO PORTRAIT OF MARY
KINGSLEY. SHE EXPRESSED HER FEELINGS FOR
THE "CIVILIZED" LIFE IN ENGLAND BY SAYING,
"I WOULD MUCH SOONER WADE THROUGH A
SWAMP UP TO MY NECK IN MUD OR CLIMB THE
PEAK OF THE CAMEROON, THAN GO THROUGH
THE TREADMILL LIFE [OF A SOCIETY LADY IN
LONDON]."

AN ARTICLE PUBLISHED IN 1896 DESCRIBED
KINGSLEY: "THE EXPLORER HERSELF IS A
SLIGHT FAIR WOMAN, NOT VERY ROBUST IN
APPEARANCE, BUT SHOWING IN EVERY MOVE-
MENT ENERGY AND DETERMINATION. SHE
TAKES THINGS PHILOSOPHICALLY, DOES
NOT DISTURB HERSELF ABOUT TRIFLES, HAS
ABUNDANCE OF THAT USEFUL QUALITY A SENSE
OF HUMOR, AND ABOVE EVERYTHING THE
SPIRIT OF ADAPTABILITY."

MARY KINGSLEY, A SELF-DESCRIBED Cockney girl with no education, became the nineteenth century's foremost authority on West Africa. She made two lengthy solitary expeditions, in 1893–94 and in 1895, through the swamps and on tributaries of the Congo River to collect freshwater fish for the British Museum. The books she wrote about her travels with the Fang cannibals were widely acclaimed, and she became a popular lecturer. After her death from fever in South Africa at the age of thirty-eight the Mary Kingsley Society—which later became the Royal African Society—was founded in her honor. Although she contributed what contemporaries esteemed to be invaluable studies on the geography and fauna of the Congo region, it is her enlightened views concerning the validity of the belief systems of the African tribes for which she is remembered today.

Mary's life began under a particularly dark cloud as judged by Victorian standards: she was born just four days after her father married her mother, who had been a servant in his house. To escape the opprobrium, her father simply abandoned his family for years at a time to live abroad. What time he spent at home was almost worse since he "had a perfect horror of highly educated women, so that I was not permitted to study subjects out of the ordinary course of [an] English education." Of her youth she said, "I cried bitterly at not being taught things." But when her father was away Kingsley went into his library and was able to absorb an education far beyond what most girls of her day were exposed to. The only formal training she ever had was the German lessons her father paid for so she could translate articles for him.

Despite his discouragement, she inherited her father's love of adventure and his scholarly interest in foreign cultures. After her parents died she used part of her small inheritance to take a trip to the Canary Islands. While there she heard about white men who made their living trading with the natives in West Africa. With no ties and very little money, she thought this sounded like something she could do. Mary later wrote to a friend that the real reason for her trip was that she was "dead tired and feeling no one had need of me any more after Mother and Father died within six weeks of each other in '92 and my brother went off to the East, [so] I went down to West Africa to Die." But she clearly enjoyed all the adventures that came her way.

The area Kingsley determined to explore, and came to love, would soon be immortalized in Joseph Conrad's novella of madness and terror, *Heart of Darkness*. The Congo then was viewed as a fearful place, called "the white man's graveyard" for the variety of lethal diseases it harbored. Mary was advised to get to know the missionaries: they at least would give her a funeral when she died. She was also warned about the supposed murderous nature of the African people. Indeed, she prepared herself for the worst by carrying a small, sharp dagger to kill herself with, should the need ever arise.

Kingsley quickly saw the value of being a trader as she traveled alone without any protection, relying on the goodwill of the natives she encountered. Traders were the link between disparate worlds, since barter was something everyone could understand and appreciate. Mary also strongly believed that the English should be involved in Africa not as colonial overlords but as trading partners.

With trading as her means, her goal was to collect fish, insects, and reptiles for the British Museum. "My aim," she explained, "in visiting West Africa . . . was to get together a general collection of fishes from a West African river north of the Congo, for the terrific current of this river makes a great impression on distribution." She collected several new species, three of which were named for her—*Ctenopoma kingsleyae, Mormyrrs kingsleyae,* and *Alestus kingsleyae.*

Although she was profoundly unorthodox in where and how she traveled, Mary was entirely conventional when it came to her appearance. Even in the swamps she wore stays and a long black wool dress, declaring, "you have no right to go about Africa in things you would be ashamed to be seen in at home." And her Victorian propriety saved her life. One day while walking on a trail in the jungle she crashed into a fifteen-foot pit lined with pointed poisoned stakes. Although bruised, she landed safely, prompting her to praise "the blessings of a good thick skirt!"

Kingsley relished the beauty, excitement, and danger of traveling in the jungle. Describing the difficulties of using elephant trails, she said:

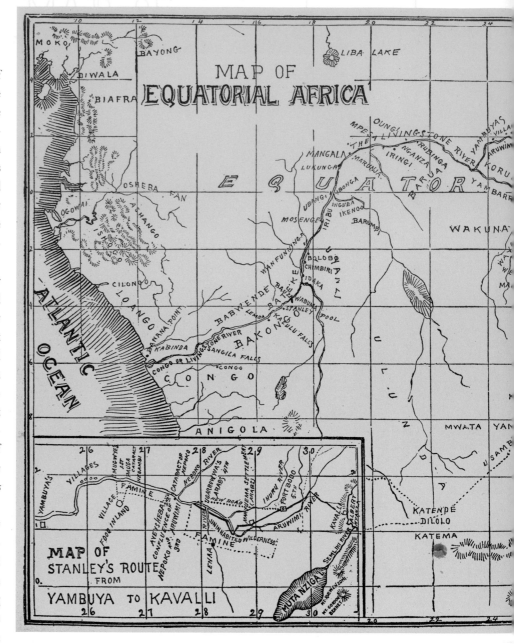

> Several times [we] came across stretches of shallow swamp where elephants
> had been rolling and bathing . . . passing over these places was difficult, for their
> great footmarks, in which you could have placed a bamboo armchair, were filled
> with water, and the rest of the ground was rolled hard and slippery; above all
> those elephants left their ticks behind them. I will not enlarge upon this subject,
> nor on the leeches, but I shall never forget either . . . an experience in the great
> tidal swamp we struck south west of Ndorko which connected with the Rembwe. We

waded two hours through it, up to our chins all the time, and came out with a sort of astrakhan collar of leeches, which we removed with trade salt.

Collecting fish in tidal areas brought with it the serious threat of getting trapped at low tide in the pools that were home to crocodiles. She related the following account of one such entrapment:

> You cannot get out and drag your canoe across stretches of mud that separate you from it [the river] because the mud is too unstable a nature and too deep... most of your attention is directed to dealing with ... crocodiles and mangrove flies, and with the fearful stench of the slime around you. . . . [O]n one occasion . . . [when] a mighty Silurian . . . chose to get his front paws over the stern of my canoe, and endeavored to improve our acquaintance, I had to retire to the bow, to keep the balance right, and fetch him a clip on the snout with a paddle, when he withdrew, and I paddled to middle of the lagoon, hoping the water there was too deep for him or any of his friends to repeat the performance.

Kingsley made the first ethnographic studies of the Fang, or as she called them to lessen their fearsome reputation, the "Fan." She wrote of her first meeting with them, "I must say that never—even in a picture book—have I seen such a set of wild wicked-looking savages as those we faced this night, and with whom it was touch and go for twenty of the longest minutes I have ever lived." But, she was quick to point out, "One by one I took my old ideas derived from books and thoughts based on imperfect knowledge and weighed them against the real life around me, and found them either worthless or wanting." She described the Fang as "full of fire, temper, intelligence and go, . . . but, I ought to confess, people who have known him better than I do say he is a treacherous, thievish, murderous cannibal. I never found him treacherous or thievish, and I like him better than any African, as a tribe, I have yet met. He is a cannibal, not from superstitious motives like the negro tribes; he just does it in his common sense way. Man's flesh, he assures

KINGSLEY RELISHED THE RISKS SHE TOOK, WRITING, "WHILE I WAS IN THE ISLANDS I HEARD VERY DREADFUL ACCOUNTS OF THE DANGER AND HORRORS OF TRAVELLING IN WEST AFRICA, AND I FELT I MUST GO—JUST FEMININE CURIOSITY. . . . I WAS INFATUATED WITH THE PLACE, AND SPENT A LONG TIME THERE, IN KA CONGO, WANDERING UP AND DOWN. THIS WILL BE TAKEN FOR A SIGN OF INSANITY ON MY PART, FOR THE DISTRICT IS CONSIDERED ONE OF THE WORST IN WEST AFRICA."

MARY ESPECIALLY LOVED THE MANGROVE SWAMPS AND TRIED TO CONVEY HER FEELINGS FOR THIS DIFFICULT LANDSCAPE TO HER READERS AT HOME. SHE WROTE: "I SHALL NEVER FORGET ONE MOONLIT NIGHT I SPENT IN A MANGROVE SWAMP. I WAS NOT LOST, BUT WE HAD GONE AWAY INTO THE SWAMP, SO THAT THE NATIVES OF A VILLAGE WITH AN EVIL REPUTATION SHOULD NOT COME ACROSS US WHEN THEY WERE OUT FISHING. WE HAD GOT WELL IN, ON TO A LONG POOL OR LAGOON; AND DOZED OFF AND AWOKE. . . . I DREAMILY FELT I HAD SOMEHOW GOT INTO A WORLD THAT WAS ALL LIKE THIS . . . NOW AND AGAIN THE STRONG MUSKY SMELL CAME THAT MEANT A CROCODILE CLOSE BY, AND ONE HAD TO ROUSE UP AND SEE IF ALL THE CREW'S LEGS WERE ON BOARD."

me, is very good, and he wishes I would try it."

Her first night in a Fang village was spent in the chief's hut, where she observed that "every hole in the side walls had a human eye in it and I heard new holes being bored in all directions; so I deeply fear the chief, my host, must have found his palace sadly draughty." Later that same evening,

[I] curled up on the boxes with my head on the tobacco sack, and dozed. Waking up I noticed the smell in the hut was violent . . . knocking the ash off a smoldering bush-light that lay burning on the floor, I investigated, and tracked it to . . . bags . . . I shook its contents out in my hat, for fear of losing anything of value. They were a human hand, three big toes, four eyes, two ears, and other portions of the human frame. The hand was fresh, the others only so so, and shriveled. Replacing them I tied the bag up, and hung it up again. I subsequently learnt that although the Fans will eat their fellow friendly tribes . . . yet they like to keep a little something belonging to them as a momento. This touching trait in their character I learnt from Wiki [her guide] . . . still it's an unpleasant practice when they hang the remains in the bedroom you occupy.

She summed up her understanding of their beliefs, saying,

It is impossible . . . to touch upon the immense variety of ceremonial surrounding soul affairs in this . . . "land of the living thronged with the dead;" and you must remember that, of the throng of spirits, these dead men's souls are only a very small section for almost everything in West Africa has a soul, trees, rivers, weapons &c., thus among the Congo-Française tribes, it is held that in the matter of medicine, the soul of the medicine combats with the soul of the disease, and so on.

Mary's denunciations of the efforts of Christian missionaries to convert the natives did not win her any support at home. Most Europeans at the time believed that Africans were a race that had not developed beyond childhood. Kingsley presented the Africans as people similar to Europeans, with equally valid—and moral—belief systems, who furthermore were less materialistic and more spiritual than the Europeans. The missionaries, she said, acted as if the Africans were an empty jug they could fill with their "second-hand rubbishy white culture." She realized their teachings were having a devastating effect on the lives and culture of the native Africans.

Mary undertook her third trip to Africa in 1900, knowing it would probably be her last. She volunteered to nurse South African Dutch colonists—the Boers—captured by the English, in their squalid detention camps. Four months after she arrived she caught a deadly fever and was buried at sea.

BEBE BWANA

MAY FRENCH SHELDON
AMERICAN EXPLORER • 1847–1936

IN THE LAST HALF of the nineteenth century, Africa was still the "dark continent," with large areas of its territory unmapped. Tribes in many regions had not been subdued, and from their initial contacts with Arab slavers and Western explorers, they were often (and wisely) hostile to foreigners. Diseases against which outsiders had no immunities had been named but not cured. Roads and even trails were almost nonexistent. But these very obstacles made Africa an irresistible challenge to adventurers. Most, of course, were men, but one of the more remarkable, unconventional, and brave of these explorers was a middle-aged American woman by the name of May French Sheldon, who in 1891 planned and led an expedition to East Africa. For her it was not enough just to follow the trail of the male explorers. Her aim was to prove that women could do whatever men could do.

MAY SHELDON IN A TRAVELING PALANQUIN THAT SHE HELPED TO DESIGN.

eccentric. Sheldon had her own ideas on how to express the respect she felt for the natives. For instance, in order to "meet the men of tribal importance in their own sultanates, as a woman of breeding should meet the highest officials in any land, under any circumstances, and be civil and polite for favors granted," she adopted a ceremonial costume which, among other things, consisted of a spangled ball gown and a voluminous blond wig.

The astonished (and perhaps amused) natives renamed her Bebe Bwana, "Woman Master," and a delighted London press took up the title in satirical articles. But there was a seriousness to her travels. Unnoticed by *Punch* (which had a field day lampooning her), May contributed learned papers on little-known topics such as the navigation of Lake Chala, and she made some of the first ethnographic studies of African

For her trek from the port of Mombasa, across the territories of some thirty-five tribes, up to the towering peak of Kilimanjaro, May engaged 138 porters. Thinking her at best eccentric or more likely mad, the British authorities in East Africa tried to prevent her departure. Possibly they had good reasons for this, but the one they put forth merely infuriated her: they declared that East Africa was no place for a lady. That was bad enough but worse was to come. What she saw as she moved inland of the relations with the natives caused her to comment that the British and German policies were "unnecessary, atrocious, and beyond the pale of humanity."

She was right, but an impartial observer would have to admit that the British, at least, had a point in thinking her

women and children. It is the latter work which today stands out as a major accomplishment. Along with her contemporary Mary Kingsley, Sheldon was among the first white people to describe Africans and African culture sympathetically.

On the basis of her first successes, May organized a second expedition to the Belgian Congo in 1894 and a third to Liberia in 1905. She went on, she explained, because exploration gave her "very much thought, and imagination thrilled my brain with the ineffable pleasure, which I had craved, and sought for years, of being the first to visit a place undefiled by the presence of man before."

Recognition of her pioneering studies came in 1892 in the form of election, then a very rare honor for a woman, to membership in the Royal Geographical Society.

Walk Straight on Following Your Heart's Desire

ALEXANDRA DAVID-NÉEL

FRENCH EXPLORER • 1868–1969

ABOVE: ON HER JOURNEY TO LHASA, DAVID-NÉEL CROSSED ON FOOT MANY HIGH MOUNTAIN PASSES SUCH AS THIS ONE AT KUM ZUM.

OPPOSITE: ALEXANDRA DAVID-NÉEL SITTING OUTSIDE THE HERMITAGE 13,000 FEET HIGH IN THE HIMALAYAS. IT WAS HERE THAT SHE SPENT TWO YEARS STUDYING TIBETAN BUDDHISM WITH A HERMIT CALLED THE GOMCHEN OF LACHEN.

THE GREAT GREEK POET Kaváfis has told us that life is a journey, not a destination. For Alexandra David-Néel, the French explorer, life was both: she experienced a series of fascinating and transformative journeys through exotic lands, culminating in reaching the forbidden city of Lhasa in Tibet. But for her, the journey was also an inner quest, searching for enlightenment through the teachings of Buddhism. And her true destination was within.

Alexandra David began her life in Paris. As a child, she "craved to go beyond the garden gate, to follow the road that passed it by, and to set out for the Unknown." As she writes in her book, *My Journey to Lhasa,* "this 'Unknown' fancied by my baby mind always turned out to be a solitary spot where I could sit alone, with no one near, and as the road toward it was closed to me I sought solitude behind any bush, any mound of sand, that I could find in the garden."

As a young woman seeking her true path, she studied philosophy and religion, becoming attracted to the beliefs of the Theosophical Society. She also began to make journeys: she traveled on foot through the mountains of Switzerland at the age of seventeen. Later, in Paris, she appeared to settle down, studied music, and eventually became an opera singer. But her wanderlust did not die, and she used her singing to make travel possible; during her twenties she toured throughout Asia and spent a year in India. At thirty-six, she married Philip Néel, an engineer, and settled in Tunis. But the mundane life of a businessman's wife left her feeling depressed and empty. With the encouragement of her husband, Alexandra set off alone in 1911 to return to India. She planned to be gone for eighteen months. Her husband waited twenty-four years for her return.

David-Néel traveled through India and up into the region of Sikkim, a small, mountainous country surrounded by India, Nepal, Bhutan, and Tibet. There she met Sidkeong Tulku, the sovereign of Sikkim; her close relationship to him opened doors for her to Buddhist monasteries. While in Sikkim, she also met the Dalai Lama, who was impressed with her knowledge of Buddhism and encouraged her to learn to speak Tibetan. The monks of Sikkim awarded Alexandra the great honor of appointing her a female lama and presented her with the traditional garnet-colored robe. It was during this time that she met Aphur Yongden, a young monk who was assigned to her as a servant. The pair became inseparable and David-Néel eventually adopted the young man as her legal son. They would be together until his death in 1955.

In 1914 her life's path led her to the solitary spot she had yearned for as a child, a hermitage thirteen thousand feet up in the Himalayas. For two years, she lived sequestered in a cave and studied with the hermit called the Gomchen of Lachen. This holy man taught Alexandra the art of *tumo* breathing. The practice of

tumo is a spiritual one, a meditation on the fire that burns within the self. It is said to raise the body temperature sufficiently to allow one to live in the harsh cold of the mountains without protection. While meditating, David-Néel would breathe out anger, pride, and laziness and breathe in pure spirit. During meditation, she also found herself detaching from her past life and discovered inner resources of great courage.

Upon leaving the hermitage in 1916, she journeyed to Japan, Korea, and western China to visit Buddhist holy sites. She settled in a Himalayan monastery and remained there for two and a half years, until February 1921, translating a Tibetan Buddhist manuscript. But always she was "haunted by the song of the wind in the solitude," and yearned to return to the mountains of Tibet. Indeed, the secret city of Lhasa provided a metaphor for her own internal quest; it was a place protected by many obstacles and hardships, a destination never before reached by a Western woman. For her, it was a place that, once glimpsed, would reveal a golden, transcendental splendor. It would take her three more years to attain this vision.

The story of her journey to Lhasa is one filled with cold, illness, and hardships. Alexandra was turned back in her first attempt to reach Tibet in 1922 because foreigners were forbidden to enter the kingdom. This only served to intensify her determination. On her second attempt, with Yongden, she took unmarked mountain pathways to avoid detection. In 1923 they began their journey on foot across the Gobi Desert. They followed meandering rivers and crossed mountain passes at eighteen thousand feet. David-Néel traveled through lands that no Westerner had ever seen before, collecting information about the people and geography of the region. In November she discovered the source of the Po River. Upon reaching the border of Tibet, Alexandra and Yongden abandoned their belongings and, dressed as a beggar and a monk, thus continued through the Himalayas. In February 1924 David-Néel and Yongden finally beheld the golden rooftops of the Potala Palace, at the center of Lhasa. They entered the holy city of Lhasa during a New Year's festival and a fortuitous rainstorm. The chaos it created allowed them to mingle with the crowd, and they successfully remained hidden for two months. Alexandra shared her experience of her journey in *My Journey to Lhasa*, which was published in 1927.

In May 1925 she returned to a world eager for her story. Now a celebrity, David-Néel settled with Yongden in Digne, in the south of France. She wrote more than thirty books and articles on the subject of Buddhism, serving as a bridge of understanding between the cultures of East and West. Her travels and stories inspired James Hilton, author of the best-seller *Lost Horizon*, with his vision of Shangri-La. In 1969 France recognized her achievements as an explorer by bestowing upon her the country's highest award, the Legion of Honor, commemorating her triumphs on a bronze medal. Alexandra chose the inscription "Walk Straight on Following Your Heart's Desire."

David-Néel was one hundred years old when she decided to renew her passport for a planned journey to America. It was not to be. In the summer of 1969, with her health failing, she told her secretary that God had spoken to her and revealed to her "the nothingness of all that was myself." Her journeys, both inner and outer, were nearing completion. Alexandra died on September 8, 1969, just short of her 101st birthday.

The pageant moved in a fairy setting. Under the blue luminous sky and the powerful sun of central Asia the intensified colours of the yellow and red procession, the variegated bright hues of the crowd's dresses, the distant hills shining white, and Lhasa lying on the plain at the foot of the huge Potala capped with glittering gold—all these seemed filled with light and ready to burst into flames. Unforgettable spectacle which alone repays me for my every fatigue and the myriad dangers that I had faced to behold it!

OPPOSITE: DAVID-NÉEL TRAVELED TO MANY REMOTE AREAS AND HOLY PLACES IN THE EARLY PART OF THE 1900S. HERE IN THE MOUNTAINS OF CHINA, A EUROPEAN WOMAN WAS CLEARLY AN UNUSUAL SIGHT. THE CARTS IN THE FOREGROUND CONTAIN HER PERSONAL ITEMS, INCLUDING A WASHTUB.

As a woman I was first of all interested in the life of these other women of the plains and forest. Being a woman, and a solitary traveler, I was able to win their confidence and by the greatest tact, patience and perseverance make them my friends. . . . I listened to them with a feeling of awe and admiration, always with interest and often with profound respect.

TOP LEFT: DELIA AKELEY STANDING UNDER THE TUSKS OF THE FIRST ELEPHANT SHE SHOT DURING HER COLLECTING EXPEDITION FOR THE AMERICAN MUSEUM OF NATURAL HISTORY. SHE ONCE WROTE: "I'M ALWAYS FRIGHTENED IN THE JUNGLE—ALWAYS PREPARED FOR A VIOLENT DEATH. I NEVER GO WITHOUT TAKING ALONG THE MEANS TO END IT QUICKLY IF I AM MORTALLY HURT. BUT I LOVE IT."

LEFT: PROGRAM FROM A LECTURE ON ONE OF AKELEY'S AFRICAN EXPEDITIONS.

ABOVE RIGHT: IN HER NOTEBOOK, DELIA LISTED THE SUPPLIES SHE PLANNED TO TAKE ON HER SOLO EXPEDITION TO THE BELGIAN CONGO, INCLUDING BAKED BEANS, SARDINES, AND MARMALADE.

OPPOSITE: DELIA AKELEY IN HUNTING GEAR.

Congo Dreams

DELIA JULIA DENNING AKELEY

AMERICAN EXPLORER OF AFRICA

1875–1970

WHEN DELIA Denning was a girl of thirteen, she ran away from her parents' farm in Beaver Dam, Wisconsin, and never saw her family again. Making her way to Milwaukee, she met a young taxidermist and sculptor named Carl Akeley. Delia was fascinated by his work and began helping him to prepare and mount his specimens. She continued to assist him when he went to work for the Field Museum in Chicago, and when he was hired by the American Museum of Natural History in New York to create the Hall of African Mammals, Delia, still his assistant, was by then his wife.

In 1905 and again in 1909–1911, the Akeleys went on museum-sponsored expeditions to Africa to hunt the animals they would exhibit. On these expeditions Delia not only had to manage the camp, care for her often ailing husband, and hunt food for themselves and the porters, but she also had to shoot and preserve the specimens destined for the museum. She did all this and found time to observe the animals around her. She developed a fascination for monkeys and in her observations determined that they communicated with each other, thus anticipating the much later work of primatologists.

She divorced Carl soon after the end of World War I and began to plan her own expedition back to Africa. While sponsorship for expeditions did not come easily for women, Delia's previous success on her expeditions convinced the Brooklyn Museum of Art to commission her to collect specimens and artifacts in central and eastern Africa. Akeley returned to Africa in 1924 at the head of her own expedition:

> *Finally in the summer of 1924, I was in a position to organize an expedition of my own and return to Africa for the purpose of living with the natives. . . . Ever since my first experience with the primitive tribes of Central Africa twenty-two years ago, I have had the firm conviction that if a woman went alone, without armed escort, and lived in the villages, she could make friends with the women and secure authentic and valuable information concerning their tribal customs and habits.*

At the age of fifty, Delia became the first woman explorer to cross Africa from coast to coast. It took her eleven months to tra-

verse Kenya, starting from Lamu on the Indian Ocean, move through Uganda into the Belgian Congo, and float down the Congo River to Boma and on to the Atlantic coast. Describing her expedition to Kenya collecting specimens along the Tana River, Delia said:

> *The first part of my journey was made in dugout canoe, traveling inland up the Tana River from the Indian Ocean. I hunted in the thorn scrub along the banks for specimens, preserving and caring for the skins myself. I made photographs and developed the negatives. Securing camels from the Somali, a hostile, nomadic tribe, I proceeded across the arid desert country which lies between the Tana River and Abyssinia, marching by moonlight to avoid the heat of the day.*

Intrigued by the elusive pygmies, whom she had heard were living in the Ituri Forest in the Congo, she continued on her journey in search of them. Though extremely shy of white men, who had treated them very badly, they readily accepted the visit of a woman. Akeley lived with them in the forest for several months and took fifteen hundred photographs and thousands of feet of film of the pygmies, almost all of which have sadly disappeared.

ABOVE: DELIA STANDING BEHIND AN ELEPHANT SHE HAD JUST SHOT FOR THE AMERICAN MUSEUM OF NATURAL HISTORY.

LEFT: AKELEY'S EXPEDITION WITH PORTERS STOPPING TO REST IN THE SHADE. THE FEATHERS ON THEIR HATS HELPED TO CAMOUFLAGE THEM WHEN HUNTING.

Delia witnessed the devastating changes Africa underwent in the later part of the twentieth century, as wild animals were hunted to the edge of extinction and jungles and savannas were torn down to make way for the burgeoning human population. Her work in educating people about the Africa she loved lives on in the museum exhibits she helped create.

MRS. CARL
AKELEY

(Mary L. Jobe Akeley)

Wife of the Great
African Explorer
& Scientist, the late

CARL
AKELEY

presenting in

MOTION PICTURES
& COLORED SLIDES

AFRICA

Three Separate Lectures on The Bright
Side of the Once Dark Continent. The
Accounts of Her Expeditions with her
Famous Husband and On Her Own.

ILLUSTRATED BY HER OWN AND CARL
AKELEY'S FAMOUS GORILLA MOVIES

From Canada to the Congo

MARY LEONORE JOBE AKELEY

AMERICAN EXPLORER • 1878–1966

FEW OF THE VISITORS to the magnificent Hall of African Mammals at the American Museum of Natural History have ever heard of the woman who helped make it possible. But the work of Mary Jobe Akeley, Carl Akeley's second wife, has given millions their best and most authentic view of African wildlife.

Born on a farm in Ohio in 1878, Mary Jobe grew up to be a tall, strong, and determined woman. Farm life endowed her with stamina and endurance, qualities that would later serve her well in both the Canadian Rockies and the Belgian Congo. She graduated from Scio College in Ohio in 1897, went on to Bryn Mawr, and eventually received a master's degree in history and English from Columbia University. Although she decided to pursue a career in education, her real love was exploring. When not teaching, Mary rushed off to the Canadian Rockies where, over the course of more than ten expeditions, she mapped the mountains and studied the Native American tribes. On one expedition, in 1913, she rode horseback for thirteen hundred kilometers to photograph and study the Gitskan and Carrier Indians. She noted, "They told me I was the only white woman to witness the potlatch [ceremony of gift exchange]." The Indians gave Jobe the name Dene-Sczaki, or "man-woman," in tribute to her abilities.

Maps of the west at that time had large blank spaces labeled "terrain features unknown." Mary filled in one of them. In 1914 she set off into the Canadian wilds to find a magnificent peak she had heard tales of but had never seen on any map. "Here was a chance," she wrote, "to see what on the government maps was only a blank white spot." Why do it? She said that the challenge of discovery "gave immeasurable satisfaction . . . these things thrilled us. They were sufficient reasons for us going." This excitement of discovery comes out in all her writings. Climbing toward the peak of what would later be called Mount Sir Alexander, she wrote, "A huge ice peak, sheer and terrible, rose straight in front of me. . . . As I looked the great ice-field above us was rent by a mad avalanche, which plunged down over the rock cliffs directly in our path." In honor of her epic struggle to explore and map the wilder parts of British Columbia, she was elected to the Royal Geographical Society in 1915, just two years after they opened their doors to women.

Believing strongly that the education of young girls should include learning to live with nature, Mary went on to start a summer camp for girls in Mystic, Connecticut. For sixteen years, she brought in explorers to lecture about their experiences, and through one of these she met Carl Akeley, the renowned explorer, naturalist, inventor, sculptor, and taxidermist, who was then on the staff of the American Museum of Natural History in New York.

Jobe became the second Mrs. Carl Akeley in 1924. It was perhaps as much a partnership as a romance. Almost immediately after the wedding, the Akeleys began planning a major expedition to Africa. Their goal was to collect the speci-

ABOVE: MARY JOBE AKELEY, CONTEMPLATING THE SUNSET OVER A RIVER. SHE WROTE: "AS A LITTLE GIRL, IN THE HILLS OF EASTERN OHIO . . . I USED TO TRAMP THREE MILES A DAY TO SCHOOL OVER THE STICKY CLAY ROADS IN SPRING AND THE FROZEN CLODS IN WINTER, AND I SELDOM MISSED A DAY. AND ALWAYS I WAS DREAMING DREAMS. THE OFTEN DISAGREEABLE PRESENT I PUT ASIDE. THE FUTURE HELD ME ENTHRALLED. HISTORY AND GEOGRAPHY BECAME MY FAVORITE STUDIES. I SOON LEARNED ABOUT STRANGE PEOPLES AND ABOUT EVERY RIVER, LAKE AND MOUNTAIN. . . . I DETERMINED TO DO THINGS IN THE GREAT WORLD FAR BEYOND OUR QUIET FIRESIDE."

OPPOSITE, TOP: AKELEY IN AFRICA, SURROUNDED BY A GROUP OF NATIVES.

OPPOSITE, BOTTOM LEFT: AKELEY EXPLORED AND MAPPED THE WILD MOUNTAIN RANGES OF BRITISH COLUMBIA. HERE, A GROUP WORKS TOGETHER AT THEIR CAMPSITE.

mens necessary to complete the last six dioramas of the Hall of African Mammals. They sailed in 1926, with a team of botanists, artists, and supporters. Tragedy struck, however, when Carl Akeley died suddenly soon after their arrival in Africa.

After Akeley's burial at the site of his last effort, Mary returned to New York in 1927, heartbroken but resolved to finish their African hall; the American Museum agreed and appointed her special advisor and assistant to the Hall of African Mammals.

Not only did Akeley leave his project uncompleted, but he left bitter enmity between Jobe and his first wife. Delia Akeley felt that the great project for the American Museum of Natural History was at least partly hers. She had contributed many of the specimens and had worked hard for years with Carl developing the African Hall. The mutual hostility between the two women was painful for their friends and colleagues, but, ironically, it may have worked to the benefit of the preservation of the African legacy.

What Carl and Delia had begun, Delia and Mary continued in their separate ways. They both collected material for the hall's dioramas, and for both it was meticulous and arduous work. Animals had to be observed and photographed in their natural habitat in order to accurately position them, and then they had to be killed. The animals had to be measured, have plaster casts made of their bodies, be painstakingly

skinned and preserved with their cleaned bones, and then hermetically sealed and packed for shipping back to New York. In addition, since each diorama was to have as many as fifty plants and other natural elements, these also had to be photographed, collected, casted, and then preserved and packed. Finally, artists were put to work in New York painstakingly painting the backgrounds for each scene. The success of this effort is apparent in the powerfully realistic scenes that have continued to draw crowds to the Hall of African Mammals ever since it opened in 1936.

Jobe received many honors in recognition of her efforts but she was not content to sit back and bask in her achievements. She not only led several more expeditions after finishing the hall but broadened the scope of her activities to promoting game parks, a biological research station, and a sanctuary in the Belgian Congo open only to scientists and dedicated to protecting the gorillas and the pygmies. It took until 1967 for Dian Fossey to succeed in establishing the scientific research center that Mary had sought.

Mary Jobe Akeley made her last expedition to Africa when she was sixty-eight. She died in 1966 in Mystic, Connecticut. In recognition of her work, the Geographical Board of Canada named a mountain, "Mount Jobe," in her honor.

TOP: AKELEY CROSSED THE WAHPUTIK ICE FIELD DURING ONE OF HER EXPEDITIONS IN THE CANADIAN ROCKIES IN THE EARLY 1900S.

ABOVE: MARY AND CARL AKELEY WHILE ON AN AFRICAN EXPEDITION.

LEFT: MARY AND CARL SHOT MANY ANIMAL SPECIMENS THAT WERE TO BE DISPLAYED IN THE AMERICAN MUSEUM OF NATURAL HISTORY'S HALL OF AFRICAN MAMMALS.

OPPOSITE: THE CANADIAN ROCKIES.

Strolling on Alone, Hatless

FREYA MADELINE STARK

ENGLISH EXPLORER • 1893–1993

FREYA STARK was celebrated in her lifetime as the quintessential explorer. Though often suffering from poor health, she sallied forth, usually alone, by camel, by horse, or by foot to explore what she called the "blank spots on the maps" of Persia, Arabia, and Turkey. Not only were her accounts of her travels inspiring and witty, but she laced her observations of the people and land with fascinating historical vignettes. She wrote more than fourteen books of history, exploration, and memoir.

Freya's parents were first cousins who loved to travel and led unconventional lives, traits they passed on to their eldest daughter. Born in Paris, she was carried over the Dolomites by basket before she could walk; though she was raised like a nomad, she eventually learned to call both the English moors and the Italian mountains home. Freya entered university—her first formal education—just as World War I was starting.

In 1921, Freya moved to San Remo, Italy, where she decided to raise vegetables to support herself. There she met an old Capuchin monk who taught her Arabic. She wanted to learn Arabic because, she presciently said, "the most interesting things in the world were likely to happen in the neighborhood of oil." Eventually she mastered Arabic enough "to go out and practice in its own habitation." In 1927 she sailed East. "The life I left behind me," she recalled, "had given, without my knowing it, some of the necessary ingredients for travel. In the first place I learnt to rely on myself . . . perhaps this is the most important of all assets a traveller can possess, for it minimizes barriers . . . and endurance."

Soon after her arrival in Lebanon she had a transformative experience in the desert. She wrote, "Camels appeared . . . I stood in ecstasy among them . . . I never imagined that my first sight of the desert would come as such a shock of beauty and enslave me right away." After seven months in Lebanon and Syria she sailed home realizing that "the whole of my future must be rearranged."

ABOVE: FREYA STARK IN ARAB DRESS.

RIGHT: STARK PHOTOGRAPHED THIS CARAVAN IN THE WADI HADHRAMAUT, ARABIA, IN 1935.

It is, I believe, a fallacy to think of travellers' qualities as physical. If I had to write a decalogue for journeys, eight out of ten virtues should be moral, and I should put first of all a temper as serene at the end as at the beginning of the day. Then would come the capacity to accept values and to judge by standards other than our own. The rapid judgement of character; and a love of nature which must include human nature also. The power to dissociate oneself from one's own bodily sensations. A knowledge of the local history and language. A leisurely and uncensorious mind. A tolerable constitution and the capacity to eat and sleep at any moment. And lastly, and especially here, a ready quickness in repartee.

Stark returned to the Middle East in 1929, determined to make it her home. Not having much money, she boarded with an Arab shoemaker's family, an unorthodox thing for a young Englishwoman to do. Some people thought that she was a spy while others defended her as merely an eccentric. But her daily associations with Arabs helped her to master Arabic. Soon she began to tackle Persian to prepare for her first expedition.

She was to make two expeditions to Persia, crossing the "blank spot" between Luristan in western Persia, to the Valley of the Assassins on the Caspian coast. Traveling toward the Caspian, Freya looked for archaeological ruins and dug whenever possible. The months she spent in Persia, in "the unmapped hills and rivers, the saucer plains enclosing little worlds whose voice is never heard beyond their borders," resulted in her first book, *The Valley of the Assassins*. Exploration, she found, causes "that tightening of the heart, which comes with the remoteness of beauty, just beyond the possible footsteps of man."

Back in England after her Persian expeditions, Stark was awarded some of the most prestigious awards in the field of exploration. The Royal Geographical Society bestowed upon her the Back Grant, and she was the first woman to receive the Burton Medal of the Royal Asiatic Society. During this time she also discovered that she could be an immensely popular lecturer, endearing herself to English audiences with remarks like "I used to walk on ahead of my miserable guide, because even a bandit would stop and ask questions before shooting when he saw a European woman strolling on alone, hatless."

Freya next set her sights on southern Arabia, an area that had been recently engulfed in tribal warfare. For that reason, and because of its remoteness and harsh deserts, the region had been effectively cut off from the West. Interested in discovering and exploring the early centers of the spice and incense trade, she organized two expeditions between 1935 and 1938. On the first she caught measles and had to be evacuated just short of her goal. Over the years while on the trail, she also suffered heart attacks, malaria, and dengue fever and was near death many times.

During World War II, Stark worked for British intelligence in Aden, Cairo, and Baghdad. Her major coup was establishing what she called a fifth column—the Brothers and Sisters of Freedom—a semisecret pro-British support group of local citizens in Egypt. After the war, and a brief detour into marriage, Freya set her sights on Turkey. She would write three books about her years of exploration there. Using historical personalities such as Alexander the Great as her guide, she explored ancient routes. When she was in her late seventies, a television crew from the BBC took her on an expedition down the Euphrates River to revisit places she hadn't seen in fifty years. Dauntless, she kept planning expeditions: to Afghanistan to see a newly discovered archaeological site and, at age eighty-six, a horseback trip around the Annapurna mountain range in Nepal.

Despite a lifetime marred by ill health, Stark lived to be one hundred years old. Her last years were spent in Italy in the mountains she had loved since her childhood. She managed to have an immensely successful life, despite the lack of financial or governmental support for her explorations. She transformed her often solitary experiences into books that combined the vast sweep of history with tangible descriptions of the landscape, communicating the sense of wonder it inspired in her. "The lure of exploration," she said, "still continues to be one of the strongest lodestars of the human spirit, and will be so while there is the rim of an unknown horizon in this world or the next."

DESERT QUEEN

GERTRUDE MARGARET LOWTHIAN BELL
ENGLISH EXPLORER • 1868–1926

GERTRUDE BELL rose to international prominence during World War I as one of the most powerful women in the British Empire. She had lived in the Middle East for years learning Arabic and Persian; discovering, exploring, and excavating archaeological ruins in the desert; founding the archaeological museum in Baghdad; and, most important, forging a network of relationships with the Bedouin tribes throughout the Arabian deserts. At the outbreak of the war Gertrude was recruited by British intelligence and quickly rose to the senior position of Oriental Secretary to the British High Commissioner. Her numerous books and articles, hundreds of letters, and thousands of photographs are a rich chronicle of the first decades of the twentieth century when the Levant changed from a mosaic of medieval desert fiefdoms to a region of modern states.

Born into a wealthy family, Bell grew up in the English countryside. Like most girls of her class she was tutored at home until she made the unusual decision to go to Oxford University. After she graduated, she traveled to Persia (Iran) in 1892 to visit an uncle who was then the British ambassador. Her first book, *Persian Pictures,* was about her impressions of that country. Gertrude was an active, intelligent girl and traveling to Iran whetted her appetite for adventure. Over the next few years she traveled around the world twice; her climbing exploits in the Alps earned her recognition as a mountaineer. But she longed to return to the Middle East and finally did so in 1901. Her first expedition was in 1905 through the Syrian deserts, a trip that resulted in her second book, *The Desert and the Sown.*

Bell became an accomplished archaeologist and published monographs on her discoveries in the desert along with thousands of her photographs. She excavated and drew the plans of the ruins of Byzantine and Christian churches, then spent several years searching for ancient ruins in the desert, labor that laid the groundwork for her role in World War I. She knew the lay of the desert so well that the Royal Geographical Society awarded her its Gold Medal for exploration.

As the Oriental Secretary to the British High Commissioner, Bell was influential in establishing Iraq as a nation, with her friend Faisal as the king. In her position of authority, she drafted many of the laws for Iraq and was instrumental in setting laws regarding education for women. Despite her tremendous achievements, however, her personal life was troubled, and in 1926 Gertrude committed suicide in Baghdad.

ABOVE: BELL TAKING MEASUREMENTS OF UKHAIDIR, A SIXTH-CENTURY PALACE SHE DISCOVERED IN IRAQ WHILE MAPPING ARCHAEOLOGICAL SITES IN MESOPOTAMIA.

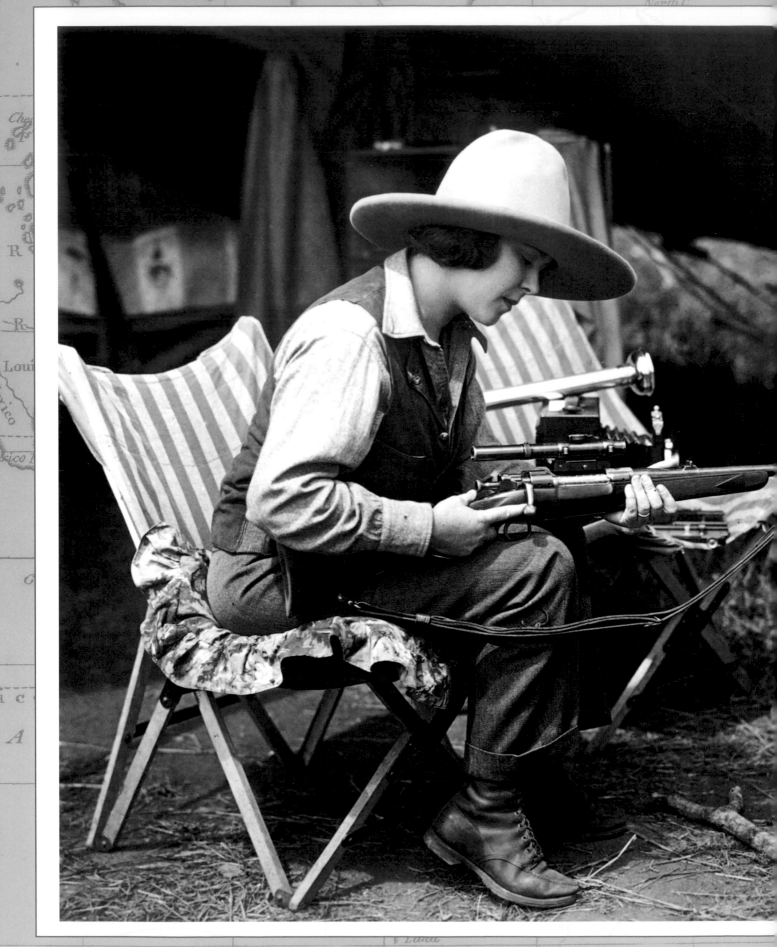

She Lived Adventure

OSA LEIGHTY JOHNSON

AMERICAN FILMMAKER • 1894–1953

IN THE FIRST HALF of the twentieth century Osa and Martin Johnson were two of America's most celebrated explorers. They traveled to remote South Sea islands and trekked in unmapped parts of Africa to create some of the first documentary films about wild animals and tribal peoples.

Born and raised in Chanute, Kansas, Osa Leighty was fifteen when she went to a lecture given by a young photographer, Martin Johnson, about his recent adventures in the South Seas with the novelist Jack London. It was a fateful meeting: Osa was just sixteen when she married Martin. They immediately embarked on a tour of the Midwest—Martin lectured and Osa sang—to raise money for a film they wanted to make about the cannibals on Malekula Island in the Pacific Ocean.

Martin had heard stories about the fierce "Big Nambas" of Malekula—the same people the English entomologist Evelyn Cheesman would stay with twenty years later. Relations between white colonials and the local tribesmen were then at an all-time low. The whites often raided the shores of the islands to kidnap men to work on their plantations. In retaliation the Big Nambas caught and killed as many foreigners as they could. When the Johnsons arrived in Malekula in 1917, they met some seemingly friendly natives of the Big Nambas tribe who invited them off the relative safety of the beach—and their boat—into the jungle. Busy with their cameras, the Johnsons did not realize their danger. Suddenly they were seized as prisoners. The miraculous appearance of a British gunboat in the bay far below caused the Big Nambas to release them. The Johnsons ran for their lives, crashing through the jungle, stumbling down the cliff side, and racing across the sand with angry, perhaps hungry, warriors in hot pursuit and managed to reach their boat with their precious canisters of film intact. The film that came from this encounter, *Among the Cannibal Isles of the South Pacific,* turned out to be a great success.

TOP: OSA IN CAMP WITH A LEOPARD SHE SHOT AND HER DOG.

ABOVE: OSA FILMS GAME IN THE ABERDARE MOUNTAINS OF KENYA.

OPPOSITE: OSA CHECKS HER GUN IN CAMP.

The couple returned to the South Seas in 1919 with a large support staff—a safety precaution—to make their next film, *Cannibals of the South Seas.* Bravely, they returned to the scene of their near disaster the year before and set up a movie projector and screen on the beach. The Big Nambas were astonished not only to see a film, which was a novel experience for them, but to see themselves projected on the screen. They invited the Johnsons—this time as real guests —to their village. Included in the footage Osa and Martin shot for *Cannibals of the South Seas* were scenes of a cannibal feast, which guaranteed the success of the film in America.

Back in New York, they fortuitously met Carl Akeley, husband first of Delia and then Mary Jobe Akeley, who had just invented a new movie camera for use in the field. Akeley suggested the Johnsons turn their attention to Africa and use his camera there to film wildlife. He pointed out that this type of film would have invaluable educational uses as well as serve as an important document of the animals he realized

OSA JOHNSON WROTE LYRICALLY: "FOR DAYS WE MARCHED BEHIND OUR ANCIENT GUIDE OVER SOME OF THE ROUGHEST COUNTRY I'VE EVER CROSSED. FOR ANOTHER DAY WE CLIMBED STEADILY, AND THEN, COMPLETELY WITHOUT WARNING, WE WERE AT THE EDGE OF A HIGH CLIFF OVERLOOKING ONE OF THE LOVELIEST LAKES I HAVE EVER SEEN . . . A TANGLE OF WATER-VINES AND LILIES—GREAT BLUE AFRICAN LILIES—GREW IN THE SHALLOWS AT THE WATER'S EDGE. WILD DUCKS, CRANES AND EGRETS, CIRCLED AND DIPPED. ANIMALS MORE THAN WE COULD COUNT, STOOD QUIETLY IN KNEE-DEEP WATER AND DRANK. IT'S PARADISE."

would soon be endangered.

Martin and Osa traveled to Africa to search for and film the continent's great herds of elephants, zebras, wildebeests, and other animals. They trekked for weeks through the northern Kenyan territory, an area unfortunately already hunted out, until they chanced upon a volcanic crater where thousands of animals congregated around a vast pool of water, a place they aptly named "Paradise." Their first African film, *Trailing African Wild Animals,* was a huge success; they decided to return to Paradise for an extended period of time to make films of big-game animals.

After filming in Paradise for four years, the Johnsons went to the Serengeti Plain for a year to film lions. "We worked with lions; we ate and slept with their roars all round us. At times, with good reason, we feared the great tawny cats, but . . . grew, as Carl said we would, to respect and love them." Obtaining pictures of lions at the kill was difficult since the beasts generally ate at night. To get night

ABOVE: OSA WITH THE WIVES OF A BIG NAMBA LEADER ON MALEKULA ISLAND, VANUATU (FORMERLY THE NEW HEBRIDES) DURING THEIR EXPEDITION TO THE SOUTH PACIFIC.

OPPOSITE: THE JOHNSONS, SURROUNDED BY THEIR PYGMY FRIENDS IN THE BELGIAN CONGO ON A STOP DURING THEIR "FLYING SAFARI" IN 1934.

images they had to build a blind near a kill. Once a lion was feeding they would whistle loudly to get the animal to look up, then shine lights and quickly film it. This was a simple and, as Osa discovered, a very dangerous technique, when she went alone one night to film by a kill site, taking her flashlight, camera, and gun. She waited in a blind by a dead zebra, but as the hours passed she fell asleep. Suddenly she awoke with a start, "hair feeling," she recalled, "like needles of ice." She sensed—and smelled—a lion a few feet away on the other side of her flimsy blind. The lion sniffed around her for some time, then went to feast on the zebra. Osa continued, "He wasn't going to leave that kill for anyone. For some unaccountable reason, or lack of reason, I decided to bolt the blind. Had I thought twice I should have known better, but I acted on impulse." Hearing the lion growling behind her and catching sight of hyenas lurking ahead of her, she ran in a blind panic. Seeing something ahead in the dark, she realized, with enormous relief, that she had found the campsite. Later that morning she went back to the blind to retrieve her

camera and film. The film she shot that night was used in the film *Simba, King of the Beasts*.

The Johnsons explored next the Ituri Forest in the Belgian Congo. Their film *Congorilla* documents the elusive forest-dwelling pygmy tribes and the mountain gorillas. Their last major expedition together was to northern Borneo, where they stayed for two years, canoeing and rafting on the rivers. They were the first to explore the Kinabatangan River region and the first to enter the lands of the Tenggara headhunters and document their lives. As in Africa, they spent much time trying to film elusive animal life, including elephants, crocodiles, and orangutans.

After Martin's tragic death in a plane crash in 1937, Osa continued her travels, and in Africa made the films *I Married Adventure* and *Jungles Calling*. She also wrote several best-selling books about her experiences. The teenage bride who had braved cannibals in the South Seas, the woman who had spent years filming wildlife in Africa, and the wife who had survived the plane crash that killed her husband, died peacefully in her sleep in a New York City hotel in 1953.

An Independent Explorer

SUE HENDRICKSON

AMERICAN EXPLORER • B. 1949

For more than one hundred years, fossil hunters have scoured the earth looking for the bones of strange beasts that died millions of years ago. Museums have vied for the best finds and have underwritten costly expeditions to build their competitive collections. Most observers would agree, however, that the race has been won, at least for the time being, by fossil hunter Sue Hendrickson. In 1990 she discovered the largest, most complete, and best preserved *Tyrannosaurus rex* to date. At 67 million years old, it is also the oldest known fossil of this formidable creature. Hendrickson's discovery in the wind-swept badlands of the Cheyenne River Indian Reservation in South Dakota caused a sensation. The dinosaur, named Sue for its discoverer, was eventually bought at auction by the Field Museum in Chicago for a record-breaking $8.36 million.

Finding a fossil is both an art and a game of chance. Sue discovered Sue the *Tyrannosaurus rex* one very hot day while she was walking in the South Dakota desert. Noticing some "bone scraps" on the ground, she scanned the rock face above her. There, sticking out of the rock, were three large vertebrae. As she later recalled, she immediately realized that "they were definitely from a carnivore and definitely big, which for that area could mean only one thing," *Tyrannosaurus rex!*

Although the year's field season was almost over, her team did not want to leave such a potentially

OPPOSITE AND ABOVE: SUE HENDRICKSON WITH THE *TYRANNOSAURUS REX* SHE FOUND WHILE FOSSIL HUNTING IN SOUTH DAKOTA IN AUGUST OF 1990. IT WAS ULTIMATELY NAMED SUE, AND IS HOUSED TODAY AT THE FIELD MUSEUM IN CHICAGO.

TOP: A GREAT DOG LOVER, SUE BROUGHT HER DOGS, SKYWALKER AND TORMENTA, WITH HER TO HONDURAS IN 1997.

important find. With only picks and shovels, they went to work. Thirty feet of rock lay between them and their quarry. "Fossil hunting," Hendrickson remarked laconically, "is physically tedious, hard and uncomfortable work. People who love fieldwork are considered nuts. You have to have a high tolerance for pain. I totally love what I do and couldn't do anything else."

Sue's life belies the notion that the age of the intrepid explorer is over. She is independent and unaffiliated to university or institution. Alone, she has roamed deserts and mountains, seeking remains of the ancient past. Despite the fact that she holds no degree, she has become a recognized expert in fossil entomology and has made spectacular paleontological finds, including Sue. And as though these activities were not enough, she has also been searching underwater for historically important shipwrecks.

Born and raised in the suburbs of Chicago, Hendrickson was at heart a child of the wild. She remembered herself as the only girl who cried when it was time to go home at the end of summer camp. Ruminating on her future, ten-year-old Sue "wanted to be a vet and a missionary, and because I always liked languages, I thought I'd be a translator. But whatever it was I knew that I would be traveling."

By the age of seventeen she had dropped out of school to live and travel on her own. Casting about for a means of supporting herself, she did not realize that what she really enjoyed doing would lead to her life's work. "I liked to look for things, and at a young age I got rewarded for digging through garbage. Even into adulthood I would walk with my head down and I always found things."

The first things Sue began finding were in the ocean. Her father had taught her to swim, but for her, swimming was not just a hobby or sport; it became a means to a larger end. "When I left home," she recalled, "I realized I needed to be outside. I am ecstatic when I am outside and away from people and finding things." She eventually made her way to the Florida Keys, where she took up diving to earn a living. At first she collected shells and tropical fish to sell. As she remembers those days, they were marked by "being underwater for eight to nine hours crawling under coral heads searching for 'neat little critters.'"

But "neat little critters" soon began to lose their attraction. Much more exciting were the remains of wrecked ships. To compensate for her lack of an academic background, she developed the habit of "latching on to the expert in the field that I loved and learning everything from him, soaking it up like a sponge."

A turning point in her life came the day she saw a man selling pieces of amber, the several-million-years-old fossilized tree sap in which small insects are often preserved. Hendrickson became intrigued by these insects and was soon on her way to the Dominican Republic where she "went up into the mountains to look for amber, and that is when I became hooked on fossils. I began to thoroughly educate myself about amber. Eventually my curiosity was stronger than my timidity and I found an entomologist who educated me about the insects." She began collecting amber for museums. Eventually she became recognized as an expert on amber and many of her pieces were exhibited by the American Museum of Natural History.

In 1985 Sue began fossil hunting. "Amber is what started me with fossils," she recalled. From amber's "micro-fossil people," she moved to what she called "mega-fossil people," the paleontologists. Not only did she love being out in the wilds looking for fossils, but she had a real flair for finding them, an intuitive understanding of where they would be.

Hendrickson's underwater work has taken her around the world. She has participated in major marine excavations in the Philippines, Egypt, and Cuba. "I have dived thousands of hours," she said. "There is always something exceptionally beautiful and new. The *San Diego* shipwreck in the Philippines was the best shipwreck of my life. It sank in 1600 while fighting pirates. It was intact fifty-two meters down. Other divers and typhoons hadn't touched it. We found four hundred-year-old chicken eggs, human bones, and intact ceramics."

Sue has been diving in the harbor of Alexandria, Egypt, since 1992, exploring Cleopatra's sunken palace. "We are cleaning, mapping, recording and documenting the ruins. Our goal is to put glass tunnels underwater so people can walk through the palace. It is more impressive to leave it under water." She has also been working in Cuba since the late 1970s with a Cuban marine archaeologist as his international spokesperson. Using magnetometers she has been helping map the coastal waters around the island to document its wrecks; so far, her team has discovered twelve. She dreams of finding the ship that sank in 1521 carrying the treasure Cortés had looted from the Aztec lord Montezuma.

Discovery of an object is, of course, wonderful, but what really excites Hendrickson is what that discovery can teach us. "I went through an evolution. At first I wanted to keep everything. Then I wanted to match up the best pieces to the best scientist and the best museums. Having it isn't what is thrilling, finding it is thrilling. When the discovery is documented that is thrilling. That is the moment. It gets you through the long dry periods. The moments keep coming and that's what keeps me going." It is explorers like Sue Hendrickson who remind us how little we know about the world and how much is left to be discovered.

ABOVE: DIVING IN THE PHILIPPINES IN 1996, HENDRICKSON EXPLORES THE WRECK OF A CHINESE VESSEL THAT WENT DOWN AROUND 1600.

BELOW: HENDRICKSON, SCUBA DIVING IN THE WATERS OFF CUBA, HOVERED OVER A CANNON FROM A SPANISH WRECK.

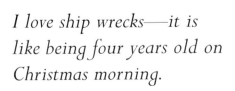

I love ship wrecks—it is like being four years old on Christmas morning.

A Life in the Field

ANNIE MONTAGUE ALEXANDER

AMERICAN NATURALIST • 1867–1950

"AS YOU MAY KNOW," Annie Alexander wrote to a friend, "the death of my father in 1904 when we were in Africa together was a terrible shock to me. I felt I had to find something to do to divert my mind and absorb my interest and the idea of making collections of West Coast fauna as a nucleus for study gradually took shape in my mind." Annie was to find her diversion in collecting fossils and amassing a collection, numbering in the tens of thousands of specimens, of mammals, birds, amphibians, and plants. This formed the core collection of the Museum of Vertebrate Zoology, which she founded in 1908 at the University of California at Berkeley.

Alexander grew up on the island of Maui in Hawaii. Her father was a successful sugarcane planter who not only bequeathed her a fortune but instilled in her a love of adventure. He taught her how to ride, shoot, and camp in the wilds—skills she would later use in her life as a naturalist. In her youth she took many trips with him, including a sailing trip through the South Pacific, a sixteen-hundred-mile bicycle trip through Europe, and finally the fateful safari in Africa, during which they trekked more than eight hundred miles and shot many animals. Annie was such a good shot that she helped supply meat for fifty-one porters. Apparently they had a glorious time together, but six months into the expedition, her father was struck by a falling boulder and died.

In 1900 Alexander began attending lectures at the Uni-

We sleep again in the open and the freshness of the early morning puts new life into me. I like to watch for the first rays of the sun touching the range west of us, the rapid shortening of shadows until the world is ablaze with light . . . I like a show of energy in nature even when nothing happens.

versity of California on paleontology given by John C. Merriam. She wrote, "I have not missed a lecture. I like it more and more, this study of our old, old world and the creatures to whom it belonged in the past, just as much as it does to us today. Perhaps the study is all the more interesting because it is incomplete, there is so much yet to find out—I think it is wonderful." Her fascination prompted her to approach Merriam to ask him if he could help her organize her own fossil-hunting expedition in exchange for which she would donate all the specimens to the university. He agreed. She wrote of that first trip in 1901 to Fossil Lake, Oregon, "The fever for amassing these strange treasures might make of me a collector of the most greedy type." Eventually some of the fossils Annie found would be named for her, including a new species of the extinct quadruped, shastasaurus, which Dr. Merriam later named *Thalattosaurus alexandrae*. That trip began her great interest in fossils, which would result in her founding and endowing another museum, the Museum of Paleontology, in 1921.

Over the next decades Alexander spent a good part of each year on expeditions. Not only did she fund these trips, she also collected specimens—and she cooked.

We sat in the dust and sun, marking and wrapping bones . . . night after night we stood before a hot fire to stir rice, or beans, or corn or soup, creating the best dinner

we could out of our dwindling supply of provisions. We sometimes wondered if the men thought the firewood dropped out of the sky or whether a fairy godmother brought it to our door, for they never asked any questions.

At the same time she was engaged in paleontology, Annie continued studying living animals. She realized that in order to understand the most ancient animals, a collection of more recent animals was needed to trace their evolution. The best collections of vertebrates were on the East Coast, making it difficult for West Coast scientists to use them. She also realized that many animals were fast disappearing from the landscape and samples of them should be preserved in museums. By 1910, for example, the beaver once plentiful in California was nearly gone.

Annie wanted her new museum to have a collection to rival the best on the East Coast. She joined with enthusiasm in the task of collecting. Of her first trip to Alaska to hunt bears, she wrote, "My object in making this collection is to form the nucleus for a collection representing the fauna of the Western coast." With her friend and colleague Louise Kellogg, the self-taught naturalist, she went on numerous expeditions, many of them lasting months at a time, throughout the mountains and deserts of the west and to Alaska, shooting and preparing thousands of animals over the years. One of the largest of Alaskan bears was named for her: *Ursus alexandrae.* Over the course of forty years she and Kellogg gathered a collection of more than thirty-four thousand fossils, animals, and plants, of which more than sixteen thousand specimens went to the Museum of Vertebrate Zoology.

It was in character that this intrepid and persistent explorer celebrated her eightieth birthday in 1947 by going on a three-month collecting trip to Baja. It was to be her last expedition: Alexander died after a stroke in 1950. Having devoted her talents and inheritance to support scientific endeavors, Annie left a legacy in the two museums she founded and eventually endowed, in the substantial collections she created for three museums, and in the more than fifteen fossil, plant, and mammal species named for her.

This page: these photographs of Alexander on expedition record her hard work and determination. She wrote of her exploration, "Think what countless and diverse races have walked or crawled or swum on the earth and become extinct since that remote time! It is a thrilling thought to the fossil hunter that he is privileged to reach back in the world's history and uncover some of its ancient pages."

Rhapsody in Blue

STEPHANIE SCHWABE

GERMAN-AMERICAN GEOMICROBIOLOGIST • B. 1957

ABOVE: STRENGTH IS REQUIRED TO SUPPORT ALL THE GEAR NECESSARY FOR SAFE CAVE DIVING. WITH HER EXTRA OXYGEN TANKS, SCHWABE CAN WEIGH UP TO 320 POUNDS WHEN SHE ENTERS THE WATER.

OPPOSITE: DESCENDING THROUGH A CRACK INTO THE LOTHOREN BLUE HOLE CAVE SYSTEM, EAST END, GRAND BAHAMA ISLAND.

FLOATING, SWIMMING, suspended underwater far above the floor of a dark cavern, Stephanie Schwabe observes the world as it was ten million years ago. It is a world before the glaciers melted and the oceans rose, filling these caves with seawater; a world where bats hung from the ceiling of the vast chambers, and the ceaseless dripping of calcite created a forest of stalagmites. Within this realm dwell species not yet known to science. Small creatures float past her and are illuminated in her light. Today this silent world is preserved in an eight-mile system of underwater caves meandering below the surface of the busy island of Freeport in the Grand Bahamas. The portals to this ancient world are called the Blue Holes, and they lend their name to Schwabe's nonprofit organization, The Rob Palmer Blue Holes Foundation.

Steffi came to the Bahamas in 1993 with her husband, the renowned cave diver Rob Palmer, to pursue their common dream: the exploration of the Blue Holes underground caves. As diving partners and scientists, they studied the caves and came to understand their importance. "This cave system is unique in the world," Schwabe explained, "because a lot of it is still pristine." Discovered more than thirty years ago, 90 percent of the caves remain unexplored. This makes them rich natural laboratories in which to study past world climates and ocean levels, the role of living organisms in cave formation, and the destructive effects of environmental pollution.

When Palmer lost his life in a diving accident in the Red Sea in 1997, the task of carrying on the work fell to Steffi: no one was better qualified. She was, in fact, the scientist of the team all along: she had two degrees in geology and was well on her way to a Ph.D. in geomicrobiology. She was also a champion swimmer and experienced cave diver, and she had the determination, integrity, courage, and passion required of an explorer. "Cave diving is a lone activity," Schwabe said. "You have to believe in yourself and be able to rely on yourself alone."

Her childhood prepared her for this life of self-reliance. Born in Germany, she came to the United States as a child. Unable to speak English and isolated from classmates, she filled her lonely time by pursuing her curiosity about the natural world. On summer sailing trips out of Boston, Steffi would sit on the deck staring at the dark water and wonder what was below the surface. The budding scientist would lose herself in the blades of grass in the lawn, observing the tiny insects that scurried about in the ground. Schwabe learned early to look beyond the visible world, to discover the secrets that lie just beyond. Her sense of wonder continues today, when she discovers unknown species or encounters the mysteries of the past.

In 1999, Schwabe's discovery quest led her to the Black Hole of Andros. First spotted by her late husband more than twenty years earlier as he flew over in a small plane, the Black Hole was originally thought to be a very deep underwater cave system. Steffi's later discovery would be of great scientific importance concerning cave systems in the Bahamas.

Her first opportunity to explore the Black Hole came in 1998, thanks to a film

crew that supplied the necessary Cessna 206 seaplane to get them to this remote location. What was originally thought to be the entrance to a deep, clear cave turned out to be something quite different. Schwabe discovered that what was responsible for the blackness was in fact "a one-meter-thick layer of what could be called a hot, primordial soup composed of bacteria. Without a guideline, light did not penetrate this layer, nor could I see where my bubbles were heading, leaving me totally disoriented; like floating in a dark room." Because of the limitations of this small expedition, they were forced to turn back and return home with more questions than when they'd arrived.

A year would pass before Steffi had the opportunity to return to the Black Hole. Thanks again to a film crew, this time from the Discovery Channel, she was prepared to descend through the ominous soup, one ingredient of which was hydrogen sulphide, a very potent and poisonous gas. Placing a guideline in the center of the Black Hole, she began her descent into the nearly boiling hot, sulfurous black layer, slowly disappearing from view. "I had waited a long time to get to this point and I was not turning back, so I waved good-bye and continued to descend into what appeared to be hell. After what seemed like an eternity, I suddenly found myself in crystal clear, and what now seemed very cold, water."

Schwabe and her dive partner now floated about a Martian landscape composed of a slimy purple gelatinous layer of sediment. She took samples of the floor in clear plastic tubes, and measured the depth of the sediment with a meter stick. This microbial mat exceeded the full length of the stick. Because of her courage and quest for knowledge, totally new species of bacteria may have been discovered.

Steffi's hope is that The Rob Palmer Blue Holes Foundation can evolve into both a state-of-the-art cave research laboratory and an educational facility. Although she is entirely dependent on contributions to support her research, her passion for exploration and love of the work keep her going. While she admits to being a determined and outspoken advocate for the preservation of the Blue Hole cave system, the politics involved can be daunting at times. In her outrage at the careless destruction of one of the caves by developers, Schwabe wrote that "the human race has forgotten what is valuable in life. That true wealth is not money and material things, but the health of your environment and the understanding of it!"

Steffi has dedicated herself to fighting to save not only the fragile ecosystem of the Blue Holes, but other environmental causes as well. She has taken her passion to the courtroom, and begun an environmental law degree. "The idea of litigating environmental cases and using the money to support my research has a nice appeal to it. Many times I will not be able to stop industry, but I can make them pay for their errors."

You do not know where up or down is and in a cave system, that is most important to know.

To Catch a Falling Star

In the Field with Scientific Explorers

I N MAY 1893, Lord Curzon, the president of the Royal Geographical Society (RGS), wrote a letter to the *London Times,* hotly opposing the proposal that women be allowed to join as members. "We contest in toto," he huffed, "the general capability of women to contribute to scientific geographical knowledge. . . . Their sex and training render them equally unfitted for exploration."

In the past century, exploration became increasingly driven by scientific goals, rather than being motivated by the quest for riches or the propagation of faith. Men led these expeditions and published the results. In fact, their dominance began even before the explorers set forth, since men ran the scientific organizations and underwrote the expeditions. Little by little, however, women have emerged as full participants. This has seldom been an easy struggle: they have often been excluded or have found it difficult to publish their findings in scholarly journals.

The ability of women to pursue a life in natural sciences was aided by two key developments. The first was Linnaeus's introduction in 1760 of a simplified system of classifying plants. One result of the new system was that women were encouraged to study flowers both as a fashionable pursuit and as a way of improving their minds. Some women went beyond collecting flowers in presses and used this socially acceptable endeavor of collecting plants as an avenue to exploration. Naturalist Jane Colden (1724–1766), for example, roamed the American northeast, cataloging more than three hundred new plants according to the Linnaean system.

The other aid to women's participation in the sciences was Darwin's 1858 theory of evolution. From cataloging the flora and fauna, scientists now began the huge project of trying to understand how the natural world fit together in a coherent whole. These two new systems of organizing and classifying life and its evolution opened up opportunities for women to

ABOVE: DURING HER CAREER AS AN ANTHROPOLOGIST MARGARET MEAD SPENT MANY YEARS STUDYING CHILDREN AND FAMILIES ON THE PACIFIC ISLANDS OF BALI, NEW GUINEA, AND SAMOA. HERE MEAD IS SITTING ON A CANOE WITH CHILDREN FROM THE VILLAGE OF PERI ON THE ISLAND OF MANUS, IN NEW GUINEA, IN 1928. FOR HER STUDY OF CHILDHOOD IN MANUS SHE COLLECTED 35,000 DRAWINGS MADE BY CHILDREN AND HUNDREDS OF HOURS OF INTERVIEWS AND OBSERVATIONS. THIS RESULTED IN HER BOOK *GROWING UP IN NEW GUINEA.*

OPPOSITE: JANE GOODALL'S STUDY OF CHIMPANZEES IN THE WILD HAS LED HER TO FIGHT FOR THE CAUSE OF THOSE IN CAPTIVITY. HERE SHE SITS WITH GREGOIRE, A CHIMP SHE FOUND IN 1988, WHO HAD LIVED ALONE IN THE BRAZZAVILLE ZOO IN CONGO SINCE 1945. HAIRLESS, STARVING, AND NEARLY BLIND, HE REMAINED ISOLATED BEHIND A DOOR TO HIS ROOM THAT HAD RUSTED SHUT. HE WAS MERCIFULLY MOVED TO ONE OF GOODALL'S SANCTUARIES AND NOW SHARES AN OUTDOOR EXERCISE AND PLAY AREA WITH COMPANIONS.

PRECEDING PAGES: DIAN FOSSEY AND PORTERS HEADING FOR HER NEW CAMP ON THE SLOPES OF MOUNT VISOKE IN THE VIRUNGA MOUNTAINS OF RWANDA.

participate in various scientific fields as artists and collectors. They entered geology, for example, as illustrators. Orra White Hitchcock produced illustrations of rocks and fossils for publications in the 1830s and 1840s. Botany, in the days before photography, particularly lent itself to artistic endeavor. This is how Maria Martin (1796–1863) made her way in her chosen field. She was a naturalist who painted the background flowers and trees of many of John James Audubon's famous bird paintings. Still other women became collectors for wealthy individuals or institutions. Amalie Dietrich (1821–1891) virtually swept up every sample of Australia's flora and fauna she found for scientists in Europe. Mary Anning (1799–1847) indulged in her passion for paleontology by scouring the countryside around her home in Lyme Regis, England, for fossils that she also sold to support her family. Her discoveries include an ichthyosaurus in 1811 and a pterodactyl in 1828.

Almira Hart Phelps (1793–1884) was one of America's best-selling authors. Her 1829 *Lessons on Botany* sold an astonishing 250,000 copies and inspired the opening of nature centers across America. But knowing how hard it was to break through the barriers facing women, she ruefully reflected, "Females in particular are not expected to enter into the recesses of the temple of science; it is of but late that they have been encouraged to approach even to its portals, and to venture a glance upon the mysteries within."

And it wasn't only in the natural sciences that women had to overcome chauvinism. Archaeology was, in some ways, an even more difficult redoubt against the entry of women. After graduating from Smith College, Harriet Boyd Hawes (1871–1945) went to Athens to pursue her interests in archaeology. Because she was denied permission to work on established sites, she chose to excavate on Crete, which was then virtually unknown to archaeologists. Her discoveries there of Minoan sites were so sensational that she eventually became the first woman to lead a large-scale excavation in the field.

Anthropology was born in the mid-nineteenth century when missionaries and government officials and then a few scholars sought to record the strange habits of primitive peoples. Gradually, an attempt was made to understand how their societies fit together. But since many societies segregated men and women, or at least assigned to them very different daily routines, much of what actually happened was

ABOVE: LOUISE ARNER BOYD PHOTOGRAPHED THE GLACIERS OF NORTHERN GREENLAND. THIS IMAGE OF A FJORD, TAKEN IN 1933, SHOWS HER VESSEL WITH THE SNOW-CAPPED MOUNTAINS OF SUESS LAND IN THE BACKGROUND.

hidden to male observers. Clearly, there was a role for women to play in observing, recording, and analyzing native cultures. It was this work to which Alice Cunningham Fletcher (1838–1923) addressed herself. Sitting in on lectures in anthropology at Harvard University, she was inspired to do fieldwork among the Sioux, Omaha, Alaska, and Nez Percé tribes. She went on to help found the American Anthropological Association.

What Alice Fletcher had done among Native Americans, Margaret Nice set out to do among wild animals. The two endeavors were really parts of the same quest, since students of the primitive and the wild assumed that the two were closely related and that understanding one or both would lead to a fuller understanding of human social life. But because missionaries and colonial officials weren't interested in the study of animals, ethology was not as attractive a field for men. The pioneering work of Margaret Nice opened the way to studying the relationship of living beings to their environments. Konrad Lorenz, the Nobel Prize–winning scholar who is often credited with being the founder of ethology, himself paid tribute to Nice as the actual founder of the scientific field, since she made "the first long-term field investigation of the individual life of any free-living wild animal."

Women have had to push their way into the different scientific fields, sometimes going where men did not wish to go or were unable to go. As such, they have brought different perspectives or even a different sensibility to exploration. The eminent paleoarchaeologist Louis Leakey believed that women were in fact better suited to undertaking field studies of primates and other animals. He felt that women are either biologically or culturally adapted to tolerate the daily demands of children and that this made them better able to study animals with the patience and empathy needed to make good observations. Men, on the other hand, might lack patience and seek to impose themselves upon the animals, instead of observing them.

Lord Curzon and his cronies failed to block the emergence of women as scientific explorers. In 1912, after a brief initial experiment in 1892, the doors of the Royal Geographical Society finally opened to women. The Explorers Club of America began admitting women only in 1981. Today women are working in all areas of scientific endeavor. Building upon the fine example of their predecessors, women today have the entire world of science open to them.

The Collector

KONCORDIE AMALIE NELLE DIETRICH

GERMAN BOTANIST • 1821–1891

The discomforts which the heat and mosquitoes bring me are soon forgotten in the feeling of infinite happiness that enters my soul when I find with every step treasures which no one has got before me.

Becoming an explorer is easier if you are young, wealthy, highly educated, and well connected, but Amalie Dietrich was none of those. Her major achievement, amassing the single largest collection of Australia's natural flora and fauna, is a monument to her refusal to be defeated. Amalie Nelle was born in a small village in the German state of Saxony, where her father worked as an artisan. Her mother supplemented the family income by working as an herbal healer, and from her Amalie learned to appreciate plants and their healing power. It was not much of an education, but it gave her a love of plants that would sustain her through the difficult years ahead.

At twenty-four, she married Wilhelm Dietrich, an apothecary who shared his wife's interest in plants. Together they decided to become plant collectors for botanists. Amalie often traveled alone over the European countryside gathering plants, minerals, and insects. Unable to afford any other means of travel, she used a cart pulled by a large and faithful dog who gloried in the name of Hektor.

But her dedication was not shared by her husband. While she was away, he fell in love with another woman. One day Amalie returned to find that she and her young daughter had not only been abandoned but were being turned out of their house. By then forty years old, she was devastated. With a heavy heart she sold off the little her husband had left behind, her cart and her beloved dog. Later she lamented, "When I think back how I traveled through countries with good faithful Hektor. The cart so heavy, the roads often so bad; we had to suffer hunger, frost and heat and always the depressing worries about our daily bread."

On the point of despair, she learned that a wealthy German collector was looking for field naturalists to voyage to the South Pacific to acquire flora and fauna for his museum. Turning to one of the collectors for whom she had often worked, she secured a letter of introduction. In part it said that she had "an unusual talent for her profession, a sharp well trained eye for everything nature has to offer, a great certainty for identifying the collected material. On her long and mainly difficult journeys she has constantly shown great perseverance and bravery."

Taking this letter, she approached the collector, the owner of a Hamburg shipping firm who in the manner of rich amateurs was then building his own private museum. To stock it, Johann Godeffroy sent employees out on his ships throughout the Pacific region to collect for him. Being cost-conscious, he offered Amalie a job at half what he paid the men who worked for him. That was very little but Dietrich was delighted. Not only would she have a steady income, small though it might be, for the first time in her life, but she would be able to educate her daughter, to whom she devoted every penny she could spare.

So it was in 1863, at age forty-two, that Amalie left Hamburg on one of Godeffroy's windjammers, *La Rochelle,* for the long voyage around the tip of Africa for Queensland. The trip was hard and long, but she was thrilled with the prospect of a new life. As she wrote, almost unbelievingly, "I really have arrived in Australia . . . on the long sea voyage there was so much for me to experi-

ence, to see and perceive! How new everything is to me here!"

For the next ten years the outback of Australia was to be her home. She lived in the field, as she collected, preserved, and shipped her specimens off to Germany. Starting off on her first expedition, she wrote her daughter, "I have to learn to look after myself in solitude—With a truly solemn feeling I equipped myself for my first collecting trip in the new continent. I hung the vasculum over my shoulder, put flour, salt, tea and matches in it, put on my big straw hat and set out on my wanderings." She sent back so much material from this first foray that Godeffroy was able to print a sales catalog filled with her specimens.

Over those years, Dietrich amassed the largest collection then known of Australia's flora and fauna. In addition to trees, shrubs, mosses, and algae, she gathered the most extensive collection of birds ever made by a single person. And so rich was her collection of beetles, butterflies, spiders, fish, corals, and marsupials that they are still being studied today.

Amalie spent her last years in Australia in the frontier town of Bowen, where she set up a small zoo to keep the animals she planned to take back with her to Germany. When she finally returned to Europe, her menagerie of exotic Australian animals included a sea eagle and a wedge-tailed eagle, which she gave to the Zoological Gardens in Hamburg. She settled in Hamburg, close to her collections, which she was soon busy cataloging.

Then disaster struck again: the Godeffroy Company went bankrupt and the museum was sold to pay creditors. Out of a job, Dietrich again lost her home. And, though now honored by scientists and even invited to attend their august meetings, she still felt marginalized. Her difficult life had also taken its toll on her relations with her daughter. With "her coarse grey loden costume, with her weatherbeaten but intrinsically distinguished face, she was an object of admiration and curiosity to the young people" but she was estranged from her own family. The daughter she had worked so hard for did achieve a better life and married well but was embarrassed by her mother and saw very little of her after her return to Germany.

Amalie spent her last years in a charitable home for elderly women in Hamburg. Sadly, the least of her collections is all that survives. The best of her samples, the part she sent home to her patron for his museum, along with all of her field notes and letters, were lost in the fire bombings of Hamburg during World War II.

But Dietrich provided rich raw material to the scientists in Europe who were obsessed with cataloging the world's creatures. It is a final tribute to her bravery and skill that several species she discovered were named for her, including the skipper butterfly (*Cephrenes amalia*), a wasp (*Nortonia amaliae*), a species of birds, two species of algae, and a plant (*Acacia Dietrichiana*).

Amalie Dietrich's kit included:

- 1 MAGNIFYING GLASS
- 1 MICROSCOPE
- 25 RETORTS
- 6 INSECT CASES
- 10 REAMS OF PAPER
  RAGS FOR PACKING
- 6 TINS OF ALCOHOL
- 20 POUNDS OF PLASTER OF PARIS
- 20 POUNDS OF OAKUM
- 100 GLASS PHIALS WITH LARGE STOPPERS
- 3 QUIRES OF TISSUE PAPER
- 5 QUIRES OF BROWN PAPER
- 4 FLASKS OF SHOT
- 10 POUNDS OF POWDER
- 1 BOX OF PERCUSSION CAPS
- 2 BOXES OF POISON
- 4 BOXES FOR LIVE SNAKES AND LIZARDS
- 3 CASKS OF SALT
- 1 BOX OF INSECT PINS

Passionate Wanderer

ALICE EASTWOOD

CANADIAN BOTANIST • 1859–1953

IN 1865 ALICE EASTWOOD'S mother died, and because her father was unable to care for his six-year-old daughter, she was sent to live in the Oshawa convent in Toronto. During the bleak years that followed the loss of her family, Alice's only pleasures came in visits to her uncle's farm. On long rambles he taught her to recognize plants by their Latin names. These happy walks, so different from the strict life of the convent, instilled in her a lifelong love of plants, although it was a love that could not be fulfilled for many years.

When Eastwood was fourteen, her father brought her to Denver, where he had a store. To make ends meet, she worked as a nanny and a salesgirl by day while studying at night. With what little time she could squeeze in between, she hiked into the Colorado mountains to collect plants. By the time she graduated from high school in 1879, as class valedictorian, she had already collected many plants for what would eventually become the first herbarium in Colorado.

Alice went to work as a high school teacher, and despite a salary of only $475 a year, she managed to save enough money to purchase botany books. During the summers she roamed the Rockies collecting plants. "What grand times I had in the Southwestern part of Colorado," she later recalled, "wandering around alone over these beautiful mountains."

At that time, wandering off alone in the mountains was something young women simply did not do. And considering how they had to dress, one can see why: ladies were expected to wear elaborate costumes that, in themselves, made exploration almost impossible. Like other early women explorers, Eastwood quickly learned she could not ride sidesaddle on rough wilderness trails or sit astride a mule in a dress. Pants, however, were out of the question. As she later wrote about her time in the field:

> The only woman who was permitted to wear trousers was Dr. Mary Walker in Washington, and she had been a nurse in the Civil War. I had to compromise so I designed and made my own. It was a blue denim and the skirt was fastened to the waist. The skirt was open in front and behind and fastened for walking by buttons and button holes concealed by a flap. When I rode, the buttons on the front were fastened to the holes of the corresponding ones in the back so it made a perfect riding skirt and not so clumsy as the later divided skirt.

In 1887 Alice managed to get hired as the guide in the Colorado mountains for the great naturalist Alfred Russel Wallace, who along with Darwin had developed the idea of evolution. Then she got what must have seemed to her to be her first lucky break: she managed to sell a small piece of property for enough money to be able to devote herself full-time to her first love, botany.

The only outlet at the time for botanical writing in the West was a magazine published in California called *ZOE;* and Eastwood began contributing articles to it about her expeditions and discoveries. Emboldened by this modest success, she embarked upon a much more demanding task, writing a book. Privately published in the 1890s, her *Popular Flora of Denver, Colorado* was a commercial flop. Her father, who had never cared much for her crazy hobby, simply burned all the unsold copies.

But on the basis of her writings, Alice finally secured a paying job in botany, a major triumph at a time when the field was a male preserve. This came about when the publishers of *ZOE,* a couple named Bandergee, who loved botany, invited her to California to help them organize the California Academy of Sciences herbarium. At thirty-three, despite all of the obstacles she had had to overcome, she became the joint curator in botany, and the following year she was named the full curator and the editor of *ZOE.*

Eastwood's daring actions during the horrific 1906 earthquake and fire in San Francisco became legend. When the earthquake hit, forty-seven-year-old Alice rushed down to the Academy of Sciences and discovered that the fire, caused by bursting gas lines, was swiftly approaching. She climbed the shattered stairwell to the collections room. Working swiftly, she made bundles of some of the priceless specimen types and the academy's records and lowered them down by string to the ground below. She had to leave behind to the flames her own collection of botany books and her personal papers.

Used to overcoming adversity, and never one to feel sorry for herself, Eastwood rebounded from the catastrophe. As she said, "I do not feel the loss to be mine, but it is a great loss to the scientific world and an irreparable loss to California. My own destroyed work I do not lament, for it was a joy to me while I did it, and I can still have the same joy in starting it again."

Alice served as curator of botany at the California Academy of Sciences until she was ninety; this position enabled her to explore little-known regions of the West and to venture as far afield as Alaska. Despite never having received a college degree, she wrote more than three hundred articles and collected over three hundred thousand specimens. She also encouraged the research of other botanists, including Ynes Mexia's South American work and Louise Boyd's work in the Arctic. Eastwood truly was one of those indomitable women who not only created themselves by their own efforts and imagination but virtually discovered their fields of endeavor.

ABOVE: EASTWOOD ON HORSEBACK IN YOSEMITE.

TOP: EASTWOOD STANDS NEXT TO A PLANT NAMED FOR HER, *EASTWOODIA ELEGANS,* MAY 24, 1938.

FAR OFF THE BEATEN TRACK

YNES MEXIA

MEXIAN-AMERICAN BOTANICAL COLLECTOR • 1870–1938

YNES MEXIA began her career as a botanical collector when she was fifty-five years old. For the next thirteen years, she roamed through the wilder parts of Latin America to collect 150,000 plants, many of which were then unknown and a few of which are now named for her. It was Alice Eastwood who taught Mexia how to preserve plants in the field. Mexia so impressed the legendary botanist with her meticulous collecting abilities that Eastwood helped arrange her first expedition to Mexico.

At that time, botany was only just establishing itself as a serious academic field, and few institutions considered women to be suitable candidates for the available jobs. Ynes's age and lack of any field experience made her prospects dim. Nevertheless, she refused to accept defeat: she was deter- mined to carve out a new life for herself as a field collector. Once in the field, her challenges had only begun. Collecting and preserving plants was an arduous and demanding task, involving meticulous visual and statistical record keeping. With great care, she photographed and then dried each plant. As Mexia gained experience in the field, she devised her own equipment, boxes "ready to pack two on a mule, weighing with presses, dryers and paper about 75 lb. each." After drying, she would pack the specimens and ship them home. Once back in California she then had the laborious job of sorting, identifying, mounting, and labeling the plants.

By 1927, having proven herself a true professional, she was asked by several herbariums to acquire plants for their collections. In Mexico, Ynes wrote that she had come "to this

ABOVE: MEXIA
IN THE FIELD.

LEFT: YNES MEXIA
KEPT CAREFULLY
TYPED FIELD NOTES.

place because it was the farthest away, most tucked in and hidden little spot I could learn about." During the next seven months she collected thirty-three thousand plants, fifty new species, and one new genera, *Mexianthus Mexianus*, named for her. At fifty-seven, this once sick and depressed woman called herself "a nature lover and a bit of an adventuress" who "never had an accident [and] passed unharmed through localities reported to be infested with bandits, tarantulas and wild animals."

From Mexico's parched highlands, Mexia next plunged into the wetlands of Brazil, embarking upon what she regarded as her life's greatest adventure: a voyage up the Amazon. The first twenty-five hundred miles was by steamer through Brazil to Peru. From Iquitos she traveled upriver by dugout toward a gorge called the Pongo de Manseriche, or the Iron Gateway of the Amazon. She was stranded there by the yearly rains and had to stay for three months in the jungle. Finally she had a balsa raft made so she could float back the several hundred miles to Iquitos. "In the two and a half years that I was in South America . . . I had no accidents and not a disagreeable incident, and that is [a] pretty good record for Latin-American countries where it is said a woman cannot travel alone!" During those fruitful years, she collected some sixty-five thousand plants.

When Ynes made her last expedition to Oxaca and Guerro in southwestern Mexico at age sixty-eight, she had already developed lung cancer. Tragically, before she had had time to write up her field notes, she died in 1938.

But her legacy is still with us. In her thirteen years as a botanical collector Mexia had amassed a collection larger than that of any other woman and had persevered to carve out a career for herself, living a lifestyle she loved.

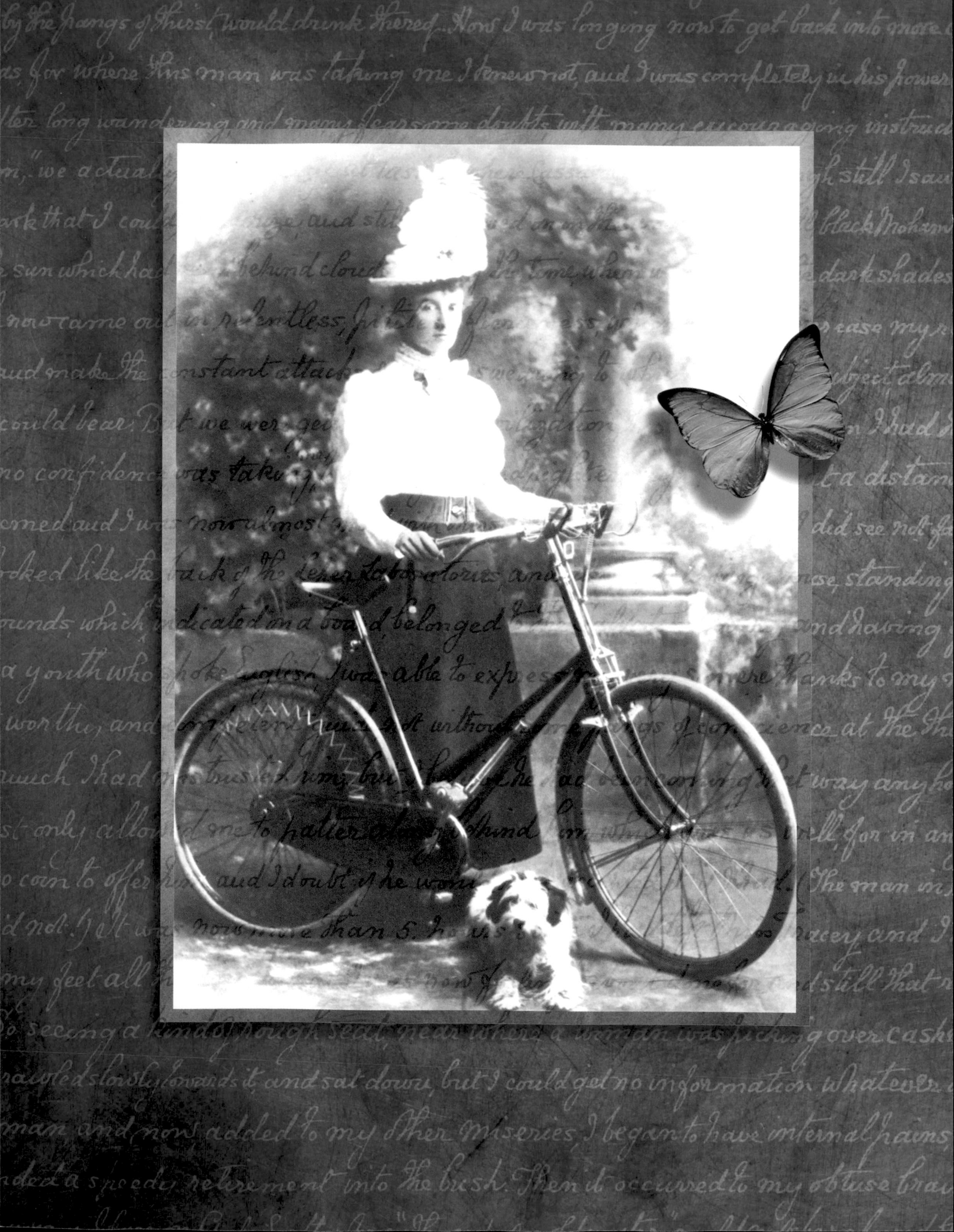

Hours That Are the Sweetest, Pass by the Fleetest

MARGARET FOUNTAINE

ENGLISH COLLECTOR • 1862–1940

Margaret Fountaine began recording her life's experiences on April 15, 1878. It was a practice she would continue for sixty-one years, until shortly before her death in 1940. In precise and measured handwriting she filled twelve enormous volumes of green leather-bound books with more than a million words, extending over 3,203 pages. Fountaine began each year on April 15, describing her joys and her disappointments, her travels and her butterflies. Illustrated with postcards, photos, sections of musical notation, and the occasional pressed flower, they paint a picture of the complex passions and conflicts of a righteous Victorian lady.

From her simple girlhood in Norwich, England, Margaret would follow her passion for butterflies across the world. These delicate insects led her through the Middle East, India, China and Tibet, Hong Kong, Australia, North and South America, across Africa, and into the Caribbean. In Florence, she chased a gorgeous orange butterfly across a hillside; in the Philippines, she searched for the rare *Magellanus;* and in Damascus, she captured the heart of Khalil Neimy, a Syrian dragoman. He was to become her "constant and untiring friend," and together they traveled "over all the loveliest, the wildest and often the loneliest places of this most beautiful Earth." For twenty-seven years they roamed exotic locations in search of elusive butterflies and together they compiled what came to be known as the Fountaine-Neimy Collection, today housed in the Castle Museum in Norwich, England. This impressive collection of butterflies, perfectly preserved and arranged by species/family, is contained in nearly two hundred drawers.

Fountaine had the eye of an artist and the precision of a scientist. Her sketchbooks are filled with exquisite and informative watercolors and illustrations of caterpillars, all meticulously labeled. In order to capture perfect specimens of butterflies, she would often collect caterpillars and carefully raise them herself, so as to avoid damaging the fragile insects with butterfly nets.

The last entry of her diaries was made on July 10, 1939. Margaret carefully lettered the next line, "April 15, 1940." She packed the journals in a black box with a note stipulating that they not be opened until April 15, 1978, exactly one hundred years after the first entry was made. At the age of seventy-seven, Fountaine died in Trinidad with a butterfly net in her hand.

ABOVE: FOUNTAINE SHARED HER PASSION FOR LEPIDOPTEROLOGY WITH KHALIL NEIMY, WITH WHOM SHE TRAVELED THE WORLD FOR NEARLY THREE DECADES.

OPPOSITE AND BELOW LEFT: MARGARET FOUNTAINE WOULD BEGIN EACH YEAR OF HER DIARIES ON APRIL 15 WITH A PHOTOGRAPH OF HERSELF. THE TWELVE VOLUMES, FILLED WITH HER LYRICAL, UNCHANGING PENMANSHIP, ARE ILLUSTRATED WITH PRESSED FLOWERS, PEN-AND-INK DRAWINGS, NEWSPAPER CLIPPINGS, AND PHOTOGRAPHS.

FOLLOWING PAGE, TOP: OVER TWO HUNDRED SPECIMEN DRAWERS ARE FILLED WITH THE FOUNTAINE-NEIMY COLLECTION OF BUTTERFLIES. BOTTOM: IN HER DIARIES, FOUNTAINE PASTED PHOTOGRAPHS OF HERSELF IN THE FIELD IN BUTTERFLY COLLECTING ATTIRE AS WELL AS AT HOME IN ENGLAND, SURROUNDED BY HER SPECIMENS.

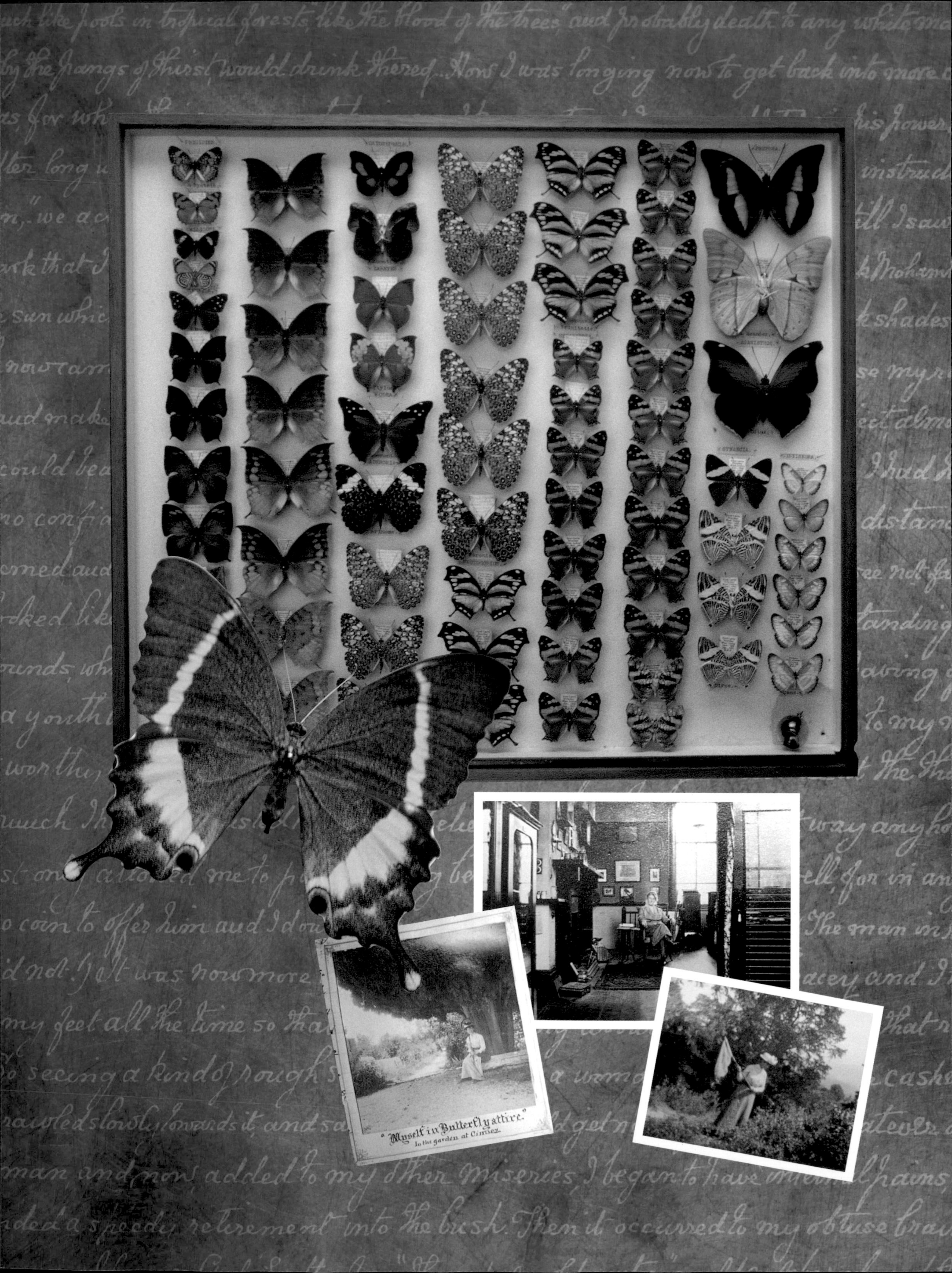
"Myself in Butterfly attire."
In the garden at Cimiez.

WINDOW ON A HIDDEN WORLD

NAOMI PIERCE
AMERICAN BIOLOGIST • B.1954

SINCE THE mid-1970s Naomi Pierce has roamed the Pacific Rim in search of elusive butterflies. She explored miles of caves in the Philippines by lantern light, searching for rare sightless crickets. In the forests of the Cameron Highlands of Thailand she hunted butterflies with the Orang Asli tribesmen. In the waters of the Bay of Thailand

she swam with sea snakes. She searched by dawn's light inside an ancient volcano, Mount Bromo, on the island of Java; on a saltbush in the outback near Mungo, Australia, she discovered two rare species of butterflies. "My favorite field camp," she recalled, "was on the edge of a rainforest in Queensland, Australia, where I stayed in an upside-down water tank. One morning I awoke to find a ten-foot carpet snake draped beside me. There were also quite a few funnel web spiders, which are actually quite dangerous, and seemed to follow me around the camp."

Since Naomi became the Hessel Professor of Biology at Harvard in 1990, and curator of lepidoptera at the Museum of Comparative Zoology, she has concentrated on caterpillars of the butterfly family Lycaenidae and their complex symbioses with ants. Some of these interactions are mutualistic ones in which caterpillars secrete food for ants in exchange for protection against predators and parasites. In others, the caterpillars mimic ant chemical communication signals and are carried into the ants' nest where they feast on the helpless ant brood.

For fifteen years at field stations in Australia, peninsular Malaysia, and Sarawak in Borneo, supported in part by the MacArthur Foundation grant she was awarded in 1988, she studied one such interdependent relationship, that of caterpillars in the Lycaenidae butterfly family with ants and acacia trees. Although the trees contain toxins that usually prevent predation, these caterpillars have evolved a tolerance for the toxins and are able to feed

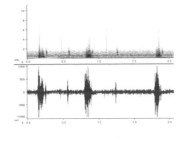

ABOVE: PIERCE USES SONOGRAMS TO PROVE THAT CATERPILLARS COMMUNICATE WITH ANTS THROUGH VIBRATIONS.

on the nitrogen-rich leaves. The caterpillars then secrete food for ants in exchange for protection against predators and parasites. Said Pierce, "This is an example of what has been called 'coevolution,' a reciprocal process in which different species evolve in response to each other."

Pierce demonstrated that the caterpillars communicate with their attendant ants through substrate-borne vibrations called stridulations. One day when she picked up one of the small caterpillars she was studying, she felt a faint buzz, almost like an electrical impulse, traveling along its back. Years after she first reported this phenomenon she was able to use sophisticated listening devices to amplify these vibrations. To her amazement she found the caterpillars produced not only one kind of call, but three distinct vibrations, which she and her students called grunts, drums, and hisses. She and her students are now making studies to determine under what conditions the sounds are made in an effort to decipher their meaning.

As biologists increasingly realize, Pierce's work in the tiny world of butterflies has significant implications for the larger effort to maintain the natural balances upon which ultimately all our lives depend. Until now we have had little way to judge the wider implications of the extinction of any given species, but as her studies show, what happens to any one species can impact disastrously on others.

Her work on the evolutionary history of Lycaenidae butterflies requires collecting fresh specimens in alcohol so their DNA can be preserved. "This has meant re-collecting hundreds of species of these butterflies from Malaysia, to South Africa, throughout South America and Australia. But," she reflected, "the great thing about studying insects is that no matter where you go, whether you speak the language or know the history or culture, you can feel completely at home with insects. It has been a great life adventure."

It Is Not Wise to Show Contempt for Crocodiles

LUCY EVELYN CHEESMAN

ENGLISH ENTOMOLOGIST • 1881–1969

FOR SCHOLARS AND EXPLORERS, the scattered and isolated islands of the South Pacific posed a fundamental puzzle: where did the people and animals who inhabited them come from, and how had they got there? Perhaps, thought entomologist Evelyn Cheesman, insects might help to answer these questions. Using the thousands upon thousands of insects she had collected during her decades in the South Pacific, Cheesman set out to "settle a few questions about the former connection of New Guinea with the other islands and archipelagos of the Pacific." She explained that "for the last ten years my work has been to follow this Papuan element [insect fauna] in the Pacific Islands back to the land of its origin; making collection on islands from which we had no material in the national collection, in order to study distribution of species in that region. . . . [M]y collection of insects made in the Territory of Papua in 1933–34 suggested to me that there must have been formerly older land connected with New Guinea."

As revolutionary as her approach was, the basis for it was laid in her childhood. Evelyn grew up in an upper-middle-class Edwardian home, full of "those carefree happy days soaking in wildlife." Her childhood home, she recalled, had "sheds and outhouses for our experiments in breeding, and Mother allowed us to bring home live things as well as moss and flowers to keep in our nursery. We had old trays on purpose for this. Mother dismissed one young nursemaid who had a tidy mind because she threw away some of our treasures as nasty messes." As a young girl, she collected glowworms to figure out what made them glow. The discovery of a frog that had been buried alive eight feet deep in a chalk pit for perhaps as long as thirty years fascinated her.

When Cheesman grew up, she desperately wanted to become a veterinarian but was told that women were not admitted to vet school. She was delighted—virtually "saved"—to be offered a job as the keeper of the then-dilapidated insect house at the Zoological Society's garden in Regent's Park, London. Once there, she became fascinated by the habits of her innumerable charges. She also discovered she also had a real flair for conveying her excitement to others. This talent would later be exhibited in the dozen books she wrote, wryly detailing her adventures collecting insects in the South Pacific.

Evelyn had always longed to go to the South Pacific. When in 1923, at the age of forty-two, she received an offer to join an expedition, she jumped at the chance. As soon as the group arrived in Tahiti, however, she announced her decision to leave: she wanted to roam and collect on her own. Traveling lightly, with only a string hammock, a few necessities, and some insect trays, she learned to rely on local people. Over the next thirty years Cheesman made eight more solo expeditions to the South Seas. Her family and friends were astonished by this arduous work,

There is always so much to endure at such camps, and that is why people—wise people—do not encamp in tropical forests.

CHEESMAN WROTE: "IT SEEMS TO BE TAKEN FOR GRANTED THAT TO GO ALONE INTO WILD PLACES LIKE NEW GUINEA, AND ENCAMP AS I HAVE DONE AT A LONG DISTANCE FROM ANY CIVILIZED PEOPLE, DEMANDS COURAGE. ACTUALLY IT IS NOT SO MUCH COURAGE THAT IS CALLED FOR BUT ENDURANCE. I SHOULD PLACE INDEPENDENCE FIRST AND THEN ENDURANCE, NEITHER OF WHICH ARE VIRTUES BUT ACQUIRED HABITS. INDEPENDENCE IS REGARDED AS AN UNSOCIABLE HABIT, ESPECIALLY IN A WOMAN, AND THE DICTIONARY DEFINES SELF-SUFFICIENT AS HAUGHTY, WHICH SHOWS PLAINLY THE GENERAL TREND OF OPINION."

since she had always been thought to be physically frail. But she proved to be much tougher than expected and her hardiness was to be a godsend during her years of solitary trekking in the South Sea islands.

There she was subjected to bouts of malaria and dengue fever, and encountered deadly vipers and ferocious spiders. Once while trekking on Gorgona Island, Evelyn tried to cross a glade heavily draped with the webs of the huge Nephila spiders. She thought she could easily break through them but instead quickly became entangled. She wrote:

> The webs clung to me, drawing sheets [of webs] after them till I was brought up short unable to advance another step. Folds within folds clung to my shoulders and arms, and when I stepped backward into what had been a space a moment before my head came against a very large sheet which enveloped my face like an eastern veil. . . . [A]s for breaking the web, all my force resulted only in cutting my fingers . . . I even tried to bite the threads but that was useless. All around hung spiders of all ages, some near my face. I did not think them handsome anymore.

Eventually she found a nail file in her pocket, which she used to painstakingly cut through the webs, strand by strand, over the next several hours, while the spiders awaited their prey. After that encounter she was never without a machete.

And it wasn't just giant spiders that were threatening. Rivers and pools teemed with crocodiles. Once as she was just about to step into a seemingly safe bathing pool, a sizable specimen rose up out of the water, jaws agape. She later recalled that as she fled, she remembered that crocodiles were perfectly capable of pursuing a horse and rider on land for quite a distance.

On her first solo expedition to the South Pacific, in 1928, Cheesman was commissioned to collect insects and small mammals for the British Museum of Natural History. During her year in the New Hebrides she often stayed with cannibals who had rarely been approached—safely—by Europeans. News of her living arrangements—a single, middle-aged white woman living and traveling with cannibals—caused a sensation back in England. She credited her ability to live with the islanders on friendly and safe terms to the fact that "it was they who were in the superior position of offering me instruction. Thus a very special kind of link was forged between us when they found that I did not attempt to press alien ideas on them."

But mutual respect did not exclude her from close contact with the cannibals' dietary practices. Once Evelyn was collecting insects with some young helpers when they got caught in a local skirmish. "The air," she said, "was suddenly full of arrows." When it was all over, she asked her "boy" whether he would have eaten her had she been killed. He replied that of course he would: eating someone had nothing to do with friendship, he explained, rather it had to do with her ghost. The cannibals believed she had a strong spirit and they did not want it haunting

them. Eating her, they believed, would take care of that danger.

Another time she was collecting specimens in the vicinity of a village that had just been attacked by an aggressive cannibal group. A number of its residents had been consumed, and the police had been summoned to arrest the offending cannibals. This was an easy task, Cheesman noted, because in her experience cannibals fell into a heavy torpor after consuming their meal. She walked into the village to see that the English police captain and his native force had already chained together thirteen suspects and were preparing to take them on the long trek to Port Moresby. The captives were singing a "Kill Song," which detailed the events that had just occurred and prepared them to die and share a similar fate. She recalled "nothing that Hides [the police officer] could tell [them] altered their belief that they were all to be killed, [but] whether they expected the white man to indulge in a cannibal feast is mere conjecture."

Cannibals proved to be a far lesser danger to Evelyn than the English officials. The worst calamity she experienced was inflicted upon her by a callous British official in Papua. She had entrusted to his care a priceless collection of orchids, ferns, mosses, and insects that she had spent six difficult months collecting for the British Museum of Natural History. He left the crates outside his headquarters to be soaked in the frequent rains, reducing her specimens to a rotting, soggy mess. She was heartbroken and the London museum never got its collection.

When World War II interrupted her fieldwork in the South Pacific, she helped the Allied forces by supplying them with detailed information on the islands she knew so well. Her maps were especially important to the Allies.

Cheesman never collected a salary for her work and lived off her writing, lectures, and collecting forays. By necessity frugal, she could live for a year in the wild on what other expeditions spent in weeks.

> On my return from any expedition, I would be driven by two necessities, first, to get money towards the next in order to provide personal wants—for I bore my personal expenses—and secondly, to share with the unprivileged my heterogeneous records. For it is indeed a rare privilege to have stayed in the wild mountain areas of New Guinea and to have intimately known the bush people who inhabit them.

The books she wrote describing her expeditions are charming, insightful, and full of lore about the people she encountered. In them Evelyn set a standard for working in wild places that has rarely been matched.

Working there presented some unusual difficulties. I had to become conversant first with local conditions, ghosts and tambu [forbidden] places as well as bush trails. . . . [T]he close proximity of members of hostile tribes resulted in most elaborate precautions being taken to prevent others using the same trail.

TOP: CHEESMAN'S NOTEBOOKS ARE FILLED WITH SKETCHES AND FIELD OBSERVATIONS FROM HER EXPEDITIONS IN THE SOUTH SEAS.

OPPOSITE TOP: CHEESMAN TOOK SHELTER FROM THE FREQUENT RAIN SHOWERS UNDER AN UMBRELLA MADE OF TREE BARK.

Expeditions on Ice

LOUISE ARNER BOYD

AMERICAN POLAR EXPLORER • 1887–1972

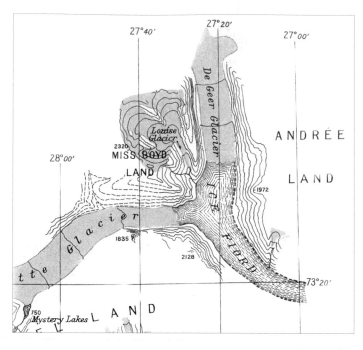

In August 1924, I visited Spitsbergen and the pack ice to the northwest in a small Norwegian tourist vessel. This trip gave me my first view of the Arctic regions and laid the foundations for expeditions subsequently carried out under my leadership.

I N RECOGNITION OF her years of exploration and her contributions to science, there is a region of Greenland named Miss Boyd Land. Louise Arner Boyd was an American polar explorer who led seven expeditions into the Arctic from 1924 to her last venture, a flight over the North Pole in 1955. Her photographic documentation of the coastline of Franz Josef Land, Greenland, and Spitsbergen made possible the first detailed maps of these northern lands. And her maps and photographs were some of the only documents of that region available to the U.S. government during World War II.

Born into a prominent San Francisco family, Boyd came from a world far different from the land of ice she would come to love. From an early age, however, she dreamed of travel and voraciously read tales of explorers. In school she studied photography, botany, geology, and topography to prepare herself for becoming an explorer. She learned how to identify and collect plants from noted botanist Alice Eastwood, who was collecting on the Boyd ranch in Mount Diablo, California; later, in the Arctic, she would make substantial collections for Eastwood, who was then the curator of botany at the California Academy of Sciences.

When Louise was young, explorers were seeking to attain the last great geographic prize—the North Pole. Though Robert Peary and Frederick Cook had each claimed to have reached this goal in 1909, the vast lands and frozen seas above the Arctic Circle remained largely unknown. Boyd had to wait until she was thirty-seven years old—until her parents had died and she had received an inheritance—before she could journey north herself. She had her first view of the far north in 1924, when she traveled to northern Norway and from there chartered a small boat to take her out to the pack ice. Entranced, she wrote, "Far north, hidden behind grim barriers of pack ice, are lands that hold one spellbound. Gigantic imaginary gates, with hinges set in the horizon, seem to guard these lands. Slowly the gates swing open, and one enters another world where men are insignificant amid the awesome immensity of lonely mountains, fjords, and glaciers."

Louise dedicated the ensuing years to planning and leading her own expeditions into the Arctic. Just as she was setting out in 1928 from Norway on board her ship, the *Hobby,* she heard that the famous Arctic explorer Roald Amundsen was missing. She volunteered her boat and joined the international search for his plane. Sailing more than ten thousand miles in three months, she scoured the Arctic ice for signs of life. As she later wrote of her frustrating and fruitless search, "Ice does such eerie things. There are illusions like mirages, and there were times we could clearly see tents. Then we'd lower the boats and go off and investigate. But it always turned out the same—strange formations of ice, nothing more." While the trip was productive for her, enabling her to make a film of the expedition and take more than twenty thousand photographs, Amundsen, sadly, was never found.

Boyd wanted to go where others had rarely been and so set her sights on the eastern coast of Greenland. There some of the ice crust is as much as two miles thick, and glacial activity has created a ragged coast broken by innumerable fjords, many choked with blocks of ice broken off the glaciers. Louise found this landscape as compelling for its beauty as it was challenging to map.

Rugged though her expeditions were, Boyd never sacrificed style: she was determined to live in as gracious a manner as possible. She wrote, "I may have worn breeches and boots and even slept in them at times, but I have no use for masculine women. At sea, I didn't bother with my hands, except to keep them from being frozen. But I powdered my nose before going on deck, no matter how rough the sea was. There is no reason why a woman can't rough it and still remain feminine."

While she believed in living as well as possible in those forbidding conditions, Louise also used her considerable resources to ensure that her expeditions had the latest and best scientific equipment. Because accurate mapping of this very difficult terrain required special tools, she studied photogrammetry, a type of photography that enabled accurate maps to be made where it was impossible to survey on foot. She was also one of the first explorers to use echo sounders. While she was primarily interested in what these sounders could tell her about geology, she discovered that they could detect schools of fish, thus inadvertently providing commercial fishermen with a tool of immense value. But it was in mapping the north that Boyd made her main contribution. Her soundings were used by the American Geographical Society to chart the sea floor near Greenland. She discovered and mapped an undersea mountain range between Bear Island and Jan Mayen Island in the Greenland Sea, which is now called the Louise A. Boyd Bank.

When she wasn't in the Arctic, or back in California planning and preparing for her next expedition, Louise explored other parts of the world. In 1934, for example, she made an extensive photographic survey of the eastern regions of rural Poland to "obtain before it was too late, views of things that are characteristic today but may be gone tomorrow." She was prescient. When the areas were

ABOVE: LOUISE BOYD, 1928. THIS ELEGANT WOMAN ONCE SAID SHE NEVER THOUGHT OF GOING ANYWHERE WITHOUT A HAT UNLESS IT WAS TO THE DENTIST.

OPPOSITE: MAP OF MISS BOYD LAND.

ON HER 1928 SEARCH FOR AMUNDSEN, BOYD WROTE: "THESE EXPEDITIONS FAMILIARIZED ME WITH CONDITIONS OF NAVIGATION IN THE POLAR SEAS AND WITH THE APPEARANCE AND BEHAVIOR OF THE DIFFERENT FORMS OF MARINE ICE AND LED ME TO THE POSSIBILITY OF CRUISING IN MORE HAZARDOUS WATERS, WHERE THE APPROACH TO LAND IS RENDERED DIFFICULT BY THE EXCEPTIONALLY WIDE BELT OF ICE."

overrun first by German and then by Russian armies, the way of life she documented was, as she predicted, gone forever.

Boyd was ostracized by other polar explorers who resented the fact that she was a woman and rich. Their attitude may have hurt her feelings, but she chose to treat them as just one more formidable obstacle. "I spared," she later wrote, "no effort or expense in order to equip every branch of our work to obtain detailed knowledge in difficult areas where time was a factor."

Hers was a lifelong mission of discovery that began in a childhood passion and took her into the frozen northlands. Louise's contributions were finally recognized when the government of Norway awarded her the Order of St. Olav for her gallant search for Amundsen. The prestigious American Geographical Society published three of her books, and the U.S. government honored her with a Certificate of Appreciation in 1949.

ABOVE AND LEFT: ON HER 1933 EXPEDITION, BOYD PHOTOGRAPHED THE MASSIVE ICEBERGS THAT FLOATED IN THE FROZEN SEA OFF GREENLAND. OF IT SHE WROTE, "[A] SEA DOTTED WITH ICEBERGS OR FRINGED WITH PACK ICE AND GREAT FLOES . . . A PICTURE OF SUCH MAJESTY AND ON SO VAST A SCALE THAT NO EXPLANATION NEED BE GIVEN BY ANY EXPLORER FOR WISHING TO REVISIT SUCH A SCENE."

Coming of Age in the South Pacific

MARGARET MEAD

AMERICAN ANTHROPOLOGIST • 1901–1978

Social anthropology, the study of man, has been in a race against time to document the language, belief systems, arts, and social organization of the world's tribal societies before they are lost forever to the global forces of industrialization and homogeneity. Among those who were seized by the need to study primitive cultures while they still existed was the young Margaret Mead, who in the early 1920s was studying at Barnard College with the noted anthropologist Franz Boas. Like others interested in fieldwork, she was looking for a little-known tribal group to study; she picked the inhabitants of Samoa in the Pacific Islands.

In the summer of 1925, when Margaret was twenty-three, she said good-bye to her family and first husband and began a long journey by train across the United States and then by ship across the Pacific, bound for Somoa in the South Seas, with, she said, "all the courage of almost complete ignorance." Until then she had never been on a ship, visited a foreign country, or even spent the night in a hotel by herself, although for the next year she would live alone in a remote Polynesian village. Nearing her destination, a kindly fellow passenger offered to store her ball gowns —a necessity for social life on board ship but useless in the lagoon she was bound for—so the cockroaches would not get at them.

Mead spent most of her first year on the tiny island of Tau, twelve sea miles from the next nearest island. One of the more devastating moments she experienced that year occurred when a hurricane washed over the island. In a letter home she wrote, "Then came the calm. It lasted only a minute, but the air seemed choked with coconut leaves so stiff they might have been wired. . . . And then the other edge of the storm, charging straight over the sea from Ofu, hit us, tearing that little calm into a thousand pieces. After that it was just a question of how long before the house went." Quickly Margaret and her companions hacked a hole in a cement water tank and crawled inside to escape the storm's fury. The village and all its crops were completely destroyed.

Mead loved her experience with the Polynesians. To express her unity with the people, she wrote as she was leaving:

> Have I not three dark spots on a white dress, spots come from the blood of the pig which was sacrificed for the birth feast of the tenth child of Mealeaga? Have I not woven polas for the great guest house of Siufaga and argued with the members of the Aumaga—the young men—on the advisability of burning down what is left of Ofu, because the people of Ofu stoned the meddlesome pastor of Tau out of the village . . . ?

Margaret returned home, published her first book, *Coming of Age in Samoa*, and became one of the youngest curators at the American Museum of Natural History, a position she held until she died. In the ensuing years Mead journeyed to New Guinea, Manus, Bali, and the American West to conduct fieldwork, observing how

different cultures raised their children. She said of those years, "Six times in the last seventeen years I have entered another culture, left behind me the speech, the food, the familiar postures of my own way of life, and sought to understand the pattern of life of another people."

Because Margaret lived closely with "her" peoples she was often affected by their beliefs. In the late twenties, for example, Mead and her second husband, Reo Fortune, were in the Admiralty Islands, living in a Manus village perched on stilts over a shallow lagoon. They were setting out from a village in a dugout canoe, when suddenly a great wail from the village caused them to turn back. Their guide's ten-year-old son had fallen down in a fit and, although Mead and Fortune did what they could, the child died. Margaret watched, fascinated, as the village tried to identify the individual whose antisocial behavior could be blamed for the child's death. Blame shifted among living and dead villagers. Finally, Mead wrote, "the general fear and terror which was spreading over the village intruded practically into our lives" and Mead herself became ill. The village decided she had to move immediately into another house to escape the bad spirit.

From 1931 to 1933, Margaret lived with three different tribes in New Guinea: the mountain Arapesh, and the Tchambuli and Mundugumor, who lived along the Sepik River. One of the most shocking phenomena she witnessed, and one that affected her deeply, was the cavalier attitude the Mundugumor showed toward children they did not want. "Women wanted sons and men wanted daughters, and babies of the wrong sex were tossed into the river, still alive, wrapped in a bark sheath." After witnessing this, Mead was determined to have her own child, and while in New Guinea she met anthropologist Gregory Bateson, the man who was to become her third husband and the father of her daughter.

With Bateson, Margaret later began her long study of Balinese culture, making photographs and films of Balinese dance techniques and activities related to child rearing, pioneering the field of visual anthropology. Their years in Bali and then again in New Guinea were interrupted by ominous rumors of war, which reached even their remote South Pacific outpost. In 1939 they decided to return to America. Mead would not return to Bali until the mid-1950s.

Margaret differed from those who sought merely to record the patterns of primitive peoples in that she wanted to use her studies on Bali, New Guinea, and Somoa to illuminate issues in our own culture. She thought that understanding the way family life evolved in a very different culture allowed her to understand the ways in which our own culture shapes us. Thus, she became one of the first social scientists to study systematically how cultural influences mold children's personalities and determine sexual attitudes. What she learned convinced her that the stages in the lives of European and American children were not so much determined by "nature" as by "nurture." Questioning the moral superiority of Americans particularly with regard to child rearing and sexual attitudes, she was one of the first "multiculturalists."

On her expeditions she collected ethnographic materials for what would become the Margaret Mead Hall of Oceanic Peoples for the American Museum of Natural History. Known for her popular books and articles and her extensive lecturing, she was elected to the National Academy of Sciences, was awarded the Presidential Medal of Freedom, and was the president of the American Academy of Sciences. Mead died of cancer in New York in 1978.

SAID MEAD, "FOR THE ANTHROPOLOGIST LIVING IN THE MIDST OF A VILLAGE, WAKING AT COCK CROW OR DRUM BEAT, STAYING UP ALL NIGHT WHILE THE VILLAGE REVELS OR MOURNS . . . [L]ISTENING FOR SOME SLIGHT CHANGE IN THE LEVEL OF CHATTER OR THE CRY OF A CHILD, FIELD WORK BECOMES A TWENTY-FOUR-HOUR ACTIVITY."

ABOVE: MEAD BROKE HER ANKLE, SO LOCAL MEN FROM MANUS IN NEW GUINEA'S ADMIRALTY ISLANDS CARRIED HER TO THE VILLAGE OF PERI, 1929.

Gold Missus

KATHARINE STEVENS FOWLER-BILLINGS

AMERICAN GEOLOGIST/CONSERVATIONIST • 1902–1997

ABOVE: FOWLER-BILLINGS WORKING AS A FIELD GEOLOGIST IN SIERRA LEONE IN 1930.

RIGHT: SHOOTING RATTLESNAKES WHILE DOING FIELDWORK IN THE LARAMIE MOUNTAINS.

OPPOSITE: FOWLER-BILLINGS AS A YOUNG GEOLOGIST IN THE ROCKY MOUNTAINS, AND IN OLD AGE (INSET), SURVEYING THE WHITE MOUNTAINS OF NEW HAMPSHIRE, WHICH SHE MAPPED AND WORKED TO PRESERVE. OF HER EARLY YEARS, SHE WRITES: "IT WAS IN THE DEPTHS OF A COPPER MINE IN BUTTE, MONTANA, THAT I WAS FIRST ACKNOWLEDGED AS A 'REAL' GEOLO-GIST. MY IRISH GUIDE, CORRECTING A MISAPPRE-HENSION OF A MINER BELOW, CALLED DOWN, 'THIS AIN'T NO YOUNG FELLA. THIS IS A "LAIDY" GEOLOGIST.' "

IN SIERRA LEONE in the spring of 1930, a slight young woman, neatly turned out in a khaki bush jacket, skirt, and pith helmet, could be seen by astonished viewers walking at the head of a long line of heavily burdened native porters. This was no movie set—Katharine Fowler had a serious purpose in mind. She was marching northwest deep into the African bush to search for deposits of iron ore and gold.

Katharine was new to Africa but she was not new to camp life. She had already spent months alone in the Laramie Mountains of Wyoming, creating a geological map for her Columbia University dissertation in geology. "I worked alone in the field, partly because there was no other woman who could and would go along," she explained. "I really enjoyed working alone, for I had learned how to have my work absorb all my interests and keep me sane."

Her interest in geology began during her New Hampshire childhood, where at the end of each school year, she could hardly wait to get back to the White Mountains. "I loved the mountain climbs and walks in the woods," she wrote. With no one to guide her, Fowler came up with the questions that would fascinate her throughout her life. "On my trips I became curious about why the mountains were there, what formed the rocks that were so different from the coastal terrain. I vowed that someday I would study geology and answer these questions. What a great training ground these explorations would prove to be for the years of field work ahead."

Answers would require study, and so she enrolled at Bryn Mawr College, which was then a haven for intellectually restless young women. There she was fortunate to have as a teacher one of the pioneer women scientists, Florence Bascom (1862–1945), who was the second woman in the United Stated to earn a Ph.D. in geology. Outside of Bryn Mawr, women were so unusual and unwelcome in geology departments that Katharine had to sit behind a screen while attending lectures at Columbia University.

For her Ph.D. work at Columbia, Fowler mapped the geological formations of a forty-by-twenty-mile region in the Laramie Mountains, detailing outcroppings of anorthosites. To make her maps, she would locate a gully, then back her old Ford motor car up the gully (it could not make the steep grade if in forward gear) to pitch her camp as high as she could. Then laboriously she would continue her way up by foot to make her sightings. One gully done, she would repeat the exhausting process on the next. In this way she covered the entire region in three months. Except for the occasional suspicious homesteader, she and her dog, Rocksie, were alone. "I did the geology of the Laramie Mts. alone," she laughed, "because men would not consider working with a woman."

In 1929 Katharine sailed to South Africa ostensibly to attend an international congress of geologists, but in truth because she wanted to begin a trek that would take her, over several months, the length of Africa from south to north, from Johannesburg to Cairo. Along the way she met, fell in love with, and became

engaged to a fellow geologist, a Scotsman by the name of Jock Lunn. After a quick wedding in London, they decided to go back to Africa to work. But marriage proved to be as much a barrier to working as a geologist in Africa as being a woman had been in America. As she later wrote, her husband's "contract forbade him to take his wife with him to West Africa [but] nothing daunted, I decided I would go to the small [neighboring] country of Sierra Leone. . . . I was lucky to 'be on the spot' and the government of Sierra Leone asked me to study their recently discovered iron areas."

In preparation for her trip, Fowler took courses in tropical diseases and had a dozen wooden crates made to hold emergency supplies of food. Then to the amazement of London tailors, she outfitted herself in specially designed clothes to protect her skin from cuts, snakes, and the heat. She was finally ready to go to "the hinterland of Sierra Leone, West Africa . . . the kind of place an explorer dreams about when he opens a map of the world and searches for a place to roam. A place where he might have unusual experiences. But a place he hesitates to go. Too near the equator. . . . Too much heat and humidity. A place reeking with malaria and disease."

Katharine led two expeditions in Sierra Leone. She earned her nickname, the Gold Missus, on the second trip, which was for the London-based Maroc Gold Company. "I was to prospect throughout the concession that they had been granted to look for new areas to mine. I would be searching the hills for the source of gold in the gravels and exploring in the bush. This was the life that I loved. I felt confident that I knew the country, the ways of the natives, and how to choose carriers. . . . There was no question of my refusing." She traveled extensively throughout the unmapped regions of Sierra Leone, living in the native villages she passed through. "My workers . . . spread tall tales about the Gold Missus who had very powerful juju and could find gold in the gravels and hills."

Fowler's marriage to Jock Lunn was undermined by their separate careers, and eventually they got divorced. At loose ends, Katharine returned to the United States in 1935. The advent of the war suddenly made geological surveys a national priority. With foreign sources of minerals either endangered or wholly cut off and with new technologies demanding rare metals, scholar-explorers like Fowler were pressed into national service. One of the minerals necessary for the war industry was mica; unaffected by cold, heat, water, acid, or electricity, it was essential for insulating the electrical wiring in airplanes. Most of the mica used by American industry had come from India, but Katharine knew that New Hampshire contained abandoned mica mines. What began with mapping mica led her to other minerals and, now a recognized expert, she was appointed an associate in geology at the Boston Museum of Natural History. Meanwhile, she also found time to marry fellow geologist Marland Billings, with whom she had two children.

After the war Katharine's knowledge of geology came into service in a new arena—conservation. She supplied scientific arguments for the preservation of entire regions of New Hampshire and Massachusetts, including the eastern White Mountains, the Saco River watershed, and Wellesley, Massachusetts. Well into her eighties she was still at work mapping, now not to find gold but to preserve our environmental heritage.

TOP: FOWLER-BILLINGS SAVED COPIES OF HER MANY PASSPORT PHOTOS.

ABOVE: A PAGE FROM HER WELL-TRAVELED PASSPORT.

A MESSAGE FROM THE RED PLANET

MEENAKSHI WADHWA
INDIAN METEORITICIST • B. 1967

EVERY DAY SOME fifty to one hundred tons of material from space fall into Earth's atmosphere. Most of the detritus is sand-size and is burned up in the atmosphere before reaching Earth's surface. Of the meteorites that do get through, about 99 percent come from asteroids. But working with a tiny part of the other 1 percent at the Field Museum of Natural History in Chicago, Meenakshi Wadhwa has been discovering the sequence of Martian geologic evolution by making comprehensive geochemical studies of Martian rocks. These rocks have come to Earth as meteorites, knocked from their home planet and hurled into space when enormous asteroids crashed into the Martian surface. "Understanding the geologic history of Mars," Wadhwa says, "will give us insight into the formation and evolution of planets in our solar system."

Meenakshi has searched for shards of Martian crust in Antarctica. In 1993 she made her first voyage to the frozen continent as a member of the U.S. Antarctic Search for Meteorites (AMSET) Expedition. Wadhwa explained that the frozen terrain "is the place to hunt for meteorites because there is no vegetation to cover them up. The dark rocks can be easily spotted on the ice. The ice sheets have been there hundreds of thousands of years so you can find a good collection of fallen debris." But finding the rocks from Mars has been a real challenge.

ABOVE: WADHWA ON A METEORITE-COLLECTING EXPEDITION IN ANTARCTICA.

I study meteorites because it gives me a unique perspective on human existence and achievement. Most meteorites formed so long ago that most of us have difficulty grasping the enormity of this time scale, and yet by studying these meteorites we can learn something about events in the distant past that have shaped our present. I think it is important to learn about our beginnings. Only humans can do that. It is a special privilege that we have.

Growing up in India, Meenakshi remembers that "rocks, minerals, and natural history" were her earliest interests. But she wasn't aware that she could make rocks the focus of her life's work until she discovered geology while attending Punjab University. "There were hardly any women undergraduates in the department. It was completely male dominated. The problem was the fieldwork. They told me that fieldwork could be strenuous and that they couldn't guarantee my safety. But I took it as a challenge." Later she discovered the possibility of studying the geology of other planets besides Earth. "I wanted to expand my horizons and apply what I learned about the earth to the solar system." She came to the United States to continue her study of galactic geology. Wadhwa's pioneering work exploring the origins of the solar system is generating very precise age dates on early events occurring "immediately after the solar system formed from the swirling cloud of gas and dust."

With the support of NASA, she is building a lab at the Field Museum to study the samples of Martian rocks that will arrive in the early part of the twenty-first century, from the NASA spacecraft missions to Mars. In 1999 the International Astronomical Union named asteroid 8356 "Asteroid Wadhwa" in her honor.

MUCURA MACHO.   Teeth —
                          Abortive.   Contraceptive.   Y-7040
                          Diuretic.   ParalysingRtm 6103
Weed, smaller leaves than hembra. Grows in shadey 1243
or sunny chacras.   7040

Woytkowski says Petiveria alliaceae L.
Harvard: Peteveria alliaceae L. Phytolacceae.
Believe this identification correct for Macho, and
Hembra.

As abortive or contraceptive: 5 leaves mashed in
cold water prevents contraception for life, according to Dona Luisa Tuesta, Puesto Yawas (GC Post)
R. Putumayo.

See Garcia Barriga : Used for teeth. (Alliaceae)

Witch Doctor's Apprentice

NICOLE HUGHES MAXWELL

AMERICAN ETHNOBOTANIST • 1905–1998

THE JOURNEY OF a society debutante from sunny California, through New York's skyscraper corporate boardrooms, to the hot, dense jungles of the Amazon, was as long and convoluted as any of the South American rivers she came to know so well. But what Nicole Hughes Maxwell most dreaded was surprising:

> The most frightening moment of my venture to collect medicinal herbs in the South American jungle was not when the Mainas caught me spying on a witch doctor ritual, nor during the terrible storm that nearly swamped our canoe on the Putumayo. It wasn't even when the jaguar came sniffing at my hammock the night I slept too far from my party. It was in New York, before I left, at lunch with top scientists and executives of a pharmaceutical company. I hate asking for money.

Raised by her grandparents in San Francisco, California, Nicole studied ballet as a child and eventually danced with the corps de ballet of the Opera Comique in Paris. There, she fell in love with and married a young U.S. Air Force officer by the name of Alfred Maxwell. They lived a peripatetic life, moving from one air force base to another. But wherever she landed, Maxwell managed to continue her education. After the end of World War II, however, her marriage broke up, and in 1947 Nicole headed for Lima, Peru, for a job with the tourist board. Her days were fairly mundane and boring, but sometimes she had an opportunity to venture away from Lima into the countryside. On one occasion, she was given the opportunity to travel upriver from Iquitos. And there an accident happened that changed her life forever.

In fact, it was an accident in both senses of the word. On her way to visit the Chayanahuita Indians off the Panapura River, she was cutting a trail through the dense jungle foliage when her swing slipped and she deeply slashed her arm with a machete. It wasn't so much the cut, although it was deep and painful, that worried her but the almost certain infection that would follow. This could kill her.

While Maxwell was imagining the worst—there was no first-aid station, and certainly no doctor, much less a hospital, for miles or even days of travel—one of her Indian guides ran out of the jungle, where he had disappeared just after her accident, carrying a gourd. When he reached her, he said she should drink what the gourd contained. Reluctantly she did. And to her astonishment, the profuse bleeding stopped. Even more miraculously, her arm healed quickly and without a scar. It was as though the accident had never happened.

As Nicole looked into the dense jungle, the thought gradually formed in her mind that what she was seeing was not a vast house of insects and microbes, but actually a million-square-mile pharmacy. Those trees, vines, orchids, and ferns were probably the natural base for incredible cures

ABOVE: DURING HER MORE THAN FORTY YEARS IN THE AMAZON RAINFOREST, MAXWELL OBSERVED THE USE OF MORE THAN 325 PLANTS TO CURE A HOST OF ILLS, FROM BURNS TO CANCER, FROM INFERTILITY TO ABSCESSED TEETH. SHE RECORDED HER DISCOVERIES ON INDEX CARDS (ABOVE AND LEFT), WHICH, SADLY, REMAIN UNPUBLISHED.

OPPOSITE: NICOLE MAXWELL ON THE TRAIL BETWEEN THE RIO NAPO AND THE RIO ALGODIN. THE VINE IS ESCALERA DE MAKISAPA (MONKEY VINE), USED BY THE CAMPA TRIBE OF SOUTHERN PERU AS A CONTRACEPTIVE.

RIGHT: MAXWELL STUDIED RITUAL DANCE IN THE PHILIPPINES IN THE 1930S.

and remedies. And from that moment Maxwell embarked upon what would be her lifelong quest to learn the secrets that generations of Indians had preserved. If she could do that, she felt, she could be of immense value to all humankind. "I could make some of those plant medicines available to my own people. . . . It was something that badly needed doing, and it was something I thought I could do."

Describing her search for a native plant called incira, Maxwell said, "I made a habit of questioning all the jungle people I met about incira. I found many who used it, but they had always drawn sap from some tree in a part of the forest distant from where we happened to be. I finally found a Coto Indian who found me the sap and a specimen. The incira is *Chlorophora tinctoria,* Moraceae. A minute amount placed on a painful or abscessed tooth will cause the molar to crumble and work its way out of the gum. At no time is there any bleeding, inflammation, evidence of infection or discomfort of any kind."

For the next forty-five years, until she was in her nineties and incapacitated by a stroke, Nicole lived on and off with indigenous tribes in the Amazon Basin—the Jivaro, Witoto, Shipibo, Yagua, Conibo, Piro, and others—and learned their extensive natural pharmacological and medicinal lore. She built an herbarium in Iquitos to cultivate and study the plants she and her helpers collected from the jungle there.

With her goal to make the therapies of the rain forest widely available, Maxwell traded her modern goods and antibiotics for the sacred and secret medicinal plants used by the witch doctors of the Amazon and Putumayo regions. She observed how they selected these plants, sometimes with herself serving as guinea pig, for treatments of arthritis, gallstones, bleeding, abscessed teeth, and hemorrhoids. In all, Nicole studied and recorded the use of more than 325 indigenous plants to treat more than one hundred ills.

One of her most astonishing discoveries was of a method of safe, cheap, effective birth control. "Primitive peoples are generally reluctant to reveal their medical lore to a stranger, and this is especially true regarding plants they use as contraceptives. They are extremely secretive about them. In fact, any plants that they believe affects the giving or withholding of life are surrounded by powerful taboos which prevent their disclosure to an outsider." Despite their hesitance, while she was staying with the Jivaro on the Corrientese River, she was told by the

TOP: A TICUNA FAMILY ON THE COLOMBIAN AMAZON.

ABOVE: A NEWSPAPER CLIPPING WITH A STORY ON MAXWELL'S WORK.

OPPOSITE: YOUNG MAINA BOYS LISTENING TO THEIR FIRST RADIO BROADCAST.

wife of a shaman about three plants: "One was used to bring on an abortion, another promoted fertility in women who could not otherwise conceive, and the third was a contraceptive with effects lasting for many years."

Armed with this discovery, Maxwell tried for many years to get a pharmaceutical company to investigate the contraceptive plants she felt could radically and positively affect the lives of millions of women. But she finally realized after many attempts that the "big pharmaceutical firms are out only for one thing: money. What counts is that women are buying the [birth control] Pill by the millions. So what if [these] plants are safer. . . . [J]ust compare a pill a woman has to take 20 times a month every month of every year . . . with something that the same woman has to buy only once. Multiply both figures by millions and you'll see if it would make sense for these business men to lay out a fortune to investigate [my] stuff and put it into production."

Another example of Nicole's discoveries was the use of plants to heal burns. "The medication that I saw heal third-degree burns on a year-old baby's arms, leaving no scarring, is one I learned on the only trip I have ever made in the company of people not native to the jungle. That was in 1966, when I took a group that included botanists, pharmacologists and one MD up the Napo River [in Peru] to visit some Witoto friends [whom] I knew I could persuade to provide the scientists with some medicines used by their tribe. The year-old baby had fallen into the cook fire and his arms were so badly burned that there was no skin at all on either inner forearm. Nothing was left but raw, red flesh . . . treatment consisted of binding on the burned areas strips of the fresh white damp bast found just under the outer skin of bast of the manioc tuber, manihot dulcis. . . . When we returned a week later I was surprised to see that healthy smooth pink-and-white totally perfect skin had grown back over all but one very small area."

Nicole soon understood the battle she was engaged in for the acceptance and recognition of her discoveries. "The scientific attitude towards my work has been one of skepticism and scorn," she said. "Botanists seem to have forgotten that the South American jungle tribes were the first to use curare, which is so important to modern surgical techniques. Quinine and all the other anti-malarial drugs have their origin in the forest of the Amazon." We have not begun to tap the resources of the jungle drugstore, but she believed that "if I keep at it, then surely I will eventually get some of these plants properly investigated and their value so clearly demonstrated that they will be available to people who need them."

I was suffering pain from arthritis in my left hand. The Indians made tea from leaves of a shrub and [I drank it] and the pain left almost immediately. . . . [A] little weed that an Indian named Yori gave me dissolves kidney stones. . . . I saw the cures for skin disease; I saw a bad case of impetigo disappear after being wiped just once with a little green bean.

Looking for the Oldest Man

MARY DOUGLAS NICOL LEAKEY

ENGLISH PALEOANTHROPOLOGIST • 1913–1996

ABOVE: MARY LEAKEY AT LAKE TURKANA EXAMINING A SKULL OF A. BOISEI THAT HAD JUST BEEN DISCOVERED BY HER SON RICHARD AND DAUGHTER-IN-LAW MAEVE.

OPPOSITE: THE EARLIEST HOMINID FOOTPRINTS YET FOUND WERE DISCOVERED BY MARY LEAKEY AND PAUL ABELL IN LAETOLI IN 1978.

MARY NICOL WAS eleven years old when her father took her into the French caves of Fond de Guame and La Mouthe to see the beautiful prehistoric paintings covering the walls. She decided then and there that her life would be devoted to learning more about early man. Eschewing formal education, she began her work as an archaeologist in England at seventeen and soon became known both as an authority on flint points and for her drawings of artifacts. At a lecture at the Royal Anthropologist Institute in 1933, the eminent Egyptologist Gertrude Caton-Thompson introduced Mary to the Anglo-Kenyan archaeologist, Louis Leakey. He was looking for someone to make drawings of artifacts for his forthcoming book. Entranced with Mary and recognizing her talents as a draftsman, he invited her to Africa to draw the stone tools he had found. She arrived in Tanzania in 1935, Leakey soon proposed to her and they were married in 1936. She spent the rest of her life working in the Rift Valley searching for signs of early man.

Mary's first view of Olduvai Gorge, a vast, bleak, windswept expanse of ravines and plains that she would explore for the next sixty years, was prophetic. "It was a place that was incredibly beautiful and where nearly every exposure produced some archaeological or geological excitement." During the ensuing years the Leakeys excavated many sites in the Rift Valley and other promising East African locations. Mary also searched for ancient cave paintings, which she documented and eventually published. "The beauty of the painting . . . together with the fascination and excitement of disentangling the figures from each other . . . made it possible to get a glimpse of the Late Stone Age people themselves, and of incidents in their lives." But it is for her discoveries of early hominids that she is best known.

Mary's spectacular discoveries made some of our earliest human ancestors practically household words. Among her well-known finds is the skull of the 16-million-year-old *Proconsul* homonid, which she uncovered in 1948. It was believed at the time to be the "missing link" between apes and humans in the evolutionary tree. Then in 1959 she found the then-oldest hominid skull, that of a 1.8-million-year-old *Zinjanthropus* of the group called *Australopithecus boisei*. Most exciting, however, was her 1976 discovery in Laetoli, Tanzania, of the oldest fossilized hominid footprints. Forever etched in stone are the tracks made one day, 3.6 million years ago, of three *Australopithecus afarensis* as they walked across a valley recently dusted with volcanic ash.

Mary's work in Africa, searching for ancient humans and collecting and studying stone tools to show how tool technology developed over time, as well as her documentation of more recent rock art, has contributed significantly to our understanding of the past. But as Mary said, "There is so much we do not know, and the more we do know, the more we realize that early interpretations were completely wrong. It is good mental exercise." Her discoveries helped create a new understanding about human evolution. Mary's legacy lives on in her three sons who share their parents' passion for paleoarchaeology.

Spirits Provided a Cure

ROSITA ARVIGO

AMERICAN ETHNOBOTANIST/NATURAL HEALER • B. 1941

W HEN ROSITA ARVIGO walked into the jungles of the Central American country of Belize in 1981, her objective was modest. Together with her husband, she planned to turn the thirty acres of jungle they had bought on the banks of the Macal River into a homestead. But soon after her arrival Rosita met the then-ninety-year-old Mayan natural healer and shaman Don Elijio, and her life was changed forever. "For every ailment or difficulty on earth, the Spirits have provided a cure—you just have to find it," he told her. Arvigo was inspired to make the finding of medicines in "nature's pharmacy" her life's work.

Don Elijio healed his patients with the extracts of medicinal plants found in the jungle. Knowing what plants to use and how to use them was lore that had been handed down from teacher to apprentice over millennia, but Don Elijio was the last in the line. Hearing his life story and watching him at work healing, Rosita realized that she was seeing an art that was both powerful and fragile—it might die with the old healer.

Fortunately, Arvigo was not just a homesteader. From her early childhood in Chicago, she had been fascinated by plants. She can still vividly recall her earliest memory, when as a four-year-old child she had watched in wonder the miracle of plants emerging from tiny seeds.

As she grew up, she had wanted to be a doctor. But it was not until she was living in Mexico that she saw how her two interests—plants and medicine—intertwined. She had moved to a small village in Guerrero in the late 1960s, where she supported herself by farming. There, late one night in 1973, a local midwife asked for her help with a particularly difficult delivery. Rosita later recalled:

> *I had never seen a birth before, and didn't know what to do. The mother suddenly began hemorrhaging. The healer hurriedly sent me outside to collect roses.*

ABOVE: MAP OF TERRA NOVA. IN 1993, THIS 6,000-ACRE AREA OF OLD-GROWTH FOREST WAS ESTABLISHED AS A PRESERVE BY THE GOVERNMENT OF BELIZE, THANKS TO THE EFFORTS OF ARVIGO.

OPPOSITE: ARVIGO WITH SHAMAN DON ELIJIO PANTI ON THE TRAIL IN BELIZE.

She made a tea out of the petals and leaves which she gave the mother. Soon the hemorrhaging stopped. The healer saved the woman's life with the flowers. I knew then that was what I wanted to be—a healer who knew the secrets of the plants.

Fascinated by what she had witnessed, Arvigo began studying herbal medicine, first with healers in Mexico, then in Chicago at the National College of Naprapathy, then in Central America. She was in a clinic she had established in the little town of San Ignacio, Belize, where she practiced a kind of massage therapy known as naprapathic medicine, when an old man walked in one day. As she later recalled, "The old man was so bent over, I thought he had come to me for a treatment." But instead, Don Elijio Panti had come to help her.

Rosita was immediately taken with the shaman and fascinated by what he knew. Discovering that he had no apprentice, she was determined to fill that role. Arvigo recalled the many meetings they had before Don Elijio agreed to this. "Taking on an apprentice is like adopting a child. It is an enormous responsibility. So he was testing me to make sure I was worth his time and effort." Finally, Don Elijio realized how serious she was, and once convinced, he spent the last ten years of his life teaching her about the local plants and their uses.

Realizing that it would take generations or perhaps centuries to rediscover what he knew, Rosita determined to do everything in her power to preserve it. Remarkably, from that little village in Belize and without much money, she managed to establish the Belize Ethnobotany Project in 1987 in collaboration with Dr. Michael Balick, an ethnobotanist and curator at the New York Botanical Garden, and got the New York Botanical Garden to sponsor it.

With this organization, she has managed not only to document Don Elijio's knowledge but also to find and record the knowledge of other healers so that today she has a database with more than twenty-five hundred plants. Of those plants, more than five hundred were identified by Don Elijio as having medicinal value. The project is currently working with the National Institutes of Health and the National Cancer Society to test the effectiveness of these plants in combating cancer and AIDS.

There is now a general recognition that our best hope for coping with many diseases arises from the discovery—or rediscovery—of treatments that occur in nature. However, the jungles in Belize, where Arvigo works, like those in many parts of the world, are disappearing at an alarming rate. Realizing how much remains to be done, Rosita urged the Belize government to establish a preserve. It responded in 1993 by setting aside some six thousand acres—less than ten square miles—of old-growth forest for the specific purpose of preserving medicinal plants. Known as Terra Nova, this was the first preserve of its kind in the world and has become a model for others. Thailand, Mexico, Guatemala, and Peru have followed the example in establishing their own plant preserves and recording traditional knowledge.

Arvigo is now working with twelve healers from different traditions to document their lore. Her days are spent walking with them through the jungle. When a medicinal plant is found, its name, its use, and any other information is recorded. If the plant is plentiful in the area, the team digs up samples. If it is rare, they take only a cutting. Specimens are then sent to the Belize Forestry Department, the Smithsonian Institution, the New York Botanical Garden, the National Cancer Institute, and Kew Gardens in London.

When Rosita hears that an area in Belize is slated for clearing, she sends her team there on a plant reconnaissance mission to dig up as many plants as they can save and to cut and dry the rest. Commercial uses for some of these plants have been developed, thus providing income for the local people and encouraging conservation.

Arvigo has sought out her own apprentice, someone to whom she can pass on the knowledge Don Elijio gave to her. Wishing to return this knowledge to the local society, she is training a fifty-year-old Mayan to carry on the work. Rosita is realizing her dream of exploring science, traditional healing, and the natural world to discover cures for the ills that plague us.

ABOVE: ARVIGO WITH HEALERS HORTENSE ROBINSON AND BEATRICE WAIGHT, MEMBERS OF THE TRADITIONAL HEALERS FOUNDATION.

OPPOSITE: ARVIGO COLLECTING A SAMPLE OF SKUNT ROOT, OR *CHIOCOCCA ALBA*, WHICH IS TAKEN AS A TEA FOR ULCERS AND VARIOUS SPIRITUAL DISEASES. ARVIGO USES CARDS TO ORGANIZE THE INFORMATION SHE'S GATHERED ON PLANTS.

After about a year and a half of tramping about in the rain forest, plants began to stand out as individuals with uses and exciting histories. The dark, mysterious forest of trees and lianas was becoming a familiar place of knowledge and healing.

Discovering the Realm of the Great Goddess

MARIJA BIRUTE ALSEIKAITE GIMBUTAS

LITHUANIAN-AMERICAN ARCHAEOLOGIST • 1921–1994

ABOVE: MARIJA GIMBUTAS. GIMBUTAS WROTE, "IT IS A GROSS MISUNDERSTANDING TO IMAGINE WARFARE AS ENDEMIC TO THE HUMAN CONDITION. WIDESPREAD FIGHTING AND FORTIFICATION BUILDING HAVE INDEED BEEN THE WAY OF LIFE FOR MOST OF OUR DIRECT ANCESTORS FROM THE BRONZE AGE UP UNTIL NOW. HOWEVER, THIS WAS NOT THE CASE IN THE PALEOLITHIC AND NEOLITHIC. THERE ARE NO DEPICTIONS OF ARMS (WEAPONS USED AGAINST OTHER HUMANS) IN PALEOLITHIC CAVE PAINTINGS, NOR ARE THERE REMAINS OF WEAPONS USED BY MAN AGAINST MAN DURING THE NEOLITHIC OF OLD EUROPE."

RIGHT: AN EARLY FIGURINE OF A GODDESS.

AS A SMALL GIRL growing up in Lithuania, Marija Gimbutas encountered the mysteries that would consume the rest of her life. "In our house," recalled Marija, "were the Fates, the witches of a continuous pagan tradition. All my servants believed in them. They were real—spinning the thread of human life. . . . The rivers were sacred, the forest and trees were sacred, the hills were sacred. The earth was kissed and prayers were said every morning, every evening." This exposure to the "preliterate" folklore of her society would later lead her on numerous expeditions in search of ancient truths. "I fell in love with what is ancient," she recalled, "because it was a deep communication and oneness with the Earth. I was completely captivated. This was the beginning of my interest in folklore."

This interest brought her, at the age of sixteen, to begin collecting stories and songs of her homeland, which had their origins in the ancient past. As the only female on several expeditions to southeastern Lithuania, she made many recordings of oral traditions; these are now preserved in the Vilnius University archives. Later, after her escape from Vilnius in the waning days of World War II, Gimbutas continued her studies first in Germany, then in the United States, where she became a recognized authority on the Balts and Slavs of the Bronze Age and of the Kurgans, the Indo-European invaders from the steppes. Because of her prodigious scholarship, which would eventually result in the publication of some 320 articles and 33 books, she was appointed professor of European archaeology and department chair at UCLA, and the curator of Old World archaeology at UCLA's Cultural History Museum.

Throughout her life, Marija never lost her fascination for the earliest of Old World cultures, echoes of which had captivated her in her youth. During the 1960s and 1970s she explored ancient sites in the rugged countryside of southeastern Europe, where she conducted excavations in Bosnia, in Macedonia, and in Thessaly in northern Greece. Some of sites she was finding, such as a seven-thousand-year-old cave in southeastern Italy, were clearly sacred spaces. But who the people were who had worshipped there was a mystery.

Gradually through her archaeological fieldwork and study of Old European artifacts preserved in museums around the world, a picture of Old Europe began to emerge. When first presented, her thesis was highly controversial. Calling upon her knowledge of linguistics, mythology, and folklore, Gimbutas posited a vast and long-lived egalitarian and matrilineal culture, based on a female deity, the Great Goddess. She believed that this pre-Kurgan culture, which lasted thousands of years, was a relatively peaceful one, given the lack of evidence of fortifications or weapons. Later, after the Kurgan invasions, which Marija laconically described as a "collision of cultures," Old Europe was gradually replaced by the culture of the invaders, with their very different belief system centered on a pantheon of warlike male gods. This reversal had profound effects on the society at the time, and, in significant ways, influences our own culture to this day.

Never one to shrink from controversy, Gimbutas postulated that future archaeologists would find that belief systems centered on the Goddess go back to the beginnings of humankind. She also believed that the religion of the Goddess did not completely die out but was absorbed by the new cultural systems. To support this idea she unearthed, in her folkloric investigations, contemporary beliefs and practices that echo those of five thousand years or more ago. And, even more controversially, she argued that a writing system had been developed in Old Europe two thousand years before the "first" written language of Sumer.

Marija stressed the multidisciplinary approach to understanding all periods of history. This was particularly important for Old Europe, where, she said, the "secular and sacred life in those days were one and indivisible." She understood the seamless fabric of human life and encouraged others to approach the study of archaeology from many angles. "This is the only thing I work for, to come to a moment where everything clicks together . . . archaeology, mythology, folklore, linguistics—all are saying the same thing."

Sadly, as Gimbutas was beginning to delve into these issues of language, of folkloric survival, and of the origins of the Goddess religion, a fatal cancer struck her. She has left behind a huge legacy. The questions she has raised by her discoveries have already given direction to the careers of numerous scholars. But most of all, she has given rise to the hope that a peaceful existence based on equality is possible. As she put it, her studies showed "that we as a civilization do not have to learn something new, in order to survive into the future, but to remember something forgotten."

IN SACRED SPACES

CRISTINA SHELLEY BIAGGI
SWISS-ITALIAN-AMERICAN
ARTIST/PREHISTORIAN • B. 1937

CRISTINA SHELLEY BIAGGI found the connecting point that fused together her interests in art, archaeology, and religion in the search for the prehistoric sacred spaces of the Neolithic Great Goddess. "We have much to learn from our ancient ancestors," she says. Profound learning also came as a result of her work with her mentor, the renowned archaeologist Marija Gimbutas. Their first meeting, while they were attending the 1985 Conference on Archaeology and Fertility Cults in the Ancient Mediterranean, was, appropriately, in Malta's famed Hypogeum, a multilayered Neolithic temple and tomb complex extending deep underground.

While researching the thesis for her Ph.D., which she received from New York University, Cristina began her year searching for and documenting the artistic similarities between far-flung Neolithic structures. Exploring ancient sites in the windswept Orkney and Shetland Islands, off the northern coast of Scotland, and in the hills of Malta, more than a thousand miles away in the Mediterranean, she discovered similarities in the remains of temples that had been covered by soil for millennia. Biaggi's discoveries confirm that "similar belief systems in ancient times were widespread. This is evidenced by similar design styles far afield from one another used in the sacred space." These sacred spaces, so alike in design and yet so far from one another, have supported Gimbutas's theory of a pan-European goddess culture.

Cristina has devoted her professional life to proving Gimbutas's Neolithic goddess theories. Inspired by the cave paintings, sculpture, pottery, and architectural remains of the Neolithic period, she hopes to increase public awareness of our ancient past.

Shark Lady

EUGENIE CLARK

AMERICAN ICHTHYOLOGIST • B. 1922

ABOVE: CLARK EMERGING FROM THE SUB-MERSIBLE *ALVIN*.

OPPOSITE: CLARK APPROACHING A SLEEPING BULL SHARK. SAYS CLARK, "I HAVE ALWAYS BEEN TOO INTRIGUED AND AWED BY SHARKS TO BE SCARED OF THEM, BUT IT'S IMPORTANT TO UNDERSTAND THEIR BEHAVIOR AND TO LEARN HOW TO BEHAVE WHEN YOU VISIT THEIR HOME."

For FIVE DECADES Eugenie Clark has been a leader in marine biology, exploration, and conservation. She has led more than a hundred expeditions to oceans around the world and has made thousands of dives. She is best known for her groundbreaking studies of shark intelligence and behavior, which have helped dispel some of the creature's fearsome reputation.

Born in New York City, Clark was raised there by her Japanese mother and grandmother; her American father had died when she was young. On Saturdays, while her mother worked selling newspapers at New York's Downtown Athletic Club, she would leave little Eugenie in the Old Aquarium. "I never tired of watching the fish," she recalled. In fact she so loved her hours by the tanks that she gave impromptu tours to other aquarium visitors. Soon she was begging her mother to get her tanks and fish of her own. "As the months passed, our small three-roomed apartment turned into a menagerie." Before long she became the youngest member ever admitted to the Queens County Aquarium Society. And, once hooked on fish, she never let go; in college she majored in zoology and specialized in ichthyology.

Like many seagoers, Clark had often wondered whether sharks were really that dangerous. "I wasn't afraid of them. I wished I could see them in person, out in the open." When she finally got her chance to work with them, she began making amazing discoveries. In 1958 she proved that sharks were not mindless killing machines, but that they were intelligent. In a large pool at the lab she founded in Cape Haze (later Mote Marine Laboratory) on the Gulf Coast of Florida, she taught lemon sharks to hit a target. This would cause a bell to ring and food would be released. She discovered the sharks could discriminate between colors and shapes to hit the food target and could quickly adjust to new placements of the target and food. In 1967 Eugenie tried the experiment again aboard Jacques Cousteau's *Calypso* off the Suakin Islands in the Red Sea. She lowered targets in the water, only one of which would give a reward. The open-water sharks learned as quickly as the penned ones had. All in all, Clark studied many of the more than 370 known species of sharks. "It's hard to decide on a favorite shark because they are all so fascinating to me, but I really like whale sharks and six-gill sharks," she says.

To study whale sharks, Eugenie often has to dive to more than two hundred meters—the creature's preferred depth—in the waters off the coasts of Mexico, Thailand, or Australia, where they can be found. One of her most exhilarating undersea moments was when she rode on a whale shark, something she strenuously discourages anyone else from undertaking. "I was crazy. We wanted to study and photograph her. She was well over forty feet long. Once I got on her, I did not want to ever let go. . . . The shark was cruising along steadily at three knots, and, after a while, I thought to myself, Why am I still holding on to the shark, getting farther away from the boat? And I finally let go."

Like other explorers, Clark has bridled at the restraints on discovery posed by the human body. The breathing helmet and, later, scuba-diving equipment pushed back some of these barriers, but what lay far below the sea's surface could only be imagined until small, maneuverable submersibles became available to scientists. Eugenie made her first submersible dive in 1987 to begin searching for what sailors (and Jules Verne) had believed would be the "monsters" waiting to be discovered deep in the sea. Since that time she has been the chief scientist in charge of more than seventy dives to depths of more than two miles, making fifty-nine of them herself. During one dive in Suruga Bay, Japan, her team indeed found and filmed a monster with which Jules Verne would have been content, the largest shark ever recorded in the deep sea, a twenty-three-foot Pacific "sleepwalker" shark swimming nearly a mile down. The sub shook when the shark slammed into the bait cage.

Despite the advances of modern technology, deep-sea exploration has unremitting perils. Once while searching for the elusive giant six-gill shark, Clark's craft became tightly wedged under a ledge in the rock cliffs more than two thousand feet down. "In the sub, I was alarmed but not really afraid. I knew we had some time to spare, but I also knew we had to use our time to figure out the problem and not waste time being scared." It was midnight—although at that depth, all time is midnight—and she, her copilot, and research assistant were cold and damp and cramped. Just when she was beginning to worry, she was finally able to free the sub and emerge from under the ledge.

For most people, however, fear comes in the shape of sharks. Eugenie explains her success with sharks by saying, "I have a good fundamental understanding of the behavior of many different kinds of sharks, and the different circumstances under which they can be dangerous. It gives me a more complete feeling around them than most people have." It is in part due to this understanding that sharks, while still feared by many, are now appreciated for the integral role they play in the ecosystems of our oceans. Clark and marine enthusiasts worldwide are calling for a moratorium on shark killing to protect this increasingly endangered animal.

Among many other accomplishments, Eugenie has discovered eleven species new to science, and her work has won the recognition it deserved; she has received numerous medals and awards, including the National Geographic Franklin L. Burr Award in 1993.

RIGHT: EUGENIE CLARK SWIMMING WITH A HOOKED NURSE SHARK IN THE RED SEA.

In Memory of Digit

DIAN FOSSEY

AMERICAN PRIMATOLOGIST • 1932–1985

ABOVE: DIAN ESTABLISHED CLOSE CONTACT WITH THE GORILLAS SHE SPENT YEARS STUDYING.

OPPOSITE: PABLO, A SILVERBACK FROM GROUP 5, HALF HIDDEN BY THE DENSE VEGETATION OF THE VIRUNGA RAIN FOREST.

THE NATIVES CALLED her Nyiramachabelli, the Lone Woman of the Forest. But far up on the slopes of Mount Visoke, in Rwanda, she was not alone. Dian Fossey shared this remote mountainside with those she came to study, and ultimately came to love: the gentle and fascinating mountain gorillas. Her primate companions became her extended family during the eighteen years of her research and observation. There was the playful blackback male she called Peanuts, with whom she achieved the first documented human touch contact in 1970; dear Uncle Bert, a giant silverback male named after a benevolent uncle back in California; the lonely silverback Tiger, separated from his group by poachers; Coco and Pucker, the babies rescued near death on their way to a zoo in Europe; and her beloved Digit. Fossey met five-year-old Digit on her first day at camp in Rwanda and described him as "a bright-eyed, inquisitive ball of fluff." She watched him grow and mature over ten years, celebrated his playfulness and affection, mourned his murder at the hands of poachers, and ultimately elevated him to immortality as an international symbol of the urgent need for animal protection. But by the end of this passionate primate story, Digit would not be the only one to be sacrificed.

Perhaps Fossey felt less lonely on the African mountaintop than she did in her first home, a world away. Raised in California by emotionally distant parents who seemed to have little understanding of their daughter's gifts and desires, she found solace and comfort in the unconditional love of animals.

She began her adult life as an occupational therapist, but at her first opportunity, she borrowed enough money to travel to Africa. It was on this trip that she first encountered famed anthropologist Louis Leakey, who would one day become her mentor. She informed him of her desire to visit the Virunga volcano country to see the mountain gorillas. It was photographer Alan Root who finally led Dian to her first sighting of the gorillas. She wrote:

> Sound preceded sight, and odor preceded both in the form of an overwhelming, musky, barnyard yet humanlike stench. The thin mountain air was shattered like window glass by a high-pitched series of deafening screams. Nothing can possibly prepare one for such a terrifying avalanche of sound. . . . Alan motioned me forward and I crept to his side. . . . There they were. . . . the last Mountain Kings of Africa. . . . "Kweli nudugu yanga!" these words in Swahili, whispered by the awestruck Manual, who was also seeing his first gorilla, summed up exactly what I was feeling. "Surely, God, these are my kin!"

It would be three years before Fossey could return to Africa again. This time, with the help of Dr. Leakey, she was offered the opportunity to carry out a field

ABOVE: DIAN IS BURIED IN THE GORILLA
CEMETERY, NEAR HER BELOVED DIGIT,
UNCLE BERT, AND A DOZEN OTHERS.

study of the mountain gorillas in the Parc des Virungas in Zaire. Finally, in January 1967, at the age of thirty-five, Dian was coming home.

Her camp in Kabara lay in a meadow at 10,200 feet up the slopes of Mount Mikeno. Reaching the camp involved an arduous five-hour climb on muddy trails that wound through a dense tangle of vegetation. Fossey hired several dozen porters to carry everything she would need to work and live over an extended period of time. Every bit of food, bedding, camera equipment, typewriters, kerosene lamps, and clothing were transported up the forty-five-degree slopes of the mountain.

Dian had the intense determination and commitment required of an explorer in this remote region. Unlike much of Africa, which is made up of open, arid plains, the Virunga rain forest receives about sixty-seven inches of rain a year, with the average day consisting of two hours of heavy downpour, often accompanied by hail. This near-constant precipitation made climbing the steep, slippery trails a daunting exercise. In addition, Fossey was plagued with a number of physical problems, such as asthma and several bouts of serious pneumonia, which made normal breathing a challenge at that altitude. On treks up the mountain, she often carried twenty pounds of equipment, including camera, lenses, notebooks, and raingear, some-times with the addition of a twenty-pound tape recorder. On these difficult climbs she stopped often, gasping for air. And yet her passion for the work she had taken on remained foremost in her life; difficulties, loneliness, and physical hardships had to be overlooked.

In July 1967, as a result of political unrest in the Congo, Dian was removed from her camp by armed soldiers only seven months after her arrival. By September, she had reestablished her study center in the Parc des Volcans in Rwanda, just one mile from the border of the Congo. The camp was located on the ten-thousand-foot-high plateau between Mounts Karisimbi and Visoke. She named it Karisoke. Fossey's contributions to the field of primate studies were the result of years of patient observation there. She became an expert tracker and could follow a gorilla group by reading the direction of broken branches along the trail and the knuckle prints in the ground. She could sometimes follow by scent.

Her approach was initially one of the hidden observer. Later, she began to announce her presence by mimicking gorilla gestures and vocalizations. Crawling low to the ground, knuckle-walking, she would belch and crunch and scratch. Nib-bling wild celery, Dian would assume a submissive posture. She once wrote of the value of her early training in occupational therapy as it applied to her slow and gen-tle approach to the mountain gorilla. She described her experience working with a patient, a mentally disturbed young man, and her ability to reach him through her nonthreatening behavior. In the same way, she was able to gain the gorillas' confidence and ultimate acceptance.

Each gorilla seemed to name itself: Old Goat, Maidenform, Geezer, Pablo,

IN THE SHADOW OF MAN

JANE GOODALL
ENGLISH PRIMATOLOGIST • B. 1934

JANE GOODALL began her forty-year study of the chimpanzees of Gombe simply by watching. She arrived on the shores of Lake Tanganyika in the summer of 1960. With no scientific background, she had prepared for her journey by speaking to wildlife experts and researchers, who gave her only disappointing news. Chimpanzees were impossible to observe. They would never get used to humans in the field. No one had succeeded in this area of animal research. And for the first three months after her arrival, their judgments seemed to be accurate.

Assigned two local scouts to help her locate the animals, Jane discovered it was impossible to observe chimpanzee families from a distance through the dense foliage. One morning she rose early and climbed to a high overlook one thousand feet above her small camp. Sitting silently on what she would later call "the Peak," she suddenly saw a group of chimps a short distance away. They stared at her, unafraid. It was the true beginning of what was to become one of the major scientific studies of the century.

Goodall's quiet presence out in the open was a message to the animals that she was harmless. Within the next few months, she made the two groundbreaking discoveries that would win her notoriety and ensure her ability to continue her research. First, she observed a male chimpanzee eating meat. Until that time it had been thought that chimpanzees were vegetarians. A short time later, she watched as the same chimp fashioned a tool from a stem of grass and poked it into a termite mound, fishing for his meal. Previous to that time, the theory was that toolmaking was what separated human beings from other animals. Her findings were at once controversial.

Jane's approach had run counter to the style of scientific observation popular at that time. Just as Dian Fossey and Cynthia Moss would do in later years, she gave her subjects names instead of numbers. She described in stories what scientists would quantify, measure, and plot out on charts. Most important, she did not begin with a theory she intended to prove. She began by just watching.

In 1986 she joined the fight to protect chimpanzees, both in the wild and in captivity. Jane's passionate efforts to improve the conditions of laboratory research animals have occupied much of her time in recent years. She travels all over the world, investigating, lobbying, and giving talks aimed at sparing these and other animals from needless cruelty. Her fame and popularity have been leveraged to help the plight of her beloved family.

What Jane Goodall began in 1960 has evolved into the longest-running scientific study of its kind. She has published numerous books, appeared in many films and documentaries, and established the Jane Goodall Institute and a children's educational program, Roots and Shoots. Through her continued efforts, she has opened the eyes and minds of millions of humans to the wonders of our closest living relative.

JOUJOU, A CHIMPANZEE WHO HAD BEEN KEPT IN CAPTIVITY IN THE BRAZZAVILLE ZOO, HAD HIS FIRST CONTACT WITH ANOTHER BEING WHEN HE REACHED OUT TO TOUCH THE FOREHEAD OF JANE GOODALL.

Macho, Beetsme, and Bonne Année. Each had a distinguishing personality and recognizable nose print. Dian's favorite, Digit, was named for his two fused fingers. On New Year's Eve of 1977 Digit was murdered by poachers while he was guarding the members of his group. His mutilated body, with both his head and hands missing, was found the next day by one of Fossey's research students. Dian wrote that when she heard the awful news, "there are times when one cannot accept facts for fear of shattering one's being. . . . From that dreadful moment on, I came to live within an insulated part of myself."

Fossey was determined that Digit's death would not be in vain. What had originally been patient scientific observation now became a full-fledged, one-woman war against the poachers who were threatening the lives and habitats of the gorillas. She established the Digit Fund to help pay for antipoaching patrols and what she called "active conservation." Many students who came to Karisoke to do primate research were enlisted in these patrols to destroy traps and guard against poachers. Dian also had numerous conflicts with Rwandan government officials. She fought those promoting tourism in her area. She often alienated her own research students. Living within that "insulated part" of herself, she cared only for the protection of the gorillas.

In 1983 she published *Gorillas in the Mist*, an account of her work with the mountain gorillas. As her fame grew, so too did her ability to influence events in Rwanda. After a successful book tour, she returned to Karisoke determined to set things right.

When Fossey was brutally murdered on December 27, 1985, she had completed her eighteenth year of primate studies and antipoaching activities. Her death surprised few of those close to her, who had become increasingly uneasy with her outspoken challenges of poachers and government officials alike. She was buried next to Digit in the gorilla cemetery near her cabin at Karisoke. And like her beloved Digit, Dian became a martyr to the cause of conservation, and a symbol of the power of passionate commitment to a beloved cause. Her work continues today through the Dian Fossey Gorilla Fund International, which sponsors ongoing research, antipoaching patrols, education, and local development.

ABOVE: DIAN HAD A SPECIAL BOND WITH DIGIT, WHOM SHE NAMED FOR HIS FUSED FINGERS. THEY INTERACTED FOR TEN YEARS, UNTIL HIS BRUTAL MURDER BY POACHERS IN 1977.

LEFT: THE WALL OF DIAN'S CABIN WAS COVERED WITH PHOTOGRAPHS OF INDIVIDUAL GORILLAS.

Echo of the Elephants

CYNTHIA MOSS

AMERICAN NATURALIST • B. 1940

ELEPHANTS, THE LARGEST of all land animals, have been hunted into near extinction. They have been a particular target for poachers because of their ivory tusks, which are highly valued as trophies and for making jewelry and medicine. Between 1973 and 1989 half of Africa's elephants were slaughtered. Into this carnage stepped a young woman from New York, whose love of animals took her to Africa on vacation. But for Cynthia Moss, Africa was not just a journey; it was a sort of pilgrimage. "I had this overwhelming sense that I'd come home," she said of her first trip there in 1967, at the age of twenty-seven. In Africa she met Ian Douglas-Hamilton, the noted ethologist, author of *Among the Elephants,* who was then conducting studies of elephant populations in Tanzania. Douglas-Hamilton was impressed enough by Moss to offer her a job. When he invited her to help him observe and record elephant behavior, she jumped at the chance. She quit her job in New York and moved to Tanzania to begin work as a field researcher.

Cynthia spent the next few years in Africa working on various animal research projects. Her goal was to begin her own study of the animals she had grown to love, because, she explained, "compared to most other animals elephants lead remarkably complex social lives. Both male and female elephants' relationships radiate well beyond the family group through a multi-tiered network of relationships encompassing the whole population." Her opportunity came in 1972 when she was asked to study the elephants in the 1,259-square-mile Amboseli National Park in Kenya. Now nearly thirty years later, Moss is still observing "her" elephants in Amboseli; indeed, her project is the longest continual observation ever made of a wild elephant population.

Cynthia's first task was to devise a way to identify individual elephants. The system she developed uses file cards with photographs of the elephants' ears. Like a human fingerprint, every elephant ear is unique, due to its pattern of holes, tears, scars, and veins. She began with six hundred cards—one for each elephant in Amboseli—and now has more than eleven hundred cards, each detailing the personality and behavior of a particular elephant. Since an elephant's normal life span is approximately sixty-five years, many elephants she began observing at the beginning of her study are still alive today. This long life span has allowed her to get to know them as individuals. It also has allowed her to document their surprisingly complex social structure and record the degree of learned behavior they exhibit. For example, during a severe drought in 1976, when more than seventy elephants died, one entire family group survived. Because this group suffered famine as did all the other elephants, Moss surmised their success was due to their cohesion; this, she decided, could only have been provided by the matriarch. As she put it, "It was Teresia's knowledge which carried them through the drought."

The matriarch, Cynthia discovered, plays the crucial role in the elephants'

ABOVE: CYNTHIA MOSS HAS BEEN STUDYING THE ELEPHANTS OF AMBOSELI NATIONAL PARK, KENYA, FOR DECADES.

OPPOSITE: ELEPHANTS IN AMBOSELI. MOSS SAYS: "AFTER YEARS OF WATCHING ELEPHANTS, I STILL FEEL A TREMENDOUS THRILL AT WITNESSING A GREETING CEREMONY. SOMEHOW IT EPITOMIZES WHAT MAKES ELEPHANTS SO SPECIAL AND INTERESTING. I HAVE NO DOUBT EVEN IN MY MOST SCIENTIFICALLY RIGOROUS MOMENTS THAT THE ELEPHANTS ARE EXPERIENCING JOY WHEN THEY FIND EACH OTHER AGAIN. IT MAY NOT BE SIMILAR TO HUMAN JOY OR EVEN COMPARABLE, BUT IT IS ELEPHANTINE JOY AND IT PLAYS A VERY IMPORTANT PART IN THEIR WHOLE SOCIAL STRUCTURE."

TOP: MOSS AND HER THREE AMBOSELI
RESEARCH ASSISTANTS. FROM LEFT TO RIGHT:
NORAH NJIRAINI, SOILA SAYIALEL, AND
KATITO SAYIALEL.

ABOVE: AN ELEPHANT FAMILY. MOSS WRITES:
"MY PRIORITY, MY LOVE, MY LIFE ARE THE
AMBOSELI ELEPHANTS, BUT I ALSO WANT TO
ENSURE THAT THERE ARE ELEPHANTS IN
OTHER PLACES THAT ARE ABLE TO EXIST IN
ALL THE COMPLEXITY AND JOY THAT ELE-
PHANTS ARE CAPABLE OF. . . . I THINK IT IS
A GOAL WORTH STRIVING FOR."

survival. She not only leads her family—which in elephant society includes close female relatives and their young, as well as males up to about ten years—to sources of water and food throughout the changing seasons but also teaches them survival skills. For example, when a baby elephant is born, it does not naturally know how to use its trunk; it has to learn this by watching its elders. Adolescent females prepare for their own motherhood by baby-sitting their younger siblings and nieces under the watchful eye of the matriarch. Perhaps one of the most poignant and unusual events Moss documented was the birth of a crippled calf and the efforts of the entire family to help it survive, which it did.

From her base at the foot of Mount Kilimanjaro, Moss continues her studies of the Amboseli elephants. In her writing and lecturing, she works to ensure their survival into the twenty-first century. "I have realized that more than anything else, more than scientific discoveries or acceptance, what I care about and what I will fight for is conservation . . . not of just a certain number of elephants, but of the whole way of life of elephants." To this end she is training local people to work with the animals and devising ways the Masai tribesmen can benefit from tourism as well as be compensated for any crop destruction elephants may cause.

Her campaign on behalf of the elephants received a devastating setback in the spring of 1999, when, despite the warnings of conservationists, several African nations lifted the ban on ivory and instituted the culling, or slaughtering, of selected numbers of elephants. Fearful that lifting the ban on the sale of ivory will bring back the heavily armed poachers, Cynthia is working with wildlife organizations and local governments to protect the borders of Amboseli and other parks. The elephants' greatest protection, however, may be the continued books, lectures, films, and entreaties of people like Moss. She has not only made these extraordinary animals come alive for us but served, literally, to keep them alive.

A SILENT LANGUAGE

KATY PAYNE
AMERICAN ACOUSTICAL BIOLOGIST • B. 1937

In 1984 Katy Payne, an acoustical biologist who had been studying the songs of humpback whales for fifteen years, decided to spend a week at the Washington Park Zoo in Oregon. She wanted to observe some newborn baby elephants. While sitting by the quiet elephant enclosure, she was amazed to feel, she recalled, "a throbbing in the air and pressure on my chest." She suspected that the elephants were making sounds she couldn't hear. Later she returned to the enclosure with a sensitive tape recorder and found that its volume meter was indeed picking up low-frequency sound. Payne was thrilled. "I discovered," she said, "that the elephants were making sounds humans cannot hear and previously no one knew existed."

Her discovery has answered many puzzling questions about elephant behavior. For example, in studying the range of their calls, she found that due to changes in atmospheric pressure in the African savanna, the low-frequency sounds they made actually had a range of up to three hundred kilometers. This ability of elephants to communicate over vast distances explains, she says, "how they found

ABOVE: PAYNE WITH RECORDING EQUIPMENT IN THE FIELD.

LEFT: KATY PAYNE.

each other when they ranged so far apart and how they maintained their distances from each other and how they coordinate their movements. Elephants eat up to 500 pounds of plants a day; if they were too close they could easily over-graze an area."

Since her discovery she has been recording elephant sounds in Africa and America in order to create an elephant dictionary. Making such a collection is no small task, Payne emphasizes, because "elephants live in a complicated acoustic world."

Her discovery has led researchers to look at the hidden communication abilities of other animals, and they have found that even crocodiles and hippopotami use sound below the audible range. For Katy, however, elephants are the most intriguing because they are highly social animals that transmit learned knowledge down the generations through their own evolving language. Hopefully her discoveries about the complex social world of elephants will aid in reinstating a worldwide ban on the sale of ivory and end the tragic policy of culling elephants.

Seeking Ancestors

ANNA CURTENIUS ROOSEVELT

AMERICAN ARCHAEOLOGIST • B. 1946

Perhaps exploring was in her blood. After all, Anna Curtenius Roosevelt's great-grandfather, President Theodore Roosevelt, had led an expedition to the Amazon in 1914 to explore and map a river that had never been explored by white men, the fifteen-hundred-mile River of Doubt. Nearly seventy years later, Anna would follow him into the jungle to explore and map the unknown story of early Amerindians.

What first drew her there was her interest in the origins of agriculture. "I wanted to be an archeobotanist," she said. "I wanted to go to South America to dig up bones and see what the people were growing and eating." But getting into the field was not easy. She had to be invited either by a host country or by the archaeologists who had professionally laid claim to a territory. Rebuffed by a Colombian archaeologist, Roosevelt was finally invited by an American archaeologist to his site to conduct her research in early maize agriculture in the Orinoco, Venezuela.

She soon found that plants, bones, pottery, and wood survive in the tropical rain forest almost as well as they do in cooler climates. Before Anna, few scientists had looked for any early remains in the Amazon because anthropologists simply assumed that the current patterns of the people of the rain forest were unchanged from those of the distant past. Because the current food staple, manioc, could not sustain dense settled populations, they argued that none had ever existed. Accounts by the first European explorers in the 1500s of vast settlements were discounted as fable. But Roosevelt wanted to see the evidence, and she looked for it in the bones that others said would have long since disintegrated in the wet climate. Anna found those bones. After geochemists analyzed the bones' chemical composition, she discovered that they belonged to people who had eaten maize, rather than manioc, as their staple. Maize can support larger populations in one place than manioc and therefore large populations could have lived in the jungle. Roosevelt's study of food was challenging the orthodox view of the settlement of the Americas.

ABOVE: ANNA ROOSEVELT RECORDING DATA AT AN EARLY POTTERY SITE. TAPERINHA, SANTAREM, BRAZIL, 1993. SHE CLAIMS, "MY MOTHER LOVED ARCHAEOLOGY. SHE GAVE ME BOOKS ON ARCHAEOLOGY, LIKE WONDERFUL STORIES BY ROY CHAPMAN ANDREWS ABOUT HUNTING FOR DINOSAUR BONES IN MONGOLIA. WHEN I WAS NINE I DECIDED I WANTED TO BE AN ARCHAEOLOGIST. MY MOTHER SAID THAT WAS FINE WITH HER."

OPPOSITE: ARCHAEOLOGISTS MAPPING THE SITE AT THE CAVE OF THE PAINTED ROCK, MONTE ALEGRE, BRAZIL.

Her National Science Foundation–funded expedition in search of evidence of complex cultures in Brazil led to her first major discovery about the Marajoara culture, c. A.D. 400 to 1300. In describing her findings she said:

The Marajoara culture was one of the outstanding nonliterate complex societies of the world. Apparently a chiefdom, it had an enormous geographic domain that dwarfs those of some famous, old-world civilizations. . . . [It had] large population centers, huge earthworks in urban settings, pottery and complex cosmology. By its scale and elaboration the culture is substantial proof contrary to the conclusion that Amazonian environments were too poor to support the development of complex culture.

Her study of museum collections also led Anna to question how far back in time humans had lived in the Amazon. She began by looking for caves and for the ancient trash dumps called shell middens. In a shell midden near Santarém, Brazil, she found the oldest pottery in the New World, dating to about seven thousand years ago. Then in 1991, on the north bank of the Amazon at Monte Alegre, in the deepest layer of human occupation in the Caverna da Pedra Pintada—Cave of the Painted Rock—she found evidence of one of the oldest sites of human habitation in the Americas, with artifacts dating back 11,200 years. Her excavations in the cave also showed that it held some of the oldest cave paintings in the Americas. They depict geometrical figures, animals, and stick figures. She was able to date them from splotches of paint found on the cave floor. "When we exposed the rock paintings in the vicinity of the cave we saw that the painters had been very sloppy. They would let the liquid paint drip down the wall of the rock as they painted. That was very helpful because then, when we came to excavate, we could look for splattered paint in the strata."

TOP: ROOSEVELT DISCOVERED WHAT IS CONSIDERED TO BE ONE OF THE EARLIEST EXAMPLES OF CAVE ART IN THE AMERICAS AT MONTE ALEGRE.

ABOVE: CROSS-SECTION DRAWING OF AN ARCHAEOLOGICAL EXCAVATION SHOWING LAYERS OF FLOORING AND HEARTHS.

OPPOSITE: POLYCHROME PAINTED BURIAL URN FROM THE MARAJOARA CULTURE, PARA, BRAZIL, CIRCA A.D. 500. FROM MONTE CARMELO ROOSEVELT WROTE, "THE CEREMONIAL ART OF THE MARAJOARA, ABUNDANT IN MAJOR MUSEUMS AND PRIVATE COLLECTIONS WORLDWIDE, IS SOME OF THE MOST COMPLEX AND ACCOMPLISHED ART IN THE WORLD, AND ITS STYLE AND ICONOGRAPHY REVEAL . . . AN AESTHETIC CULTURE OF GREAT SOPHISTICATION. THE PREDOMINANTLY FEMALE HUMAN IMAGERY SUGGESTS A POSSIBLE RITUAL EMPHASIS ON FEMALE GENEALOGY."

Roosevelt also discovered in the caves fruits, nuts, turtle shells, and the bones of deep-water fish more than five feet in length, which led her to believe these early people had used boats in the river. She believes the earliest settlers of the New World must have come up along the coast from China and Japan and crossed over the Bering Strait into North America. Rather than go inland like their contemporaries, the Clovis—the big-game hunters of the western plains—they went down the western coastlines and followed rivers inland.

Prior to Anna's discoveries in the Caverna da Pedra Pintada at Monte Alegre, archaeologists believed that the Clovis people were the ancestors of the Amerindians. Her discoveries threw this accepted belief into question and has gained her as many critics as admirers.

Her work also has implications for current management of the Amazon basin. Roosevelt has shown that the Amazon rain forest, far from being virgin territory, has been home to populations of humans who significantly altered the landscape through cutting, burning, planting, and building during an occupation of over eleven thousand years. Humans have thus played an important role in the rain forest ecological process over the millennia, making the continued presence of indigenous peoples "critical for the survival of the habitat as we know it."

When Anna began to realize that her discoveries in the Americas were going to radically change the picture of Amerindian life and history, particularly the theory that life in the Americas began with plains big game hunters, she

> *began thinking the African story of human evolution was all wrong. It was probably not the savannah where humans developed but the rainforest. There big game hunting could not have been that important and men wouldn't have been so dominant. In the rain forest today, women and children produce the most food. Evolutionists have based a lot of their thinking on the values of Western society.*

From Latin America, Roosevelt has expanded her research into Africa to explore her theory that human beings may have originated in the rain forests, rather than the savannas. There she took the radical step of looking where few had looked before—in the heart of the African jungle in the Congo. "I wanted to go to the rainforest and see if our ancestors had been there. I found evidence for early cultures at sites in the Congo basin."

Finding ancient sites is complicated in the rain forest. Unlike the African deserts that have been swept by wind and erosion—conveniently exposing early remains—the rain forests have built up substantial layers of earth over the same time period. So in order to reach prehistoric sites deep in the earth, Anna says, "I look for areas of volcanic and tectonic activity with rivers running through them to expose the strata. Then I work upriver to the headwaters to see what I can find. In Africa I work in areas where diamond miners have delved into deep earth. I look for human artifacts in their spoil heaps."

Her African work challenged the accepted scenario of early human society. Instead of arising on the savanna with mighty hunters—making modern humans genetically programmed to be violent, male-dominated, and hierarchical—early human development may have taken place in jungles, within more balanced societies relying on women as the main providers of food. As Roosevelt puts it simply, "Specialized big game hunting is not a viable life way in the rain forest."

Today Anna is the curator of archaeology at the Field Museum of Natural History in Chicago and professor of anthropology at the University of Illinois. For her research challenging the accepted canons of paleoanthropology, she has won the prestigious MacArthur Foundation award, National Endowment for the Humanities Fellowships, and the Explorers Gold Medal. While Roosevelt's conclusions are by no means universally accepted yet, evidence is accumulating to support them. Of the controversies she has generated, she says, "I like the messiness. The way things don't turn out as you expect. It's painful, but it is exciting."

In Search of Ancient Mariners

ELPIDA HADJIDAKI-MARDER

GREEK MARINE ARCHAEOLOGIST • B. 1948

ABOVE: HADJIDAKI-MARDER ON THE ISLAND OF DOKOS, 1990, DURING THE EXCAVATION OF A PREHISTORIC WRECK.

ELPIDA HADJIDAKI-MARDER'S childhood was spent in an old Venetian-style house that faced a walled harbor on the island of Crete. As she would later remember her youth, "I grew up with the sea. When I was a child I would put on my mask and flippers and jump into the water. I swam into the underwater caves and searched for anything I could find. At the same time I was reading every book on history like crazy."

These two youthful passions, the sea and the ancient Greek past, came together for Elpida in college in the late 1960s when she discovered underwater archaeology. Having discovered it, she has spent much of her life plunging into the blue Mediterranean as a pioneer in maritime archaeology.

Since 1978 Hadjidaki-Marder has been diving as a professional archaeologist and has made numerous discoveries. Her two most important discoveries are an ancient port in Crete and the largest classical shipwreck yet found; these have had a lasting impact on underwater archaeology.

When Elpida began her Ph.D. thesis on ancient harbors, she resolved to track down the harbor of Phalasarna, an ancient city on the west end of Crete that had been lost for centuries. Its location had been tentatively identified by two nineteenth-century British amateur archaeologists, but nothing was known of it; some scholars thought it was mythical. Experts warned her that nothing was left of the old port, if there ever had been one, and that the thin soil which covered the few visible remains of a town were not enough to have protected harbor installations throughout the centuries. Marks of ancient waves etched far up on the cliff sides convinced her, however, that the sea had once been much higher, and that the harbor should be sought on dry land. She said:

> I realized that the island of Crete was much lower in the sea in ancient times so the harbor I was looking for was probably now on dry land. I walked around the area where I thought it might be. It was covered with trees and brush. So I climbed up onto a little mound to get a better look around and suddenly realized, My God, here it is. I am standing on the remains of one of the old towers that used to guard the harbor. I looked and counted three more mounds marking the corners of the harbor. Then I saw something that looked like a channel that went to the sea.

Archaeologists and historians scoffed at her claim. Her site was too far from the sea, and too high up, they argued, so how could it possibly have been a harbor? A first excavation disclosed a beautiful round tower beneath the hill where she had first stood. A second identified the channel to the sea. Today Phalasarna is marked on all the tourist maps as an archaeological site, and excavations are still only beginning to uncover the many buildings that once lined the coast.

Since that day in 1986 when she stood on the mound, Hadjidaki-Marder has been working to piece together the story of Phalasarna. Ancient historians recorded that it was built in the fourth century B.C. and that over the next three centuries it was one of the most famous pirate towns on Crete, a possibility that

added even more fascination to Elpida's study. She knew that piracy had been so lucrative and so well established in the eastern Mediterranean that some pirate principalities even minted their own coins. They were certainly organized well enough that they would have been able to construct a sophisticated, well-fortified harbor to protect their ships. But by the first century, the Romans were cracking down on piracy. In 67 B.C. Pompey, the great Roman general, undertook to rid the Mediterranean of these troublesome raiders. While he ravaged the southern coast of Turkey, Pompey sent General Metellus Creticus on a "search and destroy" mission to Crete. Metellus carried out his assignment with typical Roman fury: he utterly destroyed Phalasarna and, says Hadjidaki-Marder, most likely massacred all the inhabitants. As they had done in their war with the Carthaginians, the Romans made sure that nothing was left to rebuild. Not only did they tear down the fortification walls, but they even filled in the channel that connected the harbor to the sea.

Elpida discovered that the ruins of the town were further obscured by earthquakes. From historical records, she knew that major earthquakes in A.D. 66 and A.D. 365 had raised portions of the Cretan coast by as much as nine meters (nearly thirty feet). Earthquakes strong enough to buckle huge portions of the earth's crust can also produce enormous tsunami. At least one such tidal wave probably

crashed ashore and completely covered the town with tons of silt. Thanks to the silt, the town was hidden for nearly two millennia. Just as Pompeii was preserved by its natural catastrophe, so Phalasarna has been frozen in time. Uncovering the harbor, says Hadjidaki-Marder, has taught us much about "the extraordinary engineering and architectural abilities of the ancient Greeks. They were brilliant. We had no idea they could do this."

Elpida's discovery of the largest known ancient vessel also reveals the engineering skills of the ancient Greeks. The *Alónnisos* wreck off the coast of northern Greece was first located by a fisherman. His report caught Hadjidaki-Marder's attention when she became director of underwater antiquities for the Greek Ministry of Culture. Diving over the wreck, she was stunned. As she reported, "From the moment I first saw the wreck I knew it was something special. It was like nothing I had ever seen before. It looked like an underwater mountain from above. Then I

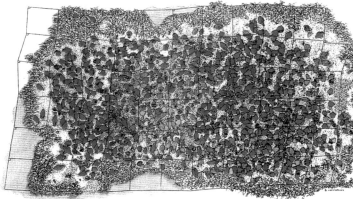

realized it was because the mountain was really a huge mound of artifacts. This was a ship that sailed at the time of the Peloponnesian Wars, about 420 B.C. at the height of Athens' greatness. And the ship was huge."

Ships displacing as much as 120 tons and measuring as much as thirty by ten meters (roughly one hundred by thirty feet) were mentioned by classical writers, but since archaeologists had recovered only ships half that size, they assumed the figures were exaggerated and that the ancient Greeks did not have the ability to build such large ships. Elpida proved the ancient writers right.

While Hadjidaki-Marder has uncovered only a small portion of the 280-square-meter (or 2,800-square-foot) site, she has determined that the ship sunk with a full cargo of amphorae filled with wine and olive oil. She has recovered sets of black-glaze Athenian pottery, plates and bowls that lay stacked on the bottom of the sea for more than two thousand years but are so beautifully preserved they look as if they were made last week. From the cargo she knows the ship was sailing from Macedonia and that it can be dated to the fifth century B.C., which is a full four hundred years earlier than known ships of comparable size.

Hadjidaki-Marder's studies bring to life the accomplishments of the ancient Greeks. Her discovery of the treasures of an ancient merchant ship and the remains of a small defiant town demolished by the Romans has illuminated a long-hidden world.

A NEW LOOK AT AN OLD WORLD

JOAN BRETON CONNELLY
AMERICAN CLASSICAL ARCHAEOLOGIST • B. 1954

THE TEMPLE known as the Parthenon, built on the Acropolis high above the city of Athens, has long been regarded as one of the great icons of Western art and culture. The sculptured relief frieze that decorated the space above the exterior colonnade was thought to represent the fifth century B.C. Athenian citizenry parading in its annual festival to celebrate the birthday of the city's goddess, Athena.

This was the accepted interpretation, but in 1996 Joan Breton Connelly, a classical archaeologist, caused a sensation with a new interpretation. "Why should the arthenon sculptures show a historic reality," she asked, "while all other Greek temples are decorated with scenes from myth?" Using new evidence for the foundation myth of Athens, a story related in a recently discovered play by Euripides, Connelly recognized the story depicted in the frieze to be that of the first king of Athens sacrificing his three daughters to save the city from defeat.

Using far-flung evidence from literature, epigraphy, and art to present exciting new insights into ancient Greek culture is what Joan does best. In 1990 she began excavating the small barren islet of Yeronisos off the western coast of Cyprus to establish its function during the Hellenistic period. After several seasons of digging, the story there began to emerge. Yeronisos, or "Holy Island," served as an important pilgrimage site for worshipers of Apollo during the first century B.C. when Cleopatra ruled Cyprus. So holy was this place that with the coming of Christianity two centuries later, it was adopted by the new Church as a place of pilgrimage.

In addition to her sensitive reinterpretation of tradition, Connelly has carefully avoided forms of excavation that would diminish or destroy the current role of Yeronisos as a major nesting site for birds and other wildlife. Concerned about the invasive procedures used in archaeological excavation, she has pioneered new ways to explore beneath the surface while maintaining the ecological balance and integrity across a site. For her years of discovery and research Connelly was awarded the MacArthur Foundation fellowship.

TOP: JOAN BRETON CONNELLY.

LEFT AND ABOVE: YERONISOS ISLAND AS SEEN FROM THE AIR, SHOWING EXCAVATIONS OF THE ANCIENT TEMPLE.

Transcending Time and Place

THE VISIONS OF ARTIST EXPLORERS

S OME EXPLORERS are inspired by the concept of the unknown, by the notion of charting the blank spots on the map or being the first to set foot in a strange land. Others find their inspiration in more personal approaches to exploration. They might not consider themselves explorers; they might not think of themselves as artists. And yet the women in this chapter are both. They have gone out into the world and experienced its unique riches. They have then brought home their experiences through their talents with paint and canvas, pen and paper, camera and film.

Spanning four centuries, these artists and explorers opened the eyes and the minds of the people they left behind. Women botanists of the eighteenth and nineteenth centuries, for example, provided exquisite illustrations of new plant and insect species to be published in books and popular magazines. Their art often gave them an income and independence and became a means to travel the world. For some, their work was an excuse to leave an unsatisfying life at home. For many, it was the expression of a lifelong passion. They may have thought of their work as serving science, but their talents transcend mere scientific representation. The composition, color, and detail of their illustrations speak of a love of the subject that goes well beyond documentation. Their devotion to the process of art—careful observation, draftsmanship, selection of material—is also evident. They captured with precision, and from a personal viewpoint, the exotic life-forms they were privileged to see.

With the invention of photography in the mid-nineteenth century, many women took to this new technology, which rendered a two-

ABOVE: *OPPOSSOMS*, PAINTED IN SURINAM BY MERIAN. PUBLISHED IN HER *METAMORPHOSIS IN SURINAM*, 1717.

OPPOSITE: MARIANNE NORTH AT HER EASEL.

PRECEDING PAGES: IN 1988, AT THE AGE OF SEVENTY-NINE, MARGARET MEE CANOED DOWN THE RIO NEGRO.

ENDING THE FIVE-HUNDRED-YEAR SILENCE

Linda Schele
American epigrapher • 1942–1998

In 1970 Linda Schele, then a twenty-eight-year-old art teacher from Alabama, went to Mexico with her husband and a group of her art students. The trip would revolutionize not only her life but the way the rest of us see the Maya culture of ancient Mexico. Before her work, the pictographs or "glyphs" that cover the Maya ruins in the Yucatán Peninsula were regarded as unreadable. Learning to read them and to understand Mayan culture became her obsession. So mesmerized was Schele by the mysterious carvings that adorned the crumbling temples of Palenque in the Yucatán region of Mexico that a two-hour tour turned into a twelve-day marathon. "It was," she said, "the most beautiful and sacred place I'd ever been to in my life." She decided from that moment to dedicate the rest of her life to studying the Mayan civilization. "I became so fascinated by the art of the Maya that I was compelled to try to understand who did it, when they did it, and why they did it."

Linda thus took the first steps on a path that would turn her into a world-renowned epigrapher—one who attempts to decipher long-lost writing systems. To share information and speed the process of understanding this ancient civilization, she began the "Maya Meetings," the annual ten-day colloquium held at the University of Texas, where scholars and amateurs gather to work on decoding the glyphs. Because of the pioneering work of Schele and her colleagues in the rain forest, a large portion of Mayan glyphs are now readable. Although she died of cancer at fifty-five, Schele left behind a remarkable legacy, giving the Maya a voice to speak to us across the centuries.

dimensional reality not experienced before. Some women traveled to the far corners of the globe toting elaborate darkrooms, bringing back pictures of ice-bound ships in the Arctic Sea, Chinese villages seemingly unchanged in centuries, and camel caravans crossing the Sahara. The readers of popular magazines could see the faces of the Inuit, Zulu, and Bedouin, and each image sparked new curiosity. Many photojournalists in the last 150 years could also be thought of as artist-explorers. Margaret Bourke-White captured visions of India and changed the way Americans thought of that subcontinent. Susan Meiselas has worked for years to produce riveting photographs of Kurdistan and its embattled people. Photojournalists Carol Beckwith and Angela Fischer captured the traditions and rituals of African cultures.

Filmmaking followed photography, and the documentary films of today can often be considered within the realm of exploration. Women were pioneers in this new form as well, making some of the very first films in the Congo and the South Seas. They are still making films underwater, in the air, in short, wherever there is something to explore.

Other explorers used words to share their visions of the world. By the eighteenth century, women writers were beginning to bring back stirring accounts of their travel, and their approach was as varied as the landscapes they explored. Through factual narrative, intimate memoirs, and even fiction, women shared their experiences with eager armchair explorers.

One common trait shared by many artists and explorers is their love of extreme situations. Having escaped predictable lives at home, they come passionately alive when facing a bruising hurricane at sea or treacherous rope bridge over a chasm. Of course, some disapproved of local customs, such as the permissive sexuality in Tahiti, and others criticized native culinary habits like cannibalism. Nonetheless, they gave us fascinating insights into the world of flying fish and whirling dervishes, sandstorms and snowstorms, mountain men and Buddhist monks. They took us around the Cape of Good Hope and across the Indian Ocean, through typhoons and tempests, past slave caravans and ritualized battles. With them, we rode on elephants and camels and yaks. With them, we ate lizards and monkey and soups made of slugs. And we were changed in the process. For these women explorers, their art was a natural extension of themselves, a reason, sometimes an excuse, to go into the wild. But what they hoped to find was often already inside. They have helped us in that interior voyage of discovery as well.

LADY OF FLOWERS

Marianne North

English Botanical Illustrator • 1830–1890

Marianne North journeyed alone in the later half of the nineteenth century to some of the more remote parts of the British Empire and beyond. Her travel was inspired by her love of botany and her desire to use her considerable artistic skills to paint exotic plants in their natural setting. She was fortunate not only to have the financial freedom which allowed her years of travel but also the courage to go where even men rarely went. She gave her work—some 832 oil paintings portraying 727 genera and more than 1000 species—and the building in which to display them, to The Royal Botanic Garden at Kew near London, where they continue to attract visitors.

Above: *Amatungala, Carissa macrocarpa, in flower and fruit,* and *Ipomoea lapathifolia,* painted by Marianne North at the mouth of the Kowie River during her visit to South Africa in 1882–83.

FLOATING THROUGH PARADISE

Margaret Ursula Brown Mee

English painter/botanist • 1909–1988

Margaret Mee was born and raised in England. She was encouraged from an early age to develop her skills as an artist by her aunt, an illustrator of children's books, and to study nature by her father, a naturalist.

It was not until she was in her early forties, however, that Mee began her great work documenting plants in the Amazon. In 1952, on a visit to South America, Margaret was captivated and inspired by the magnificent and little-known plant life of the great river basin. She mounted her first expedition in 1956 and for the next thirty-two years she traveled throughout the region, mostly by dugout canoe, often for months at a time, painting and discovering plants.

In addition to assembling one of the most important records of Amazonian plant life, Mee became a leader in the crusade to save the rain forests.

Above: A painting of tropical plant life by Margaret Mee.

The Female Voltaire

APHRA JOHNSON BEHN

ENGLISH WRITER/SPY • 1640?–1689

ABOVE: A PORTRAIT OF APHRA BEHN, BY SIR PETER LELY.

She was a most Beautiful Woman and a most excellent poet.

SIR THOMAS CULPEPPER

APHRA JOHNSON BEHN was one of England's most prolific writers during the reign of Charles II (1660–1685). She was the first English-woman to support herself by writing plays and satires; she translated scientific works, and notably, she was a pioneer in narrative fiction. But it was Aphra's experiences as an explorer that unleashed her creative abilities. She experienced a moment in history when three very different cultures came together in the South American jungles, and this experience enabled her not only to see other cultures vividly but, on returning home, to reexamine her own. Consequently, her work remains fresh today, some three hundred years later. Well might she be considered the female Voltaire.

Very little of her personal life is known beyond what she mentions in her literary publications. She came of age during a time of social upheaval in England. The return of the monarchy, a period known as the Restoration, was characterized by a relaxation of public conduct and a revival of creative thought, in contrast to the prior Puritan era. Especially important for Behn, the theaters were reopened and the public hungered for entertainment. Ambitious, talented, and beautiful, Aphra had the opportunity to work as a spy and as a playwright—arenas not usually open to women.

Unable to marry well, probably due to a lack of a dowry, Behn had to find a way to support herself. She did so by acting as a confidential agent for high officials in the British government. She worked under the code name Astrea or agent #160. Her situation was, as she admits, "Unusual with my Sex, or to my Years." It was perhaps in connection with this work, and because she spoke Dutch and French, that she traveled to Surinam, which was then a hotbed of intrigue. Fortunes were being made and lost in sugar and gold, and agents of the Spanish and Dutch were actively seeking opportunities for their nations to grab the colony. With few lines of communication, merchants and politicians often hired spies to report on their interests.

Aphra's popular story *Oroonoko or the Royal Slave* was inspired by her travels to Surinam, and possibly even to Africa, for her life at that time was shrouded in mystery. It is laced with her observations of English colonial life, the customs and habits of the African slaves and Native Americans, and with descriptions of curious plants and animals of the Amazon region.

In her plays she wrote of the hardship of traveling across the Atlantic in a small ship, ". . . a long voyage to Sea, where after a while even the calms are distasteful, and storms dangerous: one seldom sees a new Object, 'tis a deal of Sea, Sea." Once in Surinam, Behn acquired, in some mysterious way, the status of a lady, for she was housed in one of the governor's mansions for about a year; during this time she traveled throughout the countryside. Her novel *Oroonoko* can be read both as a travelogue and more significantly as one of the first powerful antislavery tracts. Her hero, Oroonoko, is a well-educated African prince who is kidnapped and sold into slavery in Suriname. There he is reunited with his beautiful royal lover, who was also captured and sold into slavery. As the story develops, Oroonoko leads an unsuccessful uprising against the evil English governor. Not being able to ensure the safety of his lover, he kills her to send her to "a better place." Doomed, Oroonoko is captured, gruesomely tortured, and executed. In her narrative Behn introduced the then-novel theme, later made popular by the French writer Jean-Jacques Rousseau, of the "noble savage."

To write her book, she drew from her experiences on an expedition she led to a native village eight days away from the colony base in Surinam. This was no light undertaking. Colonists were deathly afraid of the natives, who had on occasion, said Aphra, "[attacked colonists and] cut in pieces all they could take, getting into Houses, and hanging up the Mother, and all her children about her." Arriving at the village, Behn walked ahead with her maid, where she "saw some dancing, others busy'd in fetching and carrying of Water from the River. They had no sooner spy'd us, but they set up a loud Cry, that frightened us at first; we thought it had been for those that should kill us, but it seems it was of Wonder and Amazement. They were all naked; and we were dress'd, . . .very glittering and rich." The Indians examined all of their clothes in apparent wonder, and Behn exchanged her garters for a brilliant feathered headdress, which she eventually took back to England. In her description of their meal with the villagers she said, "They serve everyone of their Mess on these pieces of leaves; and it was very good, but too high-season'd with Pepper. When we had eat, my Brother and I took out our Flutes, and play'd to 'em, which gave 'em new wonder." Visiting the men in their council house, she was frightened by their painted faces but remarked, "However their Shapes appear'd, their Souls were very humane and noble."

She observed that many of the plantation slaves had been ritually scarred:

> [T]hose who are nobly born of that Country, are so delicately cutt [sic] and raised all over the Fore-part of the Trunk of their Bodies, that it looks as if it were japan'd, the Works being raised like high Point round the edges of the Flowers. Some are only carved with a little Flower, or Bird, at the sides of the Temples . . . and those who are so carved over the Body, resemble our ancient Picts.

Like many spies when they are no longer needed, Aphra was not paid for her work, and after returning to England she was briefly put in debtors' prison. Soon after her release she began to publish her stories, and her plays were performed on the stage. Her success led to attacks on her character. She was called wanton and loose. Later prudish generations condemned her for including sex in her plays. But the plays were then and remain today popular, in part because she took up such issues as the fate of colonial peoples and the evils of slavery, arranged marriages, and other unjust practices visited upon women. No finer tribute to her success exists than the fact that her plays are still opening in theaters in England and the United States and her novels have never been out of print.

And these People [native Americans] represented to me an absolute Idea of the first State of Innocence, before Man knew how to sin; and 'tis most evident and plain, that simple Nature is the most harmless, inoffensive and virtuous Mistress. 'Tis she alone, if she were permitted, that better instructs the World, than all the Inventions of Man. . . .They have a native Justice, which knows no Fraud; and they understand no Vice, or Cunning, but when they are taught by the White Men.

FROM OROONOKO

Metamorphosis

ANNA MARIA SIBYLLA MERIAN

DUTCH NATURALIST ILLUSTRATOR • 1647–1717

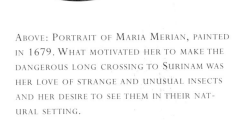

IN JUNE 1699, a fifty-two-year-old woman, accompanied by her twenty-one-year-old daughter, embarked from Amsterdam on a long ocean voyage to Surinam in the New World. Neither colonist nor missionary, wife nor whore, Anna Maria Sibylla Merian was a new type of voyager: she was a female naturalist bound for distant lands to collect, record, and paint. She was, in fact, the first painter to record the life cycles of insects in their natural habitat.

In 1647 Merian was born into a family of artists in Frankfurt. Her father was Matthäus Merian, well known for his engravings, and especially for his illustrated *Grand Voyages,* a book about the New World. Matthäus Merian died when Anna Maria was only three; soon after, her mother married the artist Jacob Marrel. From her mother, Merian acquired a love of insects and a talent for embroidery, but it was her stepfather who was the influential figure in her youth. He taught her realistic oil and watercolor painting, copper engraving, and painting on textiles. It was these skills that brought her great acclaim during her day.

As a young woman, Anna Maria studied with the painters Abraham Mignon and Johann Graff, students of her stepfather. At eighteen she married Graff with whom she had two daughters. The marriage was not a happy one and, quite unusual for her day, Merian obtained a divorce and resumed using her maiden name. In order to provide for her daughters and herself, she sold her embroidery, her drawings of flowers and insects, and occasional portraits.

Coming from a family of painters, engravers, and publishers, it was probably inevitable that Anna Maria would become an author in her own right. While she was married, her husband had published her first book, *Neues Blumen Buch,* in three parts from 1675 to 1680. Reflecting her interest in embroidery and floral design, the book was a series of painted engravings of garden flowers to be used as embroidery patterns.

A book by the scientist Johannes Goedaert, *Metamorphosis Naturalis* (1665), provided her with her next theme: the life cycles of insects. The first volume of her trilogy on European insects, *Raupen,* or *The Wonderful Transformation and Peculiar Plant Nourishment of Caterpillars,* was published in 1679. It contained fifty engravings and extensive commentary of her observations. The next two volumes of this trilogy were not published until, respectively, 1683 and 1717.

Merian's interest in caterpillars, with their astonishing changes from pupa to cocoon to winged creature, became a natural mirror for her devout Christian beliefs. So profound was her faith that in 1685 she was inspired to give up her possessions and enter a religious "retreat" with her mother and her two daughters. Emerging from the commune six years later, Anna Maria was ready for her own metamorphosis; she decided to voyage to the New World.

What motivated Merian to undertake the voyage to Surinam was primarily her love of insects and her desire to see them in their natural state. Her daughter

ABOVE: PORTRAIT OF MARIA MERIAN, PAINTED IN 1679. WHAT MOTIVATED HER TO MAKE THE DANGEROUS LONG CROSSING TO SURINAM WAS HER LOVE OF STRANGE AND UNUSUAL INSECTS AND HER DESIRE TO SEE THEM IN THEIR NATURAL SETTING.

OPPOSITE: A DEPICTION OF THE METAMORPHOSIS OF FROGS AND INSECT LIFE IN SURINAM.

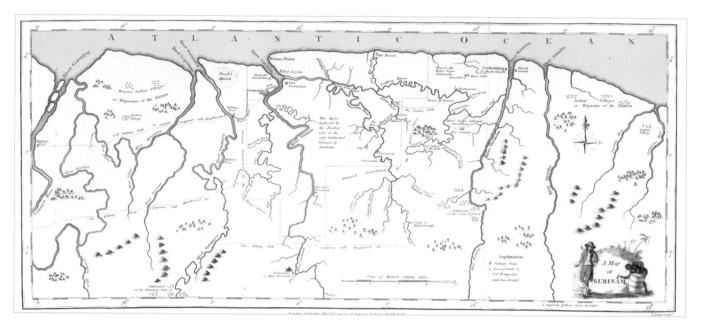

ABOVE: AN EARLY MAP OF SURINAM.

BELOW, OPPOSITE, AND FOLLOWING PAGES:
ANNA MARIA MERIAN WAS THE FIRST EXPLORER-
NATURALIST TO GIVE CREDIT TO NATIVE PEOPLES
FOR HER DISCOVERIES. "ALL [THESE CREATURES]
I MYSELF OBSERVED AND SKETCHED FROM LIFE,
EXCEPT FOR A FEW THAT I ADDED ON THE TESTI-
MONY OF THE INDIANS." SHE ALSO IDENTIFIED
THE PLANTS AND INSECTS USING THE LOCAL
WORDS, IF THEY EXISTED, AS WELL AS THE LATIN.
WHEN SHE RETURNED TO AMSTERDAM, MERIAN
BROUGHT WITH HER A NATIVE WOMAN SERVANT,
WHO PROBABLY AIDED HER IN HER MAJOR WORK,
METAMORPHOSIS OF THE INSECTS OF SURINAM.

Johanna had married a Dutch merchant with connections in Surinam, and through him, Anna Maria was able to start her own collection of South American specimens. She noticed, however, that this wealth of new fauna was not being recorded in situ. "So I was moved," Merian wrote, "to take a long and costly journey to Surinam."

Unlike her male predecessors and contemporaries, Anna Maria, though an accomplished and well-known painter and naturalist, did not receive any support or patronage for her venture. She thus became one of the first of a new breed of explorer: one without ties or obligations save to herself. To pay for passage for herself and her daughter Dorothea, she sold her collection of paintings and her plant and insect specimens and borrowed the remainder, using as collateral future sales of both paintings and specimens. She made out her will and embarked for Surinam in the beginning of summer.

Arriving there, Anna Maria and Dorothea set up house in Paramaribo. From this base and accompanied by their black slaves and native guides, the two women explored the country, usually by paddling up the rivers. For two years, until her health broke in 1701, Merian roamed the rivers and rain forests, collecting and painting insects in their natural habitat. As her reputation spread throughout Surinam native people and black slaves made their way to her home to give her special insects they thought would interest her. Mother and daughter also built up a pressed, preserved collection to take back to Amsterdam for further study or sale. The result of these years in Surinam is Maria's amazing work *Metamorphosis Insectorum Surinamensium,* with sixty colored plates and evocative commentary, which she self-published in 1705.

Merian encouraged her daughters to become painters and naturalists and to explore in search of new subjects. Her daughter Johanna moved permanently to Surinam, and there, following her mother's example, painted and collected local flora and fauna. Some of Johanna's work was included in a posthumous publication, arranged by Dorothea, of Anna Maria's Surinam paintings.

Merian's work inspired the great German explorer and scientist Alexander von Humboldt, and Carolus Linnaeus also cited her work often in his groundbreaking classification of species. Her paintings were collected by many luminaries of the day, including Peter the Great of Russia. Eventually they served as inspiration for the writer and butterfly collector Vladimir Nabokov.

P. Sluyter Sculp.

NUMB. 4621.

THE Flying=Post: OR, Post-Master.

From TUESDAY September 11, to THURSDAY September 13. 1722.

Tuesday last arrived the Mail due from Holland.

Rome, August 29.

Sunday Evening there was a Horse-Race without the Gate Pia, and the Prize being very considerable, there was a great Company of the Nobility.—Next Morning the Pope declared Mr. Maffey, who is now Extraordinary Nuncio at Paris, to be his Nuncio in ordinary at the French Court, and to assist in that Quality at the King's Coronation.—The same Day the Bavarian Minister had a private Audience of the Pope, in which he notify'd the Marriage of the Electoral Prince with the Emperor Joseph's Second Daughter, and obtained a Dispensation for his Marrying within the 4th Degree of Consanguinity.—M. Graccioli designs also to throw off the Prelatical Habit, and to get a Dispensation from the Pope for his Marriage with one of his Nieces.—Three Canons are lately come hither from Port Mahon to complain to the Pope against the English Governour; to which the Pontiff answered that he would Write to the Emperor to desire him to use his good Offices at the British Court, to obtain them speedy Satisfaction.—'Tis said that M. Cesi will be made one of the Canons of St. Peter's Cathedral, in the room of the English Abbot Howard deceased.

Leghorn, August 29. 'Tis confirmed from Lucca, that the Pretenders is actually set out Post from that Republic, but whither is not known. We hear that as long as he staid there, he kept a public Table every Day for 10 Guests, and Touched several Persons for the King's Evil, after which he put a Silver Medal about their Necks, representing *St. Edward, on one side,* and on the Reverse, *3 Ships at Sea.*—'Tis given out that Cardinal Acquaviva, in a late Audience of the Pope, told him that his Master's Squadron of Men of War now at Sea, was at his Service for the Defence of St. Peter's Patrimony and the Island of Malta, provided he would use his Interest with the Emperor to Order the Viceroys of Naples and Sicily, to permit them Entrance into their Harbors in case of need, to furnish themselves with Provisions and other Necessaries, for their ready Money.—'Tis added that the Pope told the Cardinal, he wanted Words to express his Gratitude to his Catholic Majesty for so Generous and Laudable an Offer, and that he would not fail to Write to the Emperor about the Conditions. But this News comes from a Place so suspicious that most Men of Sense treat it as a Romance.

Venice, September 4. Wednesday last the Nuncio Stampa went with a numerous Retinue to the College, to congratulate our New Doge in the Name of the Pope. There are Letters from Dalmatia which say, that the Turks sent a Bassa and a Capigi to Dulcigno, with Orders to Strangle the Captains of some Tartans who had been robbing in the Emperor's Dominions, and committed Hostilities upon the Ships of Segna; but that 3 of the Captains having timely Notice of it, fled to Barbary.

Vienna, September 5. We are told that the Electoral Pr. of Bavaria's Marriage will be certainly consummated on the 8th of next Month. The Prince of Avellino's Archdeacon having been acquitted of the Fact laid to his Charge, has having been sworn into his Office of Apostolical Prothonotary at the Nuncio's Palace, and Capt. Guide, who falsely accused him, being Condemned to Publick Whipping and then to Banishment, has cut his own Throat in Prison. The Emperor has again exhorted the Elector Palatin in very pressing Terms, to give speedy and entire Satisfaction to his Protestant Subjects, for their Grievances since the Treaty of Baden.

Bonn, September 9. Mr. Manning the King of Great Britain's Resident being recalled Home, proposes to set out To-morrow for London.

Ratisbon, September 10. The Protestant Body receives Complaints from all Parts, of the Ill Treatment the Protestants suffer in the Popish Dominions. Mons. time M. van Reck has acquainted them that on the 5th Instant, the Elector's last Placaert, enjoyning the redress of the rest of the Grievances since the Treaty of Baden, is fix'd up in all the Bailiwicks of the Palatinat.

Francfort, September 13. This Day the Elector of Cologne's Baggage passed into this place for Munich, and the Elector himself is expected every Hour in his way to the Court of Vienna. We hear that the Elector Palatin has sent his Great Marshal to meet and invite him to the Palace of Swetzingen.

Cologne, September 15. Our Elector proposes to be back again at Bon by the middle of November. Last Night a Fire broke out with so much Fury in the Village of Wesling upon the Rhine, above 3 Leagues off, that above half of the Place was consumed to Ashes before it could be Extinguished, upon which our Magistrates have ordered every Parish to get a Fire Engine, like those in Holland.

Hamburg, September 17. The Emperor has referred the Affair of the Count de Rantzau to the King of Prussia, as a Prince of the Circle of Lower Saxony, and to the King of Great Britain, as Elector of Hanover. He has likewise referred the Affair of the future Succession of the late D. of Holstein Ploen, to the Courts of Hanover and Wolfenbuttle, whose Ministers are Never-heless to act in concert therein with the Emperor's Minister the Count de Metsch.

An Account of the Inoculating the Small Pox at Constantinople, by a Turky-Merchant.

OUT of Compassion to the Numbers abused and deluded by the Knavery and Ignorance of some Persons, I am prevailed with to give a true Account of the Manner of Inoculating the Small Pox as it is practised at Constantinople and other Places in Turky with constant Success, and without any Ill Consequence whatever. I shall sell no Drugs, nor take Fees; my Design is only to perswade People of the Safety and Reasonableness of this Operation, so that it will be no way my Interest (according to the common Acceptation of the Word) that is, I shall get nothing by it, but the Satisfaction of having done Good to Mankind.

The Matter for Inoculation is always taken from a Young Person of a Sound Constitution, in the best Sort of the Small Pox, when 'tis a little past the Height. The old Nurse, who is the General Surgeon upon this Occasion, takes it in a Nut Shell, which holds enough to infect Fifty Persons, contrary to the Infamous Practice in some Places, where they fill the Blood with such a Quantity of that Matter as often endangers the Life, and never fails of making the Distemper more dangerous and violent than it needs to be: She opens the Arms, and sometimes the Legs, with a small tip of a Needle, and with the Point of the same Needle takes as much of the Matter as will lye upon it, and mixes it with the same Drop of Blood that follows the small Incision of the Needle. The Wounds are bound up with half a small Nut Shell over each of them, which are taken off in 12 or 16 Hours, and the Inflammation appears more or less, as the Blood is more or less disposed to receive the Infection: From that time the Patient is confin'd to a warm Chamber, and a low Diet; being utterly forbid the Use of Wine or Flesh-Meat. The Eruption appears generally the 7th or 8th Day. They give no Cordials to heighten the Fever, and leaving Nature to her self, the seldom or never fails of Success. The Misfortunes that have happen'd to Two Persons that have died under this Operation in London, I have reason to believe were occasioned by the Preparations given them; which is never done in Turkey.

I believe 'tis much to be doubted whether Purges, or any other Disturbance given to Nature, can ever bring the Body into a moderate Temper, which may always be done by an easy Diet and regular Hours; but as I am not a Physician, I will not pretend to dispute with those that are, concerning their General Practice in other Distempers; but they must give me leave to tell them from my own Knowledge and Observation, confirm'd by every one of our Company that has resided at Constantinople, and several Thousands of those there that have happily undergone this Operation. The Preparations serve only to destroy the Strength of the Body necessary to throw off the Infection. The miserable Gashes they give People in their Arms may endanger the Loss of them; the vast Quantity of that Infectious Matter thrown into those large Wounds may possibly give them the worst Kind of Small Pox, and the Cordials they throw down their Throats may increase the Fever to such a degree as may put an end to their Lives.

An Eastern Embassy

LADY MARY PIERREPONT WORTLEY MONTAGU

ENGLISH WRITER • 1689–1762

LADY MARY PIERREPONT Wortley Montagu was well known in early eighteenth-century England for her biting satires of literary personalities and court life. About that part of her life we know very little, because her daughter, shocked by her mother's eccentricities, burned as many of her papers as she could find after her death. As John Mullen remarked in a review of the most recent biography of her, "It was an act of literary vandalism to rank with the posthumous destruction of Byron's memoirs [but what remains is] an extraordinary travel book; glinting poetry; provoking essays; and many artful, agile letters."

It is not for Mary's famed wit and brilliant writing, but rather for what she regarded as a mere sidelight in her career, that she is included in these pages, for it was this cultured gentlewoman who found and conveyed to England the cure for what was then the world's most dreaded disease: smallpox. This scourge killed nearly one out of every four inhabitants of eighteenth-century England, among them Mary's young brother, and disfigured many others, including Mary herself. No one knew what caused it and no cures existed.

Montagu was the daughter of the earl of Kingston, who was a leading politician and a man of considerable learning. She grew up in close contact with the eminent men of the times, and from her early childhood, read and absorbed the literature then available in English and several European languages. While still a child, she began, as she later wrote, "stealing the Latin language." It was a habit she would carry over to learning Turkish and Arabic during her travels.

Despite her innate abilities, Mary was denied any formal education. As she recounted, she was expected to acquire "womanly skills," such as the art of polite conversation, drawing, a bit of music, and enough household management to preside over her prospective husband's dinner table. Her future lay in a suitable marriage to a wealthy man of her class. Nonetheless, she was inspired to begin her own writing. By the age of fourteen, she had written a book of poems; by seventeen, she had written several long odes or poetical stories on classical themes. Soon her

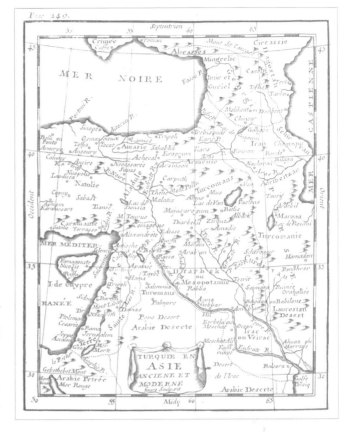

ABOVE: A MAP OF TURKEY FROM THE PERIOD.

OPPOSITE: LADY MARY WORTLEY MONTAGU IN TURKISH COSTUME (LEFT), AND (RIGHT) ISSUE OF *THE FLYING POST* IN WHICH SHE DEFENDED THE USE OF "ENGRAFTING," OR INOCULATION, TO PREVENT SMALLPOX, A PRACTICE SHE DISCOVERED DURING HER SOJOURN IN TURKEY.

BELOW: A VIEW OF EIGHTEENTH-CENTURY CONSTANTINOPLE.

essays and satires began appearing in broadsides. Men of letters began to frequent her father's house to converse with her.

Meanwhile, her father had undertaken the elaborate ritual of finding her a husband. The man who emerged from the process had the unlikely name of Clotworthy Skeffington. Whether it was the name, the man, or the process, Mary was horrified by this prospect. As she later commented, "People in my way are sold like slaves; I cannot tell what price my master will put on me." When the financial negotiations with her chosen suitor broke down, Mary did the unthinkable. In 1712 she eloped with Edward Wortley Montagu and forfeited her dowry from her father.

The marriage was hardly based on wild romantic passion. She herself compared it to the marriage her father had proposed by saying that "Limbo is better than Hell." But the husband she picked was rich, intelligent, and admired. In 1716 he was sent as British ambassador to the court of the Ottoman Empire to help negotiate a treaty to end one of the many wars between the Ottoman Empire and Austria. Accompanied by their young son and twenty servants, the couple traveled by boat, stagecoach, and horseback to Vienna and eventually on to Constantinople. To keep in touch with her many friends in England, Montagu wrote numerous descriptive and witty letters about her experiences. Later bound and published as the *Turkish Embassy Letters,* they clearly indicate her enthusiasm for new experiences and her delight in unusual customs.

One of the innovations she saw spoke to the English experience. At that time, and for generations to come, even the richest of the English suffered from cold and damp in their vast houses, and throughout the dreary winters, they went without many kinds of vegetables and fruits. As she passed through Vienna, Montagu was amazed by the variety of fresh fruits available off-season. She was told about the hothouses kept warm by the use of "stoves, which are certainly one of the greatest conveniences of life. . . . If ever I return, in defiance to the fashion, you shall certainly see one in the chamber of [your] dear sister."

Amazement arose not only on her side. In Sophia she went to a Turkish bath where the ladies were astonished by her corset. She wrote, "They believ'd I was so locked up in that machine, that it was not in my own power to open it, which contrivance they attributed to my Husband. . . . They all agreed that 'twas one of the greatest barbarities of the world, and pitied the poor women for being such slaves in Europe."

As soon as she arrived in the Ottoman capital, then still known to Europeans as Constantinople, she did as she had done in England: she contacted the leading scholars in order to learn as much about the East as possible. She also began learning Turkish. To an English friend she wrote, "I am pretty far gone in Oriental learning; and to say truth, I study very hard."

She was not content merely to remain in the great capital city. Rather, she traveled extensively in Turkey dressed in native costume—a long, flowing robe and a veil. She was often invited to dine with women in harems, a pastime she greatly enjoyed. She was amazed by the freedom of Turkish women, which she believed was in part due to their dress: being veiled allowed them to move about with greater liberty. She also attributed their freedom to their lack of concern with the notion of sin, which so constricted women in

English society. "Upon the whole, I look upon the Turkish women as the only free people in the Empire."

That any of Mary's personal writings survive at all is due to her own prescience. Before returning to England, she gave a copy of her letters to a friend in Holland, requesting him to publish them if he wished. Her daughter later tried unsuccessfully to prevent their publication, and the letters have never been out of print since.

On her travels, she witnessed a rough form of inoculation against smallpox.

> *The small-pox, so fatal, and so general amongst us, is here entirely harmless by the invention of ingrafting. . . . There is a set of old women who make it their business to perform the operation every autumn, in the month of September when the great heat is abated. People send to one another to know if any of their family has a mind to have the* [inoculation against] *smallpox . . . the old woman comes with a nut-shell full of the matter of the best sort of smallpox, and asks which veins you please to have opened. She immediately rips open [the one] that you offer to her with a large needle (which gives you no more pain than a common scratch), and puts into the vein as much venom as can lie on the head of her needle, and after binds up the little wound with a hollow bit of shell.*

Montagu returned to England just at the outbreak of the great smallpox epidemic of 1721. She was anxious to protect her daughter from the illness that had destroyed her own beauty, so in the presence of doctors she replicated the Turkish "ingrafting" to inoculate the young girl. The vaccination was immediately opposed by the clergy, however, since it was an alien practice borrowed from Muslim heretics. It was also dismissed by doctors who believed instead in bloodletting.

The controversy was carried out in a series of pamphlets written both in support of and against the practice. One said, "Posterity perhaps will scarcely be brought to believe, that an experiment practiced only by a few ignorant women, amongst an illiterate and unthinking people, shou'd on a sudden, and upon a slender Experience, so far obtain one of the Politest Nations in the World as to be receiv'd into the royal palace." But into the royal palace it came: heresy or not, the princess of Wales tried the Turkish prevention with success.

Mary herself published a rebuttal to the attacks entitled *A Plain Account of the Inoculating of the Small Pox by a Turkey Merchant*. She wrote, "Out of compassion to the numbers abused and derided by the knavery and ignorance of Physicians I am determined to give a true account of the manner of inoculating the smallpox as it is practiced in Constantinople with constant success, and without any ill consequence whatever." After being tested on six condemned criminals and on children in an orphanage, the practice began to gain adherents. But because of repeated attacks by the clergy and medical profession, the use of ingrafting died out after only about eight hundred people were inoculated. It was not until some seventy years later, when Edward Jenner reintroduced the practice, that it became the standard and successful treatment for smallpox.

Montagu traveled extensively throughout Europe alone for another twenty-three years, sending back accounts to her friends. Her open-mindedness, fairness, and truthfulness about the people and customs she encountered during her journeys make her letters as fresh and entertaining today as they were to her correspondents nearly three hundred years ago.

I was in my travelling habit, which is a riding dress, and certainly appeared very extraordinary to them, yet there was not one of 'em that shew'd the least surprise or unpertinent curiosity, but received me with all the obliging civility possible. I know no European court where the Ladys would have behav'd themselves in so polite a manner to a stranger.

VOODOO GODS
SAMANA OR
ATWOODS CAY
CROOKED I.
Plana Cays
MARIGUANA I.
Dry Rocks
Castle I.
Abraham Bay
Caicos Passage
NO. CAICOS
PROVIDENCIALES
W. CAICOS
SO. CAICOS
INAGUA I.
GREAT INAGUA
Mathew Town
Channel
TORTUGA
Port de Paix
Cap Haïtien
Gonaives
Ennery
St. Marc
Artibonite R.
Mireballais
Concepcion
Leogane
PORT AU PRINCE
Jacmel
Marigot
Saltrou
C. Falso
BEATA I.

Her Eyes Were Watching

ZORA NEALE HURSTON

AMERICAN FOLKLORIST/NOVELIST/ANTHROPOLOGIST • 1891–1960

WHILE MOST AMERICANS, black and white, were mired in the Depression, Zora Neale Hurston spent the 1930s crisscrossing the back roads of Florida and living in hamlets in Haiti, Jamaica, and the Bahamas, recording the songs, stories, dances, and rituals of African Americans. In 1936 she traveled to Haiti, on a Guggenheim fellowship, to explore the bizarre and often frightening world of voodoo. Her search was important not only because it gained her a graduate degree but because her recordings constituted an important contribution to African American studies.

Voodoo is an amalgamation of West and Central African religious traditions that were brought to the New World by enslaved Africans and practiced secretly. Hurston particularly wanted to investigate zombies, beings said to transcend death. "No one can stay in Haiti long," she wrote, "without hearing Zombies mentioned in one way or another, and the fear seeps over the country like a ground current of cold air. This fear is real and deep." But finding out about these nightmarish creatures, she was warned, would have dire consequences. "I would," she remembers being told, "find myself involved in something so terrible, something from which I could not extricate myself alive, and that I would curse the day I entered upon my search."

Today, Zora is primarily remembered as a literary star of the Harlem Renaissance, which drew the brightest black artists, musicians, and writers to uptown New York. She had made her way there by sheer talent from a childhood of segregation and deprivation in the rural South. Hurston grew up in Eatonville, Florida, one of the first incorporated black towns in America. She was proud of the fact that although her father, John Hurston, began his adult life "not owning pots to pee in, nor beds to push them under," he was three times elected the mayor of Eatonville and was a minister in the Zion Hope Baptist Church. While he passed his drive to succeed on to his daughter, their relations soured after the death of her mother. When he remarried, she desperately longed to escape, remembering, "I used to take a seat on top of the gate post and watch the world go." When she was thirteen, Zora left home to live on her own.

Almost the only opening for a young black woman at the time was to work as a maid, so Hurston took up housecleaning. Although she wasn't able to complete high school until she was twenty-seven, in 1919 she enrolled in Howard University and in 1925 she won a scholarship to Barnard College. Interested in exotic places and curious about strange customs, she studied with the eminent anthropologists Franz Boas and Ruth Benedict at Columbia University. Boas helped Zora win grants for her graduate fieldwork, and in 1928 she moved to New Orleans to begin her studies of the folkways of African American society. She was interested in the African sources of folklore beliefs as well as the ways these beliefs had changed in reaction to the trauma of slavery. These two issues led her into what would become her passion, the study of voodoo.

To penetrate voodoo's mysteries, she realized that she could not be an outside

ABOVE: ZORA NEALE HURSTON ON A FOLK-LORE COLLECTING TRIP IN A FLORIDA SWAMP.

OPPOSITE: THE MYSTERIOUS WORLD OF VOODOO HELD A FASCINATION FOR HURSTON. SHE WOULD TRAVEL TO HAITI TO BECOME INVOLVED IN THE SECRET PRACTICES OF THIS ANCIENT ART.

My search for knowledge of things took me into many strange places and adventures. My life was in danger several times. . . . Primitive minds are quick to sunshine and quick to anger.

ABOVE: HURSTON BEATING A "HOUNTAR," OR "MAMA DRUM."

Research is formalized curiosity. It is poking and prying with a purpose. It is a seeking that he who wishes may know the cosmic secrets of the world and they that dwell therein.

observer; rather she would have to become initiated in its practices. Only in this way, she thought, would the adherents come to trust her and tell her about their beliefs. As she later wrote, "In New Orleans, I delved into Hoodoo, or sympathetic magic. I studied with the Frizzly Rooster, and all the other noted 'doctors.' I learned the routines for making and breaking marriages; driving off and punishing enemies; influencing the minds of judges and juries in favor of clients; killing by remote control and other things."

The experience was a bizarre one. In one of her initiations in Louisiana, she had to lie naked on a table for days with only water to drink in order to starve herself into a condition to have visions. In another she remembered, "My finger was cut and I became blood brother to the rattlesnake. We were to aid each other forever."

New Orleans was the beginning, but she soon learned that as powerful as voodoo was there, it was only a pale relative of the original, so she determined to seek out its source. Her first stop was in the Bahamas, where, she was told, blacks had been able to preserve more of their African heritage. From there she journeyed to Jamaica and finally to Haiti.

She was determined to go wherever the trail led her. What she discovered was enormously exciting, often baffling, and sometimes frightening. Throughout the Caribbean islands Hurston found many ceremonies and celebrations that had African antecedents. For example, in the Jamaican "Nine Night" death ceremonies, the *nanas* or old nurses who presided over the rituals were reminiscent of African priestesses. The way they handled the body of the deceased and the oaths they proclaimed, she believed, were inspired by the tribal practices of central Africa.

Zora also studied the folk belief in spirits. For example, she thought *duppies* were a reaction to the trauma of slavery in the New World. The duppy is "the life force"—the spirit that causes the person (as distinct from the body) to exist. "When the duppy leaves the body, it no longer has anything to restrain it and it will do more terrible things than any man ever dreamed of." She was told that duppies

lived mostly in silk-cotton trees and almond trees. One should never plant either of those trees too close to the house because the duppies will live in them and "throw heat" on the people as they come and go about the house. One can tell when a duppy is near by the feeling of heat and the swelling of the head. A duppy can swell one's head to a huge thing just by being near. But if one drinks tea from that branch of the snake weed family known as Spirit Weed, duppies can't touch you. You can walk into a room where all kinds of evil and duppies are and be perfectly safe.

From the relatively benign duppies, Hurston moved to the far more sinister zombies. They were at the heart of voodoo. It all stems, she wrote, "from the firm belief in survival after death. Or rather that there is no death. Activities are merely changed from one condition to the other." Zombies, she was told, are "bodies without souls, the living dead." In a sense, she speculated, they resembled the transformation inherent in the process of enslavement, the move "from an educated, intelligent being to an unthinking unknowing beast" who toiled for life in the fields.

Zombies are created by a person called the *Bocor,* who performs this service for a fee either for those who bear grudges or those who need labor. The zombie goes to a targeted person and "sucks out his soul. After the person dies and is buried the Bocor goes that night and wakes the person up—but without the soul it is not human. He is taken to a ceremony and given a drop of liquid. After that he has no memory. . . . It is evident that the [drug] destroys that part of the brain which governs speech and will power. The victims can move and act but cannot formulate thought."

Zora's time in the field came to an end in 1937, when she penetrated too far into voodoo to continue in safety. Fortunately, she had broadened her studies beyond the occult to the culture of the peoples of the Caribbean. More than the place, it was the music and the dance she heard and saw throughout the area that she came to love. As she later wrote, "Folklore is the boiled down juice of human living. It does not belong to any special time, place, nor [*sic*] people. No country is so primitive that it has no lore, and no country yet has become so civilized that no folklore is being made within its boundaries."

Inspired by her exploration, Hurston published an autobiography, novels, plays, and her research on the belief systems in Haiti and Jamaica. But royalties and commissions came only sporadically. Though honored for her writing, she often had to support herself by working, as she had in her youth, as a maid. Finally, with

ABOVE: THE FIRST PHOTOGRAPHIC PROOF OF THE EXISTENCE OF ZOMBIES WAS THIS ONE TAKEN BY ZORA NEALE HURSTON. SHE WROTE, "OF MY RESEARCH IN THE BRITISH WEST INDIES AND HAITI, MY GREATEST THRILL WAS COMING FACE TO FACE WITH A ZOMBIE AND PHOTOGRAPHING HER. THIS ACT [TAKING A PICTURE] HAD NEVER HAPPENED BEFORE IN THE HISTORY OF MAN."

her health failing and financially destitute, she entered a welfare home where she died in 1960. As a pauper, she was buried in an unmarked grave.

Tragically, many of her papers were burned as trash after she died. A few were spared, thanks to a passing policeman who put out the bonfire because it had no permit. Years would go by before she was rediscovered. Zora Neale Hurston has now taken her place of honor as a pioneer in African-American southern and Caribbean cultural studies, a brave woman who traveled into danger to discover the hidden heart of another culture.

Triumph of the Will

LENI RIEFENSTAHL

GERMAN FILMMAKER/PHOTOGRAPHER • B. 1902

At last I was . . . leaving everything behind me, as though a great load were slipping from me and I was starting a new part of my life.

AT THE AGE of sixty, in 1962, Leni Riefenstahl was ready to begin a new life. She had already succeeded on both sides of the camera, both as an actress and as a director. Applauded as one of the greatest filmmakers of the pre–World War II era, she had later been damned as a friend and chronicler of the Nazis. Coming out of a long, dark period after the end of the war, she embarked on a new role: she became an explorer. "I was," she said, "magically drawn by a very specific Africa—the dark, mysterious and still barely explored continent."

Lured by the harsh desert landscape, not dissimilar to the frozen mountain landscapes where she had made films in the 1920s and 1930s, Riefenstahl explored the little-known southeastern Sudan from 1962 to the mid-1970s. It was a hostile land, barren and dry, inhabited by people who had very little, if any, contact with the outside world. "I saw black figures coming towards me, seeming to hover in the quivering light, detached from the earth as in a mirage. Africa had embraced me—

ABOVE: RIEFENSTAHL'S LIFETIME CAREER AS A FILMMAKER. LEFT, SHOOTING HER FILM *TIEFLAND* IN 1940; CENTER, FILMING THE NUBA IN KORDOFAN, SUDAN, IN 1974; AND RIGHT, MAKING UNDERWATER FILMS IN THE 1990S.

OPPOSITE: RIEFENSTAHL'S EVOCATIVE PORTRAITS OF THE NUBA OF KAU IN THE SUDAN. SHE WROTE, "AFRICA HAD EMBRACED ME— FOREVER. IT HAD SUCKED ME INTO A VISION OF STRANGENESS AND OF FREEDOM."

forever." She spent months at a time with the Kau, Masai, and Nuba peoples, photographing their dances, ritualistic knife fights, and striking body painting and tattooing. Her photography is preserved in two books, *People of Kau* and *Last of the Nuba,* both of which received wide critical acclaim.

Her journey to the Sudan was long and arduous. Leni was raised in Berlin; from an early age she dreamed of being an actress. Although her father encouraged her athletic abilities, he forbade her any career that involved the stage. But as a teenager she discovered she had a talent for dance and secretly enrolled in a ballet class. She danced in more than seventy performances in Europe before being sidelined by a knee injury. A chance viewing of the mountaineering film *Mountain of Destiny* opened a new path, which would give her skills she later used as an explorer. She met the director, the pioneering silent filmmaker Dr. Arnold Franck, who was so impressed by Riefenstahl that he wrote a film for her, *The Holy Mountain* (1925–26). Her subsequent films, all critical successes, demanded that she perform breathtaking live mountaineering stunts. In *The White Hell of Pifz Palü* (1929), she was hauled up a steep ice wall as avalanches crashed over and around her. In *Storms over Mt. Blanc* (1930), she crossed deep crevasses on flimsy ladders,

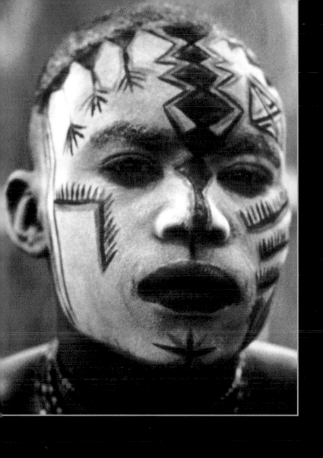

and in *The Blue Light* (1931–32), she had to climb ice walls barefoot and without ropes. The craft of filmmaking fascinated her. She said, "The editing room became a magic workshop for me."

Leni had her first encounter with her future patron, Adolf Hitler, when curiosity prompted her to attend a Nazi rally at the Sports Palace in Berlin. His speech and the enthusiastic reaction of the crowds mesmerized her. Later, after Hitler became Germany's chancellor, she jumped at the chance when he asked her to make films for him. *Triumph of the Will* (1934) and *Olympiad* (1938) achieved enormous worldwide success. But all films in Germany had to be made with the permission of Hitler's notorious minister of propaganda, Joseph Goebbels, with whom Riefenstahl had a serious falling-out. After the war, because her name and work were associated with Hitler, she was imprisoned and vilified. For years she was preoccupied with legal battles to regain the rights to and copies of her prewar films. She finally realized that because of her connection to Hitler, she would never again find either the financial backing or the opportunity to make feature films. She had to begin life anew.

ABOVE: LENI RIEFENSTAHL SHOWING THE NUBA PHOTOGRAPHS OF THEM THAT SHE TOOK ON A PREVIOUS EXPEDITION.

In her life as an actress she had played the role of an explorer; now she decided she would become one in reality. Riefenstahl first went to Africa in 1956, and while there she met some Masai tribesmen. Entranced, she determined to return to photograph them. Her opportunity came in 1962 when the German Nansen Society, which sponsored anthropological fieldwork, contacted her to make a documentary about the little-known Nuba people of Kordofan in southern Sudan.

After days of driving west from El Obeid, she found what she was looking for: "In the light of the setting sun, one or two thousand people . . . peculiarly painted and adorned, they seemed like creatures from another planet. Hundreds of spear tips danced against the blood-red ball of the sun. . . . I was among the Nuba at last." During the next years Leni would go on numerous expeditions on which she developed lasting relationships with both the Nuba and the Kau people. She delighted in showing them the photographs she took of them, in listening with them again and again to the tape recordings she made of their music, and watching with them the films she made of their lives.

By the 1970s, Riefenstahl was again ready for something new. She found it one day in 1972, while in Malindi, Kenya, on holiday. By chance, she noticed the word *goggling* written on a chalkboard and discovered it meant "snorkeling." Intrigued, she signed on for her first dive. She so loved diving that she became a certified scuba diver at the age of seventy-two.

Soon she was comfortable enough with her new milieu to begin experimenting with underwater photography and film. She photographed during night dives to capture on film marine nocturnal life. She explored the natural architecture of deep underwater caverns. She also documented the mysterious habits of large fish such as the giant stingray. Well into her nineties, Leni was still enthralled by the endless mysteries of the sea. Throughout her life, her own indomitable will more than triumphed.

SAVING A LOST WORLD

GERTRUDE ELIZABETH LOERTSCHER DUBY BLOM
SWISS CONSERVATIONIST/PHOTOGRAPHER • 1901–1993

WHEN SPANISH missionaries began to convert the indigenous Mexican peoples to Christianity in the sixteenth century, a few groups of Mayan Indians managed to escape the conquerors by fleeing into the vast jungles of Chiapas. There they eked out a livelihood and rebuilt something like their former society. Their descendants, the Hach Winik—"True People"—or the Lacandones, as outsiders called them, were able to live in hiding for hundreds of years. It was into this remote and hidden world that a Swiss woman came in 1943.

Gertrude "Trudi" Duby was raised in the Swiss Alps. While working as a journalist in the 1920s and 1930s, she was so appalled by the growing Fascist and Nazi movements in Europe that she used every opportunity to expose their destructive activities. But when she discovered in 1940 that she was on a Gestapo death list, she fled Europe for Mexico, which was then accepting European political refugees. While sailing across the Atlantic, she read French anthropologist Jacques Soustelles's book *Terre Indienne,* which described his encounters with the Lacandon Indians. The book changed her life. After reading it she declared, "My decision was made. I must also know them."

In 1943 Trudi heard that an expedition led by explorer Frans Blom was about to depart for Chiapas to search for the Lacandones. She applied to go with the expedition as a journalist and soon found herself in a small bush plane flying into the remote region. So inspired was she by the Lacandones that she decided to dedicate the rest of her life to recording their oral histories, photographing their lives, and to fighting to preserve the rain forest that is still their home. "Traveling by horse and on foot through the pueblos of Chiapas, I

ABOVE: BLOM WITH LACANDON SHAMANS. SHE SPENT DECADES IN THE YUCATÁN, PHOTO-GRAPHING THE LACANDONES. HER EXTENSIVE ARCHIVE IS NOW HOUSED IN THE CULTURAL CENTER SHE ESTABLISHED IN CHIAPAS, MEXICO.

LEFT: A LACANDON CHILD ON NAJA LAKE, 1959.

photographed all that I saw," she wrote, "I wanted to keep those impressions not only in my own memory, but put down so that other people could enjoy them."

Trudi fell in love with Frans Blom and later married him. They moved in 1960 to San Cristóbal in the Chiapan highlands, where they bought an abandoned seminary. In their large home, which they called "Na-Balom," or House of the Jaguar, they established a cultural center dedicated to Mayan studies. The center now has a library specializing in Mayan studies; it also houses Blom's archive of some fifty thousand photographs, which complements the oral histories she and others have collected and her ethnological museum.

Concerned about the widespread destruction of the rain forest in Chiapas, Trudi fought lumber companies, farmers, and cattle ranchers. She also began a reforestation program in 1975; this program has grown into a formidable effort that now plants about forty thousand saplings a year.

Blom's passion resulted in the preservation of a culture that was little known and clearly endangered. Contact with the outside world has exposed the Lacandones to diseases, including influenza, which nearly wiped them out in 1963, making Trudi's photographic document all the more poignant. She embodied a new kind of missionary zeal—not designed to change or destroy local beliefs, customs, and the environment but to help the inhabitants learn how to protect what they believe to be the essence of their lives. In this way, Blom was able to turn a personal passion into a mission to preserve one piece of the richness of our world.

Forgotten Angel

RUTH AGNES MCCALL ROBERTSON

AMERICAN PHOTOGRAPHER • 1905–1998

ABOVE: RUTH ROBERTSON'S FIELD NOTEBOOK DESCRIBES THE DAY WHEN SHE FINALLY REACHED ANGEL FALLS.

OPPOSITE: ROBERTSON IN FRONT OF ANGEL FALLS, VENEZUELA.

An orange, near-full moon came up and turned the dark mass of the canyon wall into half light, with the distant falls a silver streak down the middle. Whatever hardships this trip had given us, this particular moment seemed to make it worthwhile.

I N THE HISTORY of exploration, there are many stories of magnificent adventure and bravery. Sadly, there are also explorers whose courageous efforts have been forgotten. Daring expeditions that contributed knowledge to our world have faded away without receiving the lasting recognition they deserve. In 1949 journalist Ruth Robertson led just such a forgotten expedition.

Robertson was a reporter during and after World War II. After she returned to a desk job at the *New York Herald Tribune,* life lost its thrill. Looking to escape New York, Ruth accepted an assignment that took her to Venezuela. There she became involved in a quest that would lead her to Churún-merú, or Angel Falls, the highest waterfall in the world. Robertson had been seduced by rumors she'd heard back in New York of a "mile-high waterfall." Once in Venezuela, she convinced pilots to take her flying past the majestic cascade in order to photograph it. But these aerial glimpses were never enough: she was determined to photograph it from its base. However, no one had ever succeeded in reaching the falls on land. Four expeditions before her had tried and failed.

Angel Falls tumbles from the edge of a towering sandstone mesa called Auyan-tepui in the Guiana Highlands of southeast Venezuela. Beginning as rainfall on the flat land above, the water disappears into an underground river and finally pours out an opening in the side of the mountain. At its base, it joins the Rio Churun to meander through hundreds of miles of impenetrable, unexplored rain forest.

Ruth spent months securing funds, preparing for the journey, and organizing her team. On the evening before her departure, she "set the clock for 3:45 and eased down on the bed to rest for the couple hours left. Was I going on a fool's journey as the men had said? I had been obsessed with this idea of getting the waterfall measured for months, and the compulsion to do it had colored every day of my life."

She and her team set out on April 23, 1949, for what was to be a three-week adventure. They traveled up the Rio Acanaan in dugout canoes and camped in drenching rain. On a diet of canned sardines, pineapple, and spaghetti, she lost twenty pounds while enduring extraordinarily rugged conditions. In her book, *Churún Merú—The Tallest Angel,* she describes the relentless insect population that inhabits the jungle, including the dreaded monkey-faced tarantula.

Her team hacked their way through dense, primeval jungle and clambered over rocks. Finally, on May 12 they got their first glimpse of the Angel, a celestial sight indeed. Robertson's expedition was the first to reach the base of the falls and the first to measure it. Rising 3,212 feet above the dense jungle, Angel Falls is fifteen times the height of Niagara Falls, or twice the height of the Empire State Building. The press carried the story of her triumph around the world, unfortunately scooping her own exclusive story for *National Geographic* magazine. Today the falls are named for Jimmy Angel, the American bush pilot who first spotted them from the air. No honor or recognition has been awarded to Ruth Robertson, the intrepid explorer who risked her life to measure them.

In the Words of the Voyager

TRAVEL WRITERS

WOMEN WRITERS have enriched our lives with visions of exotic lands and inspiring accounts of their journeys around the world. They've taken us out of everyday experience and placed us in unfamiliar surroundings, thus opening our eyes and our minds. They've challenged us to accept differences, and by doing so, to understand better our own culture. In *West with the Night,* Beryl Markham showed us what it was like to fly low across the savannas of East Africa. Anne Morrow Lindbergh explored her insights and impressions while piloting her small plane along the northern route to Asia in *North to the Orient.* Robin Davidson relished solitude and simplicity in *Traveling Light,* a memoir of a trip through the world's deserts, and Diane Ackerman took us on a magical journey through the realms of the natural world in *The Moon by Whale Light.* These women went into the world with an eagerness to immerse themselves in the new, and with a willingness to see clearly from the point of view of a traveler.

In exactly the same manner as the artist feels an invincible desire to paint, and the poet to give free course to his thoughts, so was I hurried away with an unconquerable wish to see the world. In my youth I dreamed of travelling—in my old age I find amusement in reflecting on what I have beheld.

IDA PFEIFFER

visit Canton, Tahiti, and Tierra del Fuego could read about these exotic places and their strange peoples and customs. As one biographer said about her, "Ida Pfeiffer may indeed justly be classed among those women who richly compensate for the absence of outward charm by their remarkable energy and their rare qualities of mind."

Pfeiffer began her voyages when she was forty-five years old. Her first trip in 1842 to the Holy Land resulted in her first book. With its success she was able to undertake her second voyage, this time to Iceland to collect botanical and geological specimens and, again, to write about her experiences. Determined to continue traveling, she then began her first trip around the world, sailing to Brazil and continuing with an itinerary staggering even by today's standards. Her voyage took two and a half years and carried her across twenty-eight hundred land miles and thirty-five thousand miles at sea. Along the way she documented the life and customs of the people she encountered, weather events, natural phenomena, geography, and traveling conditions. Her readers were treated to tales of flying fish and sea fire. She wrote, "In the wake of the vessel I beheld a streak of fire so strong that it would have been easy to read by its light; the water round the ship looked like a glowing stream of lava, and every wave, as it rose up, threw out sparks of fire."

With her as their guide, readers crossed the equator for the first time and beheld the constellation of the Southern Cross. And with her, they weathered many a storm at sea. Of one particular storm off South America, Ida wrote:

ALONE UPON THE BOUNDLESS OCEAN
IDA REYER PFEIFFER
AUSTRIAN WRITER • 1797–1858

IDA PFEIFFER'S enthusiasm for adventure and eye for detail enabled her to create fascinating travelogues for the armchair traveler. Through her writings, people unable to

At a little past 8, the hurricane broke forth. Flash after flash of lightning darted across the horizon from every side, and lighted the sailors in their work; the agitated waves being illuminated with the most dazzling brilliancy. The majestic rolling of the thunder drowned the captain's voice. . . . Such a storm as this affords much food for reflection. You are alone upon the boundless ocean, far from all human help, and feel more than ever that your life depends upon the Almighty alone. . . . A feeling of tranquil joy always comes over me during such great convulsions of Nature. I very often had myself bound near the binnacle, and let the tremendous waves break over me, in order to absorb, as it were, as much of the spectacle before me as possible; on no occasion did I ever feel alarmed, but always confident and resigned.

Her advice to travelers considering a voyage on a sailing vessel includes a list of foods to bring along, with "a good quantity of eggs, which, when the vessel is bound for a southern climate, should first be dipped in strong lime-water or packed in coal-dust; rice, potatoes, sugar, butter. . . . I would strongly recommend those who have children with them to take a goat as well." And for added comfort, she recommends bringing a mattress.

Her readers were treated to a glimpse of her living conditions in South America: "I therefore spread out my cloak upon the ground, arranged a log of wood so as to serve instead of a pillow, and for the present seated myself upon my splendid couch. In the meanwhile, my hosts were preparing the monkey and the parrots, by sticking them on wooden spits, and roasting them before the fire." In Tahiti, she balked at the liberal sexual mores of the people, dined with Queen Pomaré

and "Prince Albert," and described the incredible shellfish living in the crystal-clear waters.

She shared her impressions of Chinese foot binding: "Four of the toes were bent under the sole of the foot, to which they were firmly pressed, and with which they appeared to be grown together; the great toe was alone left in its normal state . . . the lower portion of the foot was scarcely four inches long, and an inch and a half broad." Of her sojourn in India, she described the Taj Mahal by moonlight, introduced her readers to the antelope, and related a detailed account of a journey by ox cart and camel from Delhi to Bombay.

In Baghdad, she paid a visit to the harem of the Pasha and then joined a caravan for a two-week crossing of the desert to Tebris. On a later voyage, she stopped in Borneo and visited the Dyak tribe of headhunters deep in the rain forest, whom she found "honest, good-natured, and modest in their behavior." In Sumatra, she decided to seek out the Batak, a tribe known to be cannibals; Pfeiffer was the first European ever allowed into their territory and the first to report on their way of life.

Ida's books, published in Austria and London, opened the world to thousands of curious readers. Her descriptions were as inspiring as they were educational. Living largely through the kindness of strangers, she traveled in many dangerous and inhospitable lands, carrying with her a thirst for knowledge, extraordinary courage, and real perseverance. She brought back information about world geography, ethnography, and history, along with a collection of plants, animals, and minerals. When Pfeiffer died in Vienna at the age of sixty-two, she had traveled 20,000 miles over land and 150,000 miles at sea in sixteen years.

A LADY'S LIFE AROUND THE WORLD
ISABELLA LUCY BIRD BISHOP
ENGLISH WRITER • 1831–1904

Far from the gloom of an English winter, Isabella Bird sailed into paradise. This small, spirited lady traveler arrived in Hawaii, then called the Sandwich Islands, in January 1873. She was to experience danger and excitement, ride horseback through the countryside, climb volcanoes, and encounter unconverted, naked "heathens." But this was not the same woman who had left England six months before. Her travels had transformed her from a sickly and depressed spinster into a vital, spirited adventuress.

It was, in fact, illness that first drove Isabella to travel. This woman, who has been called one of the "most accomplished travelers of her time" by the Royal Geographical Society, began life as a frail child, the daughter of an English clergyman. Born in Yorkshire in 1831, Bird had developed a tumor on her spine by the time she was eighteen. Following surgery, her health problems continued with debilitating headaches, sleeplessness, and a general malaise. Her doctor wisely suggested a change of scene.

At first her travels were moderate in nature. From her home in the north of England, a trip to the Scottish Highlands seemed the perfect sojourn. She found herself refreshed and invigorated by this excursion but upon returning home to her confined life, the pains that plagued her returned as well, a pattern that would continue throughout her life. Isabella was by no means a flamboyant woman, and even in the remotest places she carried herself as a respectable lady. But she reveled in her freedom as she wandered across the world, observing and recording her grand adventures.

In 1854 she traveled to North America, covering six thousand miles through Canada and the United States. Her first book, *Englishwoman in America,* published in 1856, described this journey. Upon the death of her father in 1858, however, she decided to remain in Edinburgh, where the family had settled, and to attempt to lead a more pious life.

Nearly sixteen years passed while she tried to deny her longing for adventure. She filled her time at home writing articles and doing the good work of a pious Christian woman, but her health problems steadily worsened. Bird finally surrendered to her wanderlust in 1872, when she chose to embark on a voyage to Australia. She found Australia and New Zealand not at all to her liking, and after a distressing sojourn there, she boarded a ragged paddle steamer bound for California. It was during this disastrous voyage that her spirit returned.

Like Ida Pfeiffer twenty-six years before, Isabella came alive during a raging typhoon that threatened to capsize the boat. "At last I am in love," she wrote, "and the old sea-god has so stolen my heart and penetrated my soul that I seriously feel that hereafter, though I must be elsewhere in body, I shall be with him in spirit." She described the time on board as being like "living in a new world, so free, so fresh, so vital, so careless, so unfettered, so full of interest that one grudges being asleep."

She also fell in love with Hawaii. It was there that Bird learned to ride horses astride, which freed her from the crippling back pain that a sidesaddle brought. She had a special riding costume made that consisted of loose Turkish trousers covered by a full skirt. The demure skirt covering the rebellious trousers mirrored the duality of her own personality, at once respectful of convention and yet defiant.

Her trip to Hawaii was the beginning of a life that alternated between passionate travel abroad and subdued periods spent at home in

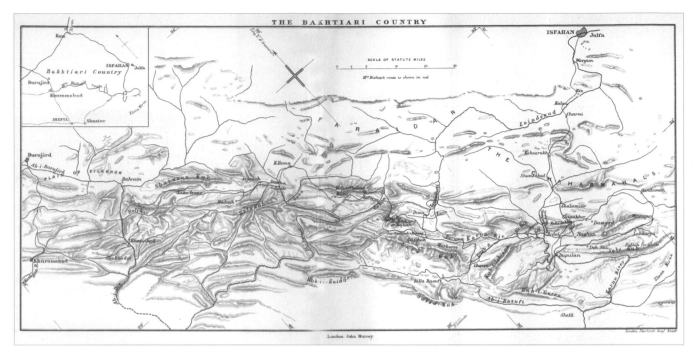

England. Isabella made a trip across America, much of it on horseback, and had a famous and seemingly romantic encounter with a rustic mountain man in Colorado, whom she would describe in her popular book, *A Lady's Life in the Rocky Mountains.* She next set off for Asia, traveling to northern Japan to see the Ainu people and becoming the first European woman ever to visit them. Ten years then lapsed during which time she married a doctor and stayed in Scot-

land. Her husband died only five years after their marriage, and she was off again, this time to Pakistan, India, and Tibet. Continuing on to Persia and Kurdistan, she joined a caravan. Her next journey took her to China and the border of Tibet.

Bird's writing paints a vivid picture of daily life in exotic and faraway places. A meal in Japan is "a stew of abominable things," including "salt and fresh fish, dried fish, seaweed, slugs, the various vegetables . . . , wild roots and berries, fresh and dried venison and bear . . . anything they can get, in fact, which is not poisonous." In Tibet, she explains, they eat "barley-meal porridge, cold balls of barley dough, broth, cheese, sour cream, and dried apricots" and sixty year old butter!

She wrote of accommodations, costume, and character; discussed politics and economics; and amazed readers with her perilous exploits. Isabella forded many a turbulent river, once nearly drowning in Tibet. In Persia she rode for six hours through rain and sleet "in mud up to the mules' knees into the filthiest village I have ever seen." In China, she describes the harrowing experience of crossing a treacherous mountain pass:

> It was then 8:30 and very dark. A snowstorm came on, dense and blinding, with a strong wind. I was dragged rather than helped along, by two men who themselves frequently fell, for we were on a steep slope, and the snow was drifting heavily. . . . Several times I sank in drifts up to my throat, my soaked clothes froze on me, the snow deepened, whirled, drifted, stung like pin points. But the awfulness of that lonely mountain cannot be conveyed in words: the ghastly light which came on, the swirling, blinding snow-clouds, the benumbing cold, the moans all round, for with others, as with myself, every breath was a moan. . . . On the whole this was my worst experience of the kind.

She was sixty-two years old at the time of this writing.

But woven throughout her tales of hardship and danger was a passion for life's intense experiences. In the end, Bird's voyages helped educate and entertain those who stayed at home, while they healed her body and her soul. Her writings paved the way for others like her who, yearning for adventure, would come to share their experiences through their writing, photographs, and films.

TOP: A MAP OF BIRD'S JOURNEY THROUGH PERSIA.

LEFT: ISABELLA BIRD IN MANCHU DRESS.

Into the Heart of Darkness

EMILY HAHN

AMERICAN WRITER • 1905–1997

I'VE SEEN crocodiles before," twenty-five-year-old Emily Hahn wrote during her journey down the Congo River, " . . . but never so close, and never so intimately. I could smell this beast: a horrible sticky, fishy smell. And it wasn't even looking at us: it just lay there and waited. I looked at the canoe and saw as if it were for the first time that we were only about six inches out of the water, and my elbow occasionally dipped in when there was a ripple . . . then without slackening in my fear, I began to shape the words to tell about the crocodile if I should get home and start to write." Emily did get home to write her story. In fact, during her long and adventurous life she wrote more than fifty books and two hundred articles, many for *The New Yorker* magazine, chronicling her adventures in Africa and China. Much of her writing was about animals, especially the apes that she kept as pets throughout her life.

Living for two years in a pygmy village in the Belgian Congo was Hahn's first exposure to a different world and one that shaped her adventurous career. But getting there was not easy. "Africa," she wrote, "was an unusual hobby for a young woman in the late 1920's and, as I learned by painful experience, most men didn't understand my ambition to go there." But Emily never worried about people understanding her ideas or schemes.

As a girl growing up in St. Louis, she was an avid reader who often acted out the adventures of the characters in books. "I drifted down river with Huck Finn, and got lost with Tom Sawyer," she wrote, "and sailed here and there, all over the world, with any number of other people, scorning the stale air of indoors." This spirit followed her to college:

EMILY HAHN WROTE: "WE WERE LOST IN A SEA OF LEAVES MOST OF THE TIME, OR STUMBLING THROUGH CLEAR SPACES FLOORED WITH BROKEN TREES, TRACES OF ELEPHANTS. NOT EVEN THE VESTIGE OF A DESERTED VILLAGE ALL THE WAY— AND A LONG WAY TOO. WE CROSSED TWO CONSIDERABLE SIZED RIVERS. THE SECOND WAS SO HIGH IT HAD WASHED AWAY THE TREE THAT SPANNED IT, AND WE CROSSED BY WADING, WITH A ROPE TO HOLD ON TO HELD OUT BY A FEW HARDY SOULS WHO WENT ON AHEAD."

when told that a course she wished to take was open only to engineering students, Hahn immediately switched her major into the all-male engineering department. Four years later, in 1926, she became the first woman to graduate with a degree in mining engineering from the University of Wisconsin.

Her college dream of going to Lake Kivu on the border of Uganda and the Belgian Congo looked to be a lot closer after she got her first job in a mining company. But Emily was disappointed. "I was," she later recalled, "put at an ordinary green metal desk that stood in an ordinary office," at a lower salary than her male colleagues. She quit her job, and after a stint in New Mexico as a trail guide, found herself in New York teaching geology and dreaming of Africa.

Her chance finally came when she met Patrick Putnam. The scion of an old Boston family, Putnam had defied custom by marrying a woman of the Mangebutu tribe during a Harvard-sponsored expedition to the Belgian Congo. He had been forced to leave the Congo by scandalized officials, but was able to return by volunteering for the Red Cross. Hahn saw this as her chance to get to Africa.

In 1930 she sailed for Africa with a load of medical supplies bound for Putnam's forest camp. She packed a costume called an elephant suit, or safari suit, and a Bible, which, she joked, was "to be found at my heart when I am found dead." After arriving in Boma, at the mouth of the Congo, she journeyed fifteen hundred miles upriver to Putnam's camp in Penge, where she was surprised to find that he had not one

but three wives, all sporting teeth filed to sharp points.

Emily worked in Putnam's makeshift field hospital for nearly two years. She learned to speak Kingwana, which came in handy when she led her own expeditions in the forest. After twenty months in Penge, however, Putnam's madness became unbearable. She left abruptly one morning when, after she asked him for help trimming her hair, Putnam shouted at her, "No member of my family is going to use halfway measures on her head anymore. And that goes for you as well as the other girls . . . clippers or nothing." His threat of subjecting Hahn to the same treatment received by his wives was a more frightening prospect to her than heading off, little prepared, into the jungle for weeks of trekking.

Of her eight-hundred-mile journey through forests and swamps to Lake Kivu, she wrote:

> I was taking a long trip on foot toward the east coast, because that was the way one had to travel in the forest. There were no roads yet through the trees; there was just a system of pathways that were—at least, half of them— elephant tracks. Apart from my head boy, Shabani, I needed a guide to figure them out. Mine was a Pygmy, whose people, of course, knew all the ways of elephants. You could always rely on a Pygmy.

In writing about her journey Emily made light of the dangers: possible encounters with cannibals, slave traders,

City Girl Feels Safer Alone in Gorilla Wilds

ABOVE: STAGING AREA OF HAHN'S BELGIAN CONGO EXPEDITION, 1932. SHE WROTE, "THE MARCH AFTER NEXT, MSABA SAYS GLOOMILY, IS NOTHING BUT A PYGMY PATH AND HE EXPECTS I WILL DIE OF FATIGUE. MAYBE SO. . . . WE STILL HAVE THREE BASKETS OF RICE IN CASE THERE'S NO FOOD IN THE FOREST."

LEFT: A NEWSPAPER ARTICLE ABOUT EMILY'S AFRICAN EXPEDITION.

OPPOSITE: EMILY HAHN'S PORTRAIT, TAKEN BEFORE SHE LEFT FOR THE CONGO.

and rogue elephants; the threat that her porters would abandon her; the danger of contracting deadly fevers; and the lack of food. In addition to her "head boy" and pygmy guide, her party consisted of her five-year-old adopted child, Matope, her pet baboon, Angelique, and twelve native porters.

Hahn was the first white woman many forest dwellers had ever encountered, and certainly she was the first leading an expedition. Anticipating a return to western society, she wrote, "I dreaded the change. I shrank from the thought of living in a white world again, where I would have to talk to people. For months I hadn't had to make conversation, and I felt that I'd lost the knack. It was all too much effort—problems to grapple with, uncomfortable clothes, and practical arrangements to make."

From Africa, Emily went on to live for nine years in China, where she was the concubine of a Chinese poet and became addicted, for a time, to opium. She fell scandalously in love with the married chief of British intelligence in Hong Kong, bore his child, and endured several years of deprivation and starvation during the Japanese occupation of the island. All of her experiences, even the most intimate, became fodder for her books and articles. Throughout her life she wrote compassionately of misunderstood cultures and of animals, especially monkeys. An outspoken advocate for female equality, Hahn died in New York in 1997 at the age of ninety-two.

At dawn, when I was on watch, I looked over the quiescent stretch of the Andaman Sea and saw on the horizon the filmy, unsubstantial image of landfall. Settled over with the peace that comes from gliding forward into a meditating world of waveless calm, I watched the tiny thickening of the horizon grow into a violet smudge.

This is the girl who did what millions dream of doing. She refused to be trapped. She walked out on her comfortable but increasingly routine life. She walked out on her well-paying New York job. She leapt from the treadmill and set off for the farthest corners of the earth.

A Stranger in the World

LEILA ELIOTT BURTON HADLEY

AMERICAN WRITER • B. 1925

In 1950, against the advice of friends and family and with her five-year-old son in tow, twenty-five-year-old Leila Hadley boarded a cargo ship in San Francisco bound for the western Pacific. "I had wanted to get away . . . I wanted to be a stranger in a world where everything I saw, heard, touched and tasted would be fresh and new." Entranced by the exotic landscapes she saw and the unusual customs of the people she encountered during her first long voyage of discovery in the Pacific, and her subsequent journeys through India, Leila wrote two award-winning memoirs about her experiences.

Born into a sophisticated family in New York, she spent her childhood summers in Scotland, where a stern Victorian grandmother set her regime. Split between these two different worlds, she never felt quite comfortable in either. Standing apart, Haley became a gifted observer and learned to share her acute observations through her lyrical writing.

Though taught to value education and learning, Leila was denied the chance to go to college and instead was rushed into marriage at age seventeen to a "suitable" young man. But the marriage did not work, and by the time she was twenty, she was divorced and had a young child. Already showing talent as a writer, she got a high-paying job in celebrity public relations. On the way to what promised to become a successful career, Hadley was nonetheless desperate to get away. She dropped out of New York society in the most dramatic way she could find: she bought a one-way ticket for herself and her son on a cargo ship bound for the Far East.

In Bangkok, a chance encounter changed her life. One afternoon she was invited aboard the *California,* a three-masted schooner then docked in the harbor undergoing repairs. The schooner's crew of four men was in the midst of a leisurely sail around the world. Leila knew this was the adventure she was looking for. She convinced the men to take her and her son along with them. She joined the crew in Singapore and quickly fell into the rhythm of life with no fixed itinerary, sailing from landfall to landfall. She chronicled their voyage through the Pacific and Indian Oceans and into the Mediterranean Sea in her first book, *Give Me the World.*

A second marriage, children, and the necessity of earning a living intervened with any further adventures. Finally, with her four children grown, and divorced

ABOVE: LEILA HADLEY'S PASSPORT, WITH HER FIVE-YEAR-OLD SON.

OPPOSITE: HADLEY IN THE RIGGING OF THE *CALIFORNIA.* IN HER BOOK *GIVE ME THE WORLD,* SHE WROTE: "THE LEVEL SPACE OF WATER BETWEEN US AND THE VIOLET SHADOW OF NANCOWRY AND CAMORTA SHOOK WITH THE GOLD OF THE SUN. SPACE ALL ABOUT, AND THE ISLANDS NOW COMING CLOSER, DARKENING, EXPANDING TO A LONG, LOW MOUND OF JUNGLY VEGETATION, WITH THE PALMS SO CLOSELY CRUSHED TOGETHER THAT NO ONE TREE WAS OUTLINED, THE WHOLE A SOLID PALISADE OF DARK QUIVERING FOLIAGE."

yet again, Hadley was able to return to Asia. Ostensibly she was going to India to find her elder daughter. As she wrote in *Journey with Elsa Cloud,* her journey began with a phone call: "[M]y daughter has been lost to me in a world I do not understand. I have been lost to her in a world she has left and has come to scorn. In more than two years I have not spoken to her. Now I have been awakened by a telephone call." Although her daughter's summons was the catalyst for Leila's journey, she was really there to discover India. She wanted to write about the essence of India, its look and feel, its customs and belief systems. Pulled by the allure of one ancient Hindu or Buddhist ceremony to the next, she found a culture incomprehensible to many westerners; through her skills as a writer, she made this world accessible.

ABOVE: HADLEY IN AN INDIAN TEMPLE.

The sights, sounds, and smells of India are captured viscerally. For example, she wanders down one dusty alleyway off a side street in the marketplace of Bangalore, "not far from the Ladies 'Urinlas' [sic]" and chanced upon an Ayurvedic dispensary. Curious about the use of the herbs she sees displayed, she inquires about their use and is told, "[T]he chilies, ginger, and pepper [are] for the effect of increasing the body's internal heat and decreasing 'body mucilage'; molasses and rose leaves arranged in alternating layers in a tightly covered jar, cooling, soothing, and excellent for constipation and piles; garlic in sesame oil for chronic disorders of the ear; white onion crushed with a little gur (jaggery) to alleviate fatigue."

Eventually Hadley reached the goal of her journey, the spiritual center of Tibetan Buddhism and the home of its religious leader, the Dalai Lama—Dharamsala. After meeting the Dalai Lama she wrote, "I feel free and light, disencumbered, as if the restrictive wrappings of worry, anxiety, depression, tiresome bindings of twentieth century acedia, have been stripped away to reveal another self—not an entirely new self, but one that is better, more comfortable."

Since her return from India in the mid-1970s, Leila has been dedicated to promoting understanding between the United States and India and Tibet. Through her writing and lecturing she has joined the ranks of those few explorers who have the skills to translate their experience to transport their readers into another world.

Inside the temple the air was dense with the sound of voices. The smell of jasmine, joss and human bodies was almost overpowering. The brilliance of the sun had temporarily blinded me, and, feeling dazed and queasy, I passively allowed myself to be jostled about. . . .

ANTARCTIC NAVIGATION

ELIZABETH ANN ARTHUR
AMERICAN WRITER • B. 1953

ELIZABETH ARTHUR was "so addicted to wilderness living" that after graduating from high school in Concord, Massachusetts, she went out west and became a wilderness guide in Wyoming. After two years leading backpacking expeditions through the Wind River Range, she decided she wanted to live year-round in the wild. She left Wyoming to homestead on a remote island on Stuart Lake in Canada.

ABOVE: ARTHUR STANDING IN FRONT OF ROBERT SCOTT'S HUT, ANTARCTICA.

Inspired by her experiences in Wyoming and Canada, Arthur began to write, explaining, "I was in love with the process of being separated from human society. Being in the natural world helped form my creative imagination." One theme, which she would carry through her novels and memoirs, was how people react to the tremendous forces of nature they encounter while living in the wilderness. She wrote about ordinary people caught in extraordinary situations, having experiences they could only have when "confronted by the extremes of the world."

Obsessed by Antarctica, Elizabeth undertook her own journey south in 1990, through the Antarctic Writers and Artists Program sponsored by the U.S. National Science Foundation. The preparation for the trip was intense, "like joining the army," she said. But when she finally arrived, she knew the waiting had been worth it. Arthur's time alone camping in a wannigan (a survival hut) at Cape Evans was, she said, "transcendent." Her resulting novel, *Antarctic Navigation,* relates the story of a woman's quest to recreate Robert Scott's last expedition to the South Pole.

Elizabeth understands the particular drive that leads an explorer to endure "a huge amount of extreme discomfort for the few moments of total transcendence." Capturing that special drive in her novels, she makes the difficult and dangerous world of exploration come alive. As her heroine recounts, "There is another Antarctica, also. The one where you go and almost die . . . where the storm and the crevasse take you inside them. I thought that would happen to me, long before I came here, I thought I would die here. But I didn't, and yet I came close enough to see the ice as few have ever seen it."

While her stories capture the intensity of exploration's hardships, she is also able to illuminate what she calls the "mystical truth that can only come from time to time," which is the ultimate goal of every explorer. Arthur's creative talent, combined with her varied experiences in the wilderness, has given her a special window into the intensely personal drives that motivate exploration. Through her writings one can viscerally feel the brittle cold of Antarctica and vicariously join in the struggle against the stinging winds roaring across a mountain ridge.

Aerial Markings

MARILYN BRIDGES

AMERICAN PHOTOGRAPHER • B. 1948

ANGING OUT of small planes as they bank and turn, Marilyn Bridges photographs the enigmatic designs and structures humans made centuries ago on the contours of the earth. Her stark black-and-white photographs have opened new vistas in exploration, allowing novel perspectives and insights on the design, nature, and intrinsic beauty of ancient and sacred sites in the Americas, Europe, Asia, and Africa.

In 1976 Bridges, then twenty-six and traveling in Peru, met the German mathematician Maria Reiche, who had been studying the Nasca Lines for thirty-seven years. Reiche introduced Marilyn to these immense drawings created more than two thousand years ago by people scraping surface rocks to reveal the lighter-colored soil beneath. Bridges quickly grasped that the best way to view these monumental designs would be from the air. When she hired her first small plane for this job, the pilot was understandably perturbed by her request that he remove the door so she could take unobstructed pictures. Here in this vast space, Marilyn's fascination with history, photography, and spiritual exploration came together and she began her lifework photographing the sacred from above.

Her work is dangerous and exhilarating. It involves soaring in small planes between mountain peaks through strong winds and updrafts, and flying low over landscapes to capture details. Because pilots were reluctant to take the risks required, she became a pilot. "I knew what I was doing was very dangerous. To take pictures I had to fly low and slow and do turns and banks to get things lined up right. I didn't know if the pilot really knew what he was doing. Now that I am a pilot, I know what is going on."

What draws Bridges to the ancient sites she has photographed in Arizona, New Mexico, South America, England, Egypt, Greece, and Indonesia is that they are or have been considered holy. She explains, "many of the sites were meant to be viewed by the Gods above." Her images of these man-made landscapes offer us a rare view of the relationships people developed with their land. Her photographs illuminate our ancestors' attempts to understand and reach their gods. She says, "Seeing from the air changes the whole way you look at the earth. I feel like I was meant to do this work.

"Being airborne must be like being reborn. As earthbound creatures, our thought and vision are quite understandably linked to the physical plane, and we ignore or at least minimize transcendental experience. . . . Seeing from above is not consistent with seeing from the ground. It is not just a matter of up and down. It took me quite some time to be able to condense information from such a large scale of vision. Seeing from a bird's perspective with human eyes initially can be confusing—one gets lost in the sweep of imagery and feels restricted by the apparent flatness of everything. But when one flies and photographs as I do, at low altitudes, shadows lift objects from the ground and . . . intimacy is regained. There is the unmistakable awareness of the warmth of contact and a vivid awareness of interrelationships."

ABOVE: MAYAN TEMPLE AT COBA.

LEFT: BRIDGES CIRCLED MONUMENT VALLEY IN A
SMALL PLANE, WAITING TO CAPTURE THE DRAMATIC
LIGHT OF THE SUNSET. BRIDGES SAYS, "I LOVE
PAINTING WITH SHADOWS. TIMING IS SO IMPOR-
TANT. I HAVE TO SHOOT WHEN THE SUN IS AT AN
ANGLE IN THE EARLY MORNING OR THE LATE
AFTERNOON. I HAVE LEARNED TO WORK QUICKLY.
IT IS DANGEROUS BECAUSE I TAKE THE DOOR OFF.
IN THE ANDES THE UPDRAFTS AND DOWNDRAFTS
CAN COME QUICKLY. SOMETIMES FEAR GOES
THROUGH ME. A LOT OF THE PILOTS I HAVE FLOWN
WITH HAVE CRASHED AND DIED. THE AIRCRAFT
EQUIPMENT ISN'T ALWAYS GOOD. BUT I HAVE TO
SHELVE THE FEAR SO I CAN GET INTO THE PHOTOG-
RAPHY. BUT IF I SENSE SOMETHING LIKE A BANK OF
DARK CLOUDS, I RETURN."

PRECEDING PAGES: CHERHILL HORSE, ENGLAND.
MARILYN BRIDGES PHOTOGRAPHED THIS PREHIS-
TORIC CARVING IN 1985.

FOLLOWING PAGE: *YARN AND NEEDLE*, NASCA,
PERU, 1979. ABOUT 250 MILES SOUTH OF LIMA,
PERU, BETWEEN THE NAZCA AND INGENIO RIVERS
STRETCHES A VAST PLAIN, BORDERED BY THE PACIFIC
OCEAN TO THE WEST AND THE ANDES MOUNTAINS
TO THE EAST. FOR THOUSANDS OF YEARS PEOPLE
OF THE NASCA CULTURE, AND PERHAPS OTHER
PREVIOUS AND SUBSEQUENT CULTURES, ETCHED
ENORMOUS DRAWINGS INTO THE HARD CRUST
OF THE EARTH. THESE DESIGNS ARE SO VAST AND
OVERLAPPING THAT TO TRULY APPRECIATE THEM
THEY MUST BE SEEN FROM THE AIR.

203

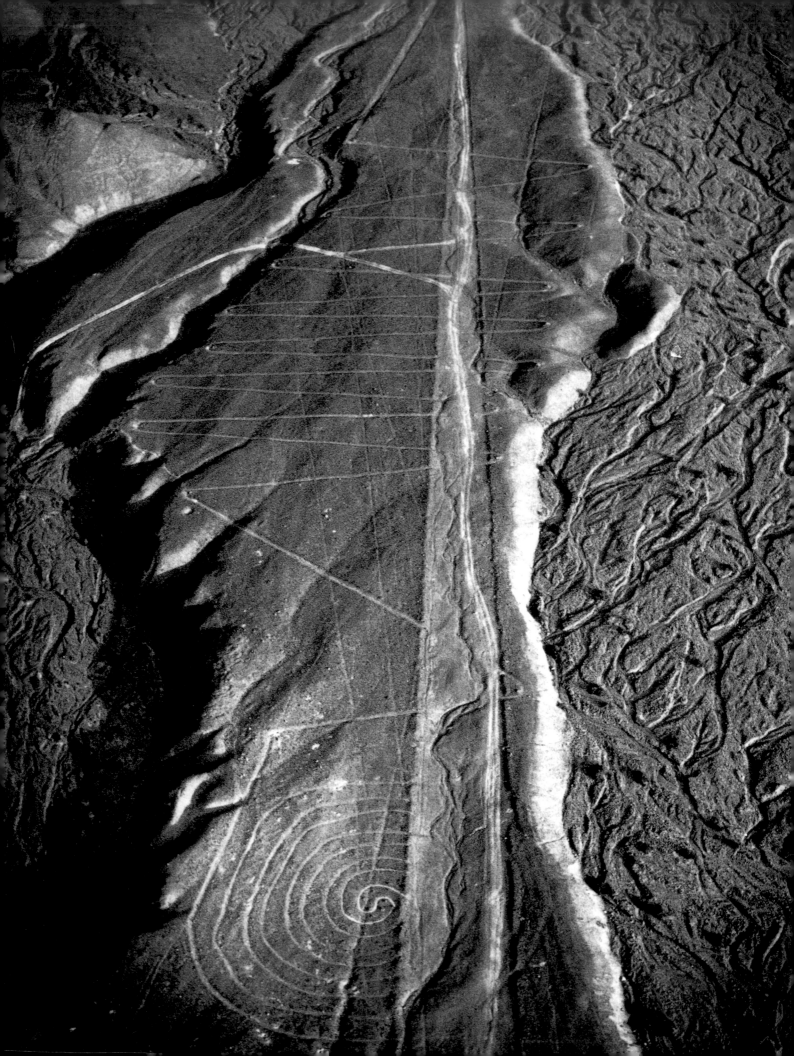

LINES IN THE SAND

MARIA REICHE
GERMAN MATHEMATICIAN • 1903–1998

ABOVE: IN 1977 MARIA REICHE USED STRING TO MEASURE THE NASCA LINES.

LEFT: OVER 30 YEARS EARLIER IN 1946, REICHE STOOD ATOP A LADDER TO GET A BETTER PERSPECTIVE ON THE ANCIENT DESIGN. SHE WROTE OF HER WORK IN THE NASCA DESERT: "THEY DIDN'T UNDERSTAND WHAT I WAS DOING, ALL ALONE UNDER THE HARSH DESERT SUN. SOME OF THEM THOUGHT I WAS A WITCH AND OTHERS CALLED ME CRAZY, BUT I WASN'T INTERESTED IN CONVINCING THEM OTHERWISE BECAUSE AT LEAST THAT WAY THEY LEFT ME ALONE."

IN 1939 A CHANCE conversation in Lima about some enigmatic designs that were carved thousands of years ago in the southern deserts of Peru led Maria Reiche, a German mathematician, to meet the historian Paul Kosok, who had recently explored them. Kosok believed that the lines might have served as a giant observatory that the ancient people used to map the heavens and, perhaps, to predict weather. Intrigued, Reiche packed a tent, some canteens of water, some fruit, and drawing materials and traveled with Kosok to explore the site. She would spend the next fifty years on the Peruvian plains, mapping and studying the vast array of lines.

In 1932 Adolf Hitler's rise to power in prewar Germany led Maria to seek a life elsewhere. She answered an advertisement for a position as a tutor in Cuzco, Peru, and while there, she went on her first archaeological dig. Fascinated by this experience, she sought out archaeologists in Peru to learn about new discoveries. This is how she heard about Kosok's recent exploration of the plains of southern Peru.

Maria's study of the lines eventually proved that Kosok was at least partially right in believing they were used for astronomical observations. Some of the lines, she realized, correlated with identifiable features in the sky, such as the forty-six-meter-long carving of a spider with the constellation Orion. Some lines indicated solstices and others could serve to predict the seasons. But beyond this functional interpretation of the lines, she came to believe that the lines had more obscure meanings, and for decades she was absorbed in untangling this deeper mystery.

Reiche was fascinated by the remarkable and unsuspected grasp of mathematical principles that the ancient Peruvians expressed through their designs. The lines are truly extraordinary and varied. They depict plants, birds, spiders, dogs, sharks, whales, a 180-meter-long lizard—unfortunately cut in half by the Pan American highway—hummingbirds, monkeys, and other fantastic creatures. These designs are overlaid and intertwined with spirals and geometric shapes. More than thirteen thousand lines cover over six hundred miles of desert, and they represent only a portion of what once existed. "I began to walk along the lines to understand their meaning," she wrote, "and noticed they formed a whole. I followed them and tried to draw them, until by reproducing them on paper I understood what I was looking at was a colossal Nasca calendar."

Reiche devoted the rest of her life to systematically surveying and mapping both the designs and the complex water channels and cisterns that crisscross the plains. This work is now preserved in the museum she established, the Museum of the Nation, in Nasca. In the 1970s, Maria also began a collaboration with Marilyn Bridges to make a photographic document of the lines.

Reich waged a constant battle against intruders who caused great damage to the lines. In an effort to preserve the site, Maria persuaded the Peruvian government to designate a large section of the plains a national park and give her guards to help patrol the boundaries. In 1994, thanks to her successful efforts, UNESCO designated the Nasca Lines a world heritage site.

However, Bridges's aerial images and Reiche's drawings together may be the only insurance the enigmatic lines have against time. Maria died at the age of ninety-five and is buried beside the lines she devoted her life to understanding.

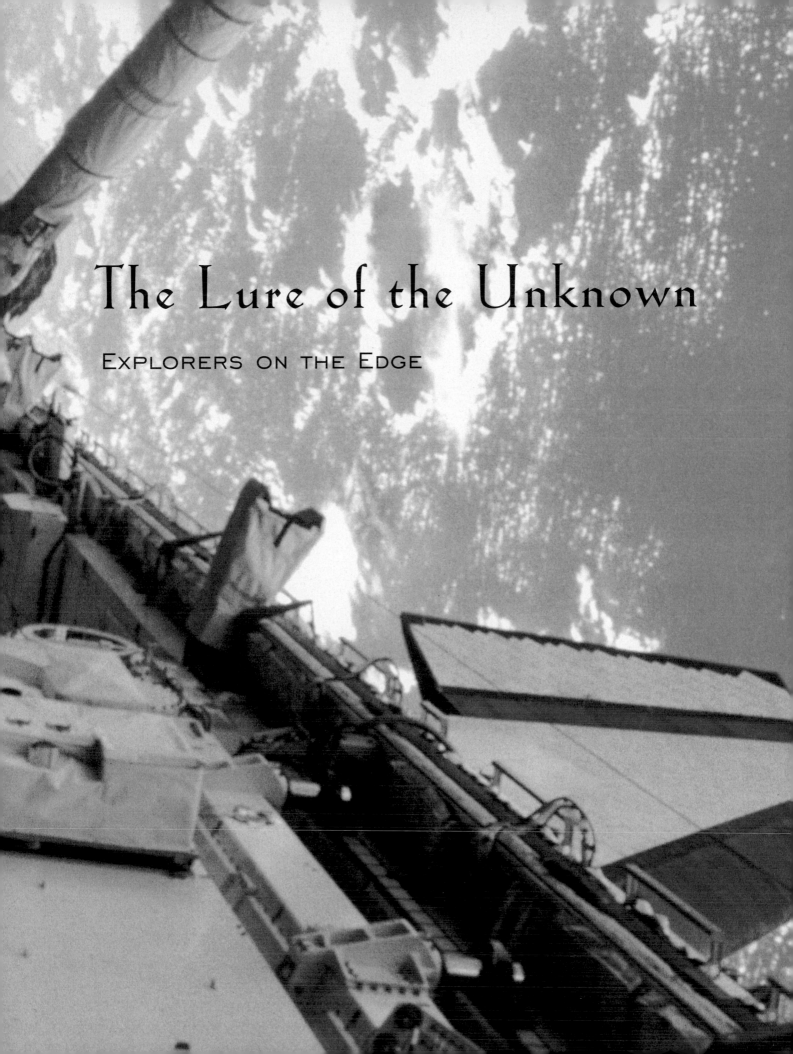

The Lure of the Unknown

EXPLORERS ON THE EDGE

V OYAGES OF exploration take many forms. Some are more dangerous than others; some are highly planned while others are almost accidental; and some are chosen for thrills while others are meant to serve art or science. Each kind of exploration is a gamble, however, where the payoff is discovery and the risk is failure. But there are types of exploration that are, by their very nature, life-threatening; we can think of them as extreme exploration. There, the penalty for failure may be absolute. Whether undertaken on foot, or in a spacecraft, a submersible, or an airplane, these are ventures into hostile environments and present the ultimate challenges of discovery.

Extreme explorers, those who choose this type of encounter with the unknown, have a passion for discovery that takes them over the edge and into the most inhospitable of regions and environments. They may be motivated by the quest for answers to scientific questions, or they may be driven by the desire to peer into an abyss of danger or beauty never seen before. Their challenges generally come in environments where the unaided human body cannot survive due to lack of oxygen, scorching heat, temperatures near absolute zero, or crushing pressures, and thus they are often heavily dependent upon technology.

We think of technology as very modern, but the reliance on technology for exploration is not itself new. The Great Age of Discovery, for example, was made possible by various innovations. Explorers like Vasco da Gama, Columbus, and Magellan profited from a revolution in shipbuilding that transformed the traditional sailing ship. Built for the Mediterranean

ABOVE: IRINA KUZNETSOVA PHOTOGRAPHING A BABY EMPEROR PENGUIN AT MIRNY STATION, ANTARCTICA.

OPPOSITE: SYLVIA EARLE FLOATS OUTSIDE THE *DEEP ROVER* SUBMERSIBLE, THE RESEARCH VESSEL SHE HELPED DEVELOP. IT IS PILOTED BY HER STEPDAUGHTER, MELANIE HAWKS.

PRECEDING PAGES: ASTRONAUT KATHRYN SULLIVAN SPACEWALKING FAR ABOVE THE EARTH ON HER 1984 NASA SPACE MISSION.

LOOKING TO THE HEAVENS

Maria Mitchell

American astronomer • 1818–1889

O N THE BASIS of her pioneering work in astronomy, Maria Mitchell in 1848 was the first woman elected to the American Academy of Arts and Sciences. The honor was well deserved, but the general view of women in astronomy in the nineteenth century was far less welcoming. Although she was a recognized authority in her field and was widely known for having discovered "Miss Mitchell's Comet" in 1847, she was refused admission to what was then the best observatory in Europe, at the Vatican, because of her sex. Annoyed but undeterred, Maria returned to the United States, where she continued her studies of sunspots, Venus, and the movements of the stars, first at home with her own telescope and later at Vassar College, where she became professor of astronomy. Like many of the women in this volume, Mitchell not only pushed forward the frontiers of our knowledge but also expanded our rights to seek knowledge.

ABOVE: A PORTRAIT OF MARIA MITCHELL PEERING THROUGH THE "LITTLE DOLLAND" TELESCOPE, PAINTED BY HERMIONE DASSEL, 1851. ON MARCH 2, 1854, MARIA WROTE, "I SWEPT LAST NIGHT TWO HOURS, BY THREE PERIODS. IT WAS A GRAND NIGHT—NOT A BREATH OF AIR, NOT A FRINGE OF A CLOUD, ALL CLEAR, ALL BEAUTIFUL. I REALLY ENJOY THAT KIND OF WORK, BUT MY BACK SOON BECOMES TIRED, LONG BEFORE THE COLD CHILLS ME. I SAW TWO NEBULAE IN LEO WITH WHICH I WAS NOT FAMILIAR, AND THAT REPAID ME FOR THIS TIME."

Sea, early ships were ill-suited for crossing the Atlantic Ocean. Small and light, they often relied upon oarsmen for power in relatively calm seas, from which they could be beached each night. In addition, their sails were poorly shaped for following the winds on long stretches of open ocean. The caravel was a striking innovation that sought to correct all these failings while keeping a shallow hull that would allow the exploration of coasts. None of the great voyages of exploration would have been possible without this innovation in design.

Technological revolution is, of course, the hallmark of our age. Without years of work on the part of scientists, engineers, and explorers to design, build, test, and launch rockets, spacecraft, scuba gear, submersibles, communications systems, and other special equipment, today's space and underwater exploration would not be possible. Explorers of the seas and heavens now must be highly skilled technically, in order to drive, guide, or utilize the vehicles and instruments upon which they depend for their very survival.

The heavens have long been thought of as a special preserve of women. The moon was nearly always regarded as a goddess, and her human priestesses were frequently charged with such astronomical tasks as predicting eclipses. But few secular women were recognized for their contributions to the study of the sky, although many must have nonetheless committed themselves to this work. Caroline Herschel (1750–1848), for example, the sister of one of the first great modern astronomers, William Herschel, herself discovered eight new comets and three nebulae and revised the then-current star map.

It was not until 1875 that Harvard University took the lead in hiring women in its astronomy department. This allowed Annie Jump Cannon (1863–1941) to enter Radcliffe as a special student in 1895 and begin cataloging the stars at the Harvard Observatory the following year. Since then, astronomy has gradually became an easier field for women to enter, and a number of outstanding astronomers are women.

While searching the skies has captivated many, a lucky few have actually entered outer space. Ever since the Wright brothers rose a few feet off the ground in 1903, sky pioneers, many women among them, have been pushing to achieve higher and farther flight. Women also trained from the first days of space exploration to become astronauts. It was not in the United States, however, but in the Soviet Union that the first women were allowed to venture aloft.

From a Russian space station, Valentina Tereshkova rode into space for seventy hours in 1963. Only twenty years later did the first American woman follow her when the physicist Sally Ride spent six days orbiting the earth in 1983. In 1999, Col. Eileen Collins became America's first female shuttle commander. This was no public relations stunt or sop thrown out to feminists: in addition to her rigorous physical and technical training, Collins spent more than five thousand hours flying thirty types of aircraft to get ready for her mission. In line behind her are a number of similarly highly trained and educated women who will take off to explore the reaches of outer space.

Space is not our only frontier. The other is virtually beneath our feet. "Deep flight" was realized first through Jacques Cousteau's participation in the invention and popularization of scuba equipment in the 1940s. Suddenly, the sea was seen in a new way. It became a place of wonder whose vastness and variety dwarfed the land we knew. Scuba limited divers to a few hundred feet, but a new breed of submersibles or mini-submarines has made possible truly deep dives. Still, explorers have visited only a small portion of the ocean, and much remains to be investigated. The bottom lands of the seas resemble the great uncharted areas that so challenged travelers in the last century. Women like the biologist Cindy Lee Van Dover are filling in some of the blanks. As the first woman pilot of the submersible *Alvin*, Cindy has ventured miles below the surface of the ocean to study the bizarre species that thrive near deep, underwater vents that spew molten minerals from the interior of the earth.

To their chagrin, today's explorers have learned that entering a new place is a process that in itself endangers that place. As the geologist Katharine Fowler-Billings lamented, once her work mapping the minerals of Sierra Leone was finished, mining companies would come and strip bare the land. But there are a few explorers who have so captured the public imagination that they can, for the first time, weigh in with some hope of success in the struggle to preserve the ecological balance of our planet. If there were no other payoff for extreme exploration, conservation would surely make it worth the risks.

No matter how far we go in this world and beyond, or how much we learn, there will always be an edge to be explored. And thanks to the courage and farsightedness of women explorers of the past and present, there will always be women in the lead, searching beyond the horizon.

WALKING IN SPACE
KATHRYN D. SULLIVAN
AMERICAN ASTRONAUT • B. 1951

ON OCTOBER 5, 1984, NASA astronaut Kathy Sullivan left Earth for eight days and became the first woman to walk, or rather float, in space. On her second mission, in 1990, she helped deploy what astronomers believe will prove to be the most significant modern "leap" into deep space, the giant Hubble Space Telescope. Her last mission was in 1992, when she was mission specialist and payload commander for a flight orbiting the earth. "Getting to fly was incredible icing on an already great cake," she says. "You can't beat the ride, the view or zero-G."

Kathy began exploring while she was working toward her graduate degrees in geology. As she then saw her career path, it led down instead of up. She joined teams from the Woods Hole Oceanographic Institute to study the Mid-Atlantic Ridge and the Newfoundland Basin in the Atlantic and the fault zones along the California Pacific coast. She has thus experienced firsthand the truth that the sea and the sky are not mutually exclusive: both make up the envelope that contains our world. From the U.S. Naval Reserve, Sullivan applied to NASA and was selected for the astronaut program in 1978.

Sullivan is proud of the work she's been able to do in her career. "The most exciting and enjoyable thing about my job at NASA was being a full-fledged member of a mission team, and making a real contribution to each one was always a real joy."

ABOVE: SALLY RIDE AND KATHRYN SULLIVAN ON A MISSION IN SPACE.

Paris Velox. 97.
VELOX FOR SYNDICAT

"My Home Is Where My Trunk Is"

ANNIE SMITH PECK

AMERICAN MOUNTAINEER • 1850–1935

LIKE ALL WOMEN in Victorian times, Annie Smith Peck was usually primly dressed in yards of material, ribbons, and stays, and had she remained in New York, she would have probably lived her entire life encased in the uniform of her social class. But that was not to be. It was not, however, until she was thirty-five and on a trip to Europe that she encountered the catalyst that would free her and would be her lifelong love. Passing through Switzerland in 1885, Annie first saw the Alps and had what the French call a *coup de foudre,* a flash of love at first sight. For her, mountains became a challenge and a guiding inspiration. She not only loved them, she wanted to dominate them. "I felt," she wrote, "that I should never be happy until I, too, should scale those frowning walls which have beckoned so many upwards, a few to their own destruction."

Nearly ten years were to pass before Peck was able to return to Switzerland to climb the mountain that changed her life, the Matterhorn. A formidable peak that straddled the Swiss-Italian border, the Matterhorn had first been climbed just thirty years previously and had already claimed a number of lives. But Annie was up to the challenge, and at age forty-five she became the third woman to reach the summit. Not only was her feat news, but she caused a sensation on both sides of the Atlantic because she climbed wearing pants. In the United States at that time, women were being prosecuted for appearing in public in "knickers." But Peck, who was an ardent suffragette, was convinced that climbing in skirts was foolhardy. When she returned home to New York she found that she was such a celebrity that the Singer Sewing Machine company included photographs of her in climbing gear with all the machines they sold.

Born and raised in Rhode Island, the only girl in a family of boys, Annie grew up competing against her brothers in outdoor sports and vying with them for academic honors in school. After graduating she began teaching elementary school but yearned for the higher education her brothers were getting. The University of Michigan had recently opened its doors to women, so in 1874 Peck enrolled. She graduated first in her class in classics and later got a master's degree in Greek. She was offered a job as a professor of Latin at Perdue University, becoming one of the first women professors in America. In 1884 she made her fateful trip to Europe to visit the ancient sites she had studied.

Upon her return, Annie accepted a chair in Latin at Smith College. To augment her small salary she began giving public lectures, illustrated by the pictures she had taken in Europe. Her posters billed Peck as a profound classical scholar, a distinguished archaeologist and an accomplished musician. These lectures became so successful that she was able to resign from her prestigious and secure position at Smith College and, despite the fact that she was approaching fifty, throw herself full-time into mountaineering.

In 1897 she went to Mexico to climb Orizaba and Popocatepetl. But she said, she wanted "to conquer a virgin peak, to attain some height where no man had pre-

ABOVE: THE *BOSTON HERALD* RAN THIS PHOTO-GRAPH WITH THE CAPTION: "MISS ANNIE S. PECK, NOTED MOUNTAINEER, WHO HAS SCALED THE HIGHEST PEAKS OF THE SOUTH AMERICAN ANDES. MISS PECK IS THE AUTHOR OF *A TOURIST'S GUIDE TO SOUTH AMERICA*; SHE RECENTLY RETURNED TO THIS COUNTRY ON BOARD THE S.S. *AQUITANIA.*"

OPPOSITE: ANNIE PECK POSED FOR A STUDIO PORTRAIT IN HER MOUNTAIN CLIMBING GEAR. OF HER PREPARATIONS, SHE WROTE: "AFTER MY LONG STRUGGLE TO OBTAIN FUNDS AND MY FEW DAYS OF HASTY PREPARATION, I WAS THANKFUL INDEED TO GO ON BOARD THE STEAMER, KNOWING THAT I COULD HAVE A LITTLE REST. . . . ON MY FOUR TRIPS TO SOUTH AMERICA, I HAVE GONE ON BOARD A PERFECT WRECK; EACH TIME A LITTLE WORSE THAN BEFORE, HAVING TAKEN PRACTICALLY NO EXERCISE BETWEEN VOYAGES."

viously stood." Annie set her sights on a mountain in
Bolivia, Mount Sorata, also known as Mount Illampu,
which was then thought to be the highest in South
America. In 1903, after years of fund-raising, she
sailed for Bolivia. She hired two Swiss guides as companions as well as an American professor who, she hoped, would
take photographs and make the necessary scientific observations to determine the height of the mountain in order to establish her record.

Peck was to be plagued, however, with climbing companions who would lose their nerve and endanger her life. Her
climb up Sorata was a harrowing experience. Halfway up, the
professor panicked and refused to leave the safety of his sleeping bag. This caused the porters to go on strike. When the
professor then announced he was leaving, Annie realized she
would have to abandon her attempt on the summit. She later
wrote of the rebellion, "Never before had I felt so helpless.
Heartsick I said nothing. It was not a question of my own
capabilities, I could climb, but certainly I could not carry up tents, sleeping bags,
etc. To manage three men seemed beyond my power. Perhaps some of my more
experienced married sisters would have done better . . . rage and mortification
filled my soul."

After raising more money, she returned in 1904 and had an even more dramatic encounter with her guides. Roped to her companions, Annie was leading a
dangerous traverse across a snow bridge sandwiched between deep crevasses.
Later, she wrote, "As I was carefully advancing, at every step thrusting the head of
my ice axe strongly into the ice above, I heard a little swish, then a shout from the
others calling me to return. I recognized the sound, it was alarming. . . . There
was indeed a danger of avalanche which might carry me a thousand feet below
[but] . . . [t]he sun had just passed to the other side of the ridge . . . therefore
the danger was diminishing; so without a pause, or a backward glance, I went
slowly onward." Peck eventually realized she would have to go back and turned to
the porter she had been tied to. "I saw to my horror and disgust the rope trailing
idly on the snow. The two men were where I had left them. On a steep and dangerous slope, on the very brink of a crevasse into which a careless step would have
plunged me, and no one on the rope! . . . There was nothing left to do but to
return to the tent."

Her next climbing attempts were on Mount Huascarán in Peru. This mountain had never been climbed before and could possibly, she thought, be the highest
in South America. Her first attempts in 1904 were thwarted by severe snowfall. In
1906 the ineffectiveness of her guides led to two unsuccessful attempts. Before
returning to New York for another round of fund-raising, Annie climbed some

smaller peaks and then turned aside from the mountain peaks to try to find, in the streams running down to the east, the source of the Amazon, a quest that, like the search for the source of the Nile, had long captivated explorers.

Riding through the mountain passes, Peck was thrown from a bolting mule and suffered broken ribs and cuts. Still she rode one hundred miles up the Marañón and Ucayali Rivers in search of the Amazon's source. Coming to the glacier that emptied into the Marañón River, Annie climbed across its crevasses to reach a summit higher than Europe's Mount Blanc.

She returned to Peru in 1908 with the backing of *Harper's* magazine. She again hired Swiss guides because she was convinced that their mountaineering expertise would make the expedition possible. But one guide suffered altitude sickness and the other collapsed with exhaustion. None could match Peck. Her sixth attempt on Huascarán was successful. Four years of effort had finally paid off. On the final assault of the summit, one of her guides raced ahead of her to summit first, a terrible breach of mountain etiquette. When she reached the summit the winds were so fierce Annie was unable to accurately measure the height. She claimed 24,000 feet; it was later adjusted to 22,205. To honor her achievement the government of Peru honored her by naming one of Huascarán's peaks "Cumbre Ana Peck."

Peck's last major climb was of Coropuna in Peru, then thought to be higher than Aconcagua, the highest mountain in South America. Annie took on the challenge in order to strike a blow for the women's suffrage movement. Competing against a team of men from Yale University, she easily reached the two highest peaks and planted flags reading "Votes for Women" before the men's team had even reached the first peak. She was then sixty-one years old.

In her sixties and seventies Peck turned her attention to encouraging good relations and commercial exchange between North and South America. To promote the numerous fledgling South American air services, she undertook a twenty-thousand-mile flying odyssey around the continent in 1930, at age eighty. She continued climbing, often in New Hampshire, and, at eighty-four, in the last year of her life, she climbed the hill of the Acropolis in Athens, where she had studied fifty years previously.

Annie was active in organizations that promoted exploration: she was elected a fellow of the Royal Geographical Society in 1917 and was a founding member of both the American Alpine Club and the Society of Women Geographers. To this day Peck retains the honor of being the only woman to make a first ascent on a major world peak.

TOP AND ABOVE: THIS SET OF CARDS DESCRIBING ANNIE PECK'S MOUNTAINEERING ADVENTURE WAS DISTRIBUTED BY THE SINGER SEWING MACHINE COMPANY AS A PROMOTIONAL ITEM. THE TOP CARD SHOWS MT. HUASCARÁN, WHICH PECK CLIMBED AT THE AGE OF 58.

Explorers of the Heavens
FEARLESS AVIATORS

THE INVENTION of airplanes opened a new arena of exploration. Not only were human beings taking a leap into the atmosphere, but for the first time explorers were utterly dependent upon a machine. The vehicle, as much as the pilot, was critical to success; making a technical mistake could be fatal. Life and death depended on knowledge of mechanics and instrumentation. The more complicated the machine, the faster and the higher it went, but also the greater the reliance of the explorer on technology. The first aviators often flew alone: Bessie Coleman, Beryl Markham, and Amelia Earhart made a career of daring solo firsts. But later explorers of the skies, such as Kathryn Sullivan, had to explore in teams, because the machines had become so complex. Expanding technology has opened a hitherto unimaginable potential for exploration: the earth shrinks below and heavens come within reach. Explorers like Sullivan are now taking the first steps into infinity.

BARNSTORMER
BESSIE COLEMAN
AMERICAN AVIATOR • 1893–1926

BESSIE COLEMAN was the first African-American woman to get an international flying license and to fly an airplane. She succeeded at a time when the United States was divided in two by strict segregation laws. Because no one in America would teach Bessie to fly, she had to go to Paris to learn. She returned to the States determined to make her life in the skies and inspire other African-American women to do the same. How she achieved this distinction is a tale of remarkable courage, determination, and hard work, one that begins with her childhood in rural Texas.

Born the twelfth of thirteen children to a woman whose mother had been a slave, Bessie learned early that some things were supposed to be beyond the reach of black people, including education. But she taught herself to read and

plunged into a segregated school, where, she remembered, "I found a brand new world in the written word. I couldn't get enough. I wanted to learn so badly that I finished high school, something very unusual for a black woman in those days. . . . I don't wish to make it sound easy but I decided I wanted to go to college too. Since my mother could not afford college, I took in laundry and ironing to save up the tuition money."

Coleman finished college about the time her older brothers returned from France, where they had been fighting in World War I. They told her many stories about their adventures, but the one that kindled her imagination was about flying. To Bessie, twenty-seven years old, working in a beauty parlor, black, and poor, the idea of flying seemed almost magical. When her brothers told her that in Paris even a woman could fly, she did not rest until she had raised enough money from friends to sail to France, where she immediately enrolled in the Ecole d'Aviation des Frères Caudron. What she saw must have both excited and alarmed her: planes flew, but they often crashed. The students joked that there were two ways out of the school—graduation or the graveyard. "It was a terrible shock to my nerves," she wrote after witnessing the not-infrequent fatal crashes, but "I kept going."

In 1921 Coleman, the only woman in her aviation class, received her pilot's license, the first black woman in the world to do so. Her return to New York was front-page news across the country. But flying cost money, and to earn money by flying in those days was difficult. There were no airlines, and mail-carrying was a completely segregated, male-only occupation. What was left to her was barnstorming.

Bessie formulated her second great ambition, to found the first flying school for African Americans. As she put it in a May 1925 interview in the *Houston Post Dispatch,* "The Negro race is the only race without aviators and I want to interest the Negro in flying and thus help the best way I am equipped to uplift the colored race." Suddenly her barnstorming had a purpose: "I decided blacks should not have to experience the difficulties I had faced, so I decided to open a flying school and teach other black women to fly. I needed money for this so I began giving flying exhibitions and lecturing on aviation. The color of my skin, at first a huge drawback, now drew large crowds wherever I went."

Like her contemporary Amelia Earhart, Coleman was most keen to get women to fly. Also like Earhart, she hit the lecture circuit, where she talked to women and children—the future aviators. But her dreams ended tragically in Jacksonville on what was a more or less routine flight. She was testing her newly purchased but aged Jenny with a copilot when the plane stalled at thirty-five hundred feet and went into a spiraling nosedive. The plane had no seat belt, and Bessie was thrown out and fell to her death. Dead at only thirty-three, Coleman had nonetheless demonstrated that the sky was no limit even to a poor black woman and that a dream can carry one beyond the greatest of barriers.

WEST WITH THE NIGHT

BERYL CLUTTERBUCK MARKHAM
ANGLO-KENYAN AVIATOR • 1902–1986

THE GREAT ADVENTURE of the first decades of the twentieth century was flying. Beginning with flimsy planes that barely cleared dirt runways and evolving into aircraft that could stay aloft as long as their fuel lasted, exploring the skies and setting records of endurance fired the imagination of generations of flyers. Those who sought the freedom of the skies in these early years of flight were heroes like Amelia Earhart, Charles and Anne Morrow Lindbergh, and Jack Harding. Into their ranks must be added an unlikely candidate, a stable girl on one of the great Kenyan plantations who had no reasonable expectation of learning how to fly, much less of owning an airplane: the young Anglo-Kenyan Beryl Markham.

Beryl's father had moved to East Africa in 1905 to farm in Njoro, then a wilderness beyond Nairobi, and took his three-year-old daughter with him. Growing up around horses, she early developed the skills as a trainer for which she later came to be known. Her work with horses and particularly with racing also put her in touch with members of the English upper classes, some of whom would later be her backers as she began to fly.

Learning to fly offered Markham a "momentary escape from the eternal custody of earth." In 1933 she became the first woman, and indeed only the eleventh pilot, in British East Africa to earn a commercial pilot's license. This commercial license was particularly important since she needed to work to support her expensive new passion for flight. Able to fly for hire, she spent thousands of hours exploring valleys and uplands, searching out animals for the safaris run by the famed white hunters, Denys Finch-Hatton and Bror Blixen.

But Markham earned fame forever in less than a day. Alone in the cramped cabin of her small Messenger plane, which she called the *Gull,* she took off from Abingdon, England, on September 4, 1936, to fly across the Atlantic Ocean. Hemmed in by fuel tanks, inhaling gas fumes, and fighting off sleep, she was "bound for a place thirty-six hundred miles from here—two thousand miles of it unbroken ocean. Most of the way it will be night."

As she flew in the dark a violent storm buffeted her plane. She struggled with the controls to keep from plummeting into cresting waves that were at times only a few hundred feet below her. Then in the first light of day, just as she sighted the coast of Nova Scotia, her engine quit. She later discovered that the fuel line had been blocked by ice. Luckily, she managed to gain some altitude before the engine stopped for good. Without power she skimmed low over a rocky beach to crash-land in a bog. It was not a glorious landing, and no cheering crowds greeted her as they did Lindberg on his arrival in Paris, but she became the first person to fly alone westward across the Atlantic Ocean. Beryl was an instant star; she was lionized by the press and was feted on both sides of the Atlantic.

After a round of public events, Markham decided to begin a new career as an author. She captured the love she felt for flying in her acclaimed memoir, *West with the Night.* So magical were her words that Ernest Hemingway said, "She has written so well . . . that I was completely ashamed of myself as a writer." Beryl's gifts are a book that will not die and an example that continues to inspire adventures.

DISAPPEARED

Amelia Mary Earhart

American aviator

1897–1937

An icon of courage, intelligence, and style, Amelia Mary Earhart is perhaps the most famous woman explorer of the twentieth century. From her earliest flights in the 1920s she set records for the highest, the farthest, and the first. She was a pioneer in commercial aviation and a champion of women pilots. At the height of her fame in 1937, she disappeared during a flight over the Pacific. The mystery of her disappearance has haunted generations.

The night I found over the Pacific was a night of stars. They seemed to rise from the sea and hang outside my cockpit window, near enough to touch, until hours later they slipped away into the dawn.

Born in Atchison, Kansas, Amelia saw her first airplane on her eleventh birthday when her father took her to the Iowa State Fair. She was not impressed. But when in 1920 she finally had an opportunity to fly, she immediately recognized her calling: "as soon as we left the ground, I knew I myself had to fly." She worked for a telephone company to pay for flying lessons and in that same year bought her first plane. Her first record, in 1922, was for high altitude by a woman pilot, when she achieved the then-remarkable height of fourteen thousand feet.

In 1928 she was working in a settlement house in Boston when she received a telephone call that changed her life. Amy Phipps Guest, a heiress who loved flying, wanted to sponsor the first woman to fly across the Atlantic. She was looking for the right American girl and Earhart had been suggested. Amelia accepted the offer and thus became the first woman to fly across the Atlantic—not as the pilot, as she wished, but as a passenger. The sponsors decided that it was too risky to entrust the valuable plane to a woman pilot. Although she was disappointed not to have actually performed as a pilot, Amelia became an instant celebrity on both sides of the Atlantic when the plane landed in Wales. From that moment on, notoriety became part of what drove her: she knew she had to fly to "prove that I deserved at least a small fraction of the nice things said about me."

Her fame also won her a publisher, George Putnam, who pushed her to break more flying records in order to sell more books. The two fell in love and married, and Amelia threw herself into setting and breaking flight records. She became the first woman to fly solo from coast to coast in 1928. She competed in cross-country air races. Later, in 1935, she became the first pilot to fly the dangerous routes over open water from Mexico to Newark and from Hawaii to California. Her aim was to garner firsts not just for herself but to prove women could fly just as easily as men could. To provide a forum for women pilots and to publicize their activities, she established the Women's Air Derby in 1929 and helped found the Ninety Nines, an organization of women pilots.

Finally she was ready to make the big jump, this time alone, across the Atlantic. "It was clear in my mind," she said, "that I was undertaking the flight because I loved flying. It was . . . proving to me, and to anyone else interested, that a woman with adequate experience could do it." To catch a tailwind, Earhart took off from Harbor Grace, Newfoundland, on May 20, 1932. She watched as the sun set through her cockpit window and saw the first stars come out. Then, she said, "something happened that has never occurred in my twelve years of flying. The altimeter, the instrument that records height above the ground, failed." Around midnight she flew into a severe lightning storm, which buffeted the small plane from side to side. To escape the storm she flew higher. But at that altitude, ice began to coat the plane. Knowing that the ice would freeze the controls and make the plane lose its airworthiness, she had to get down into warmer air. Yet without the altimeter working and in the dark with fog blanketing the water, it was hard for her to judge how close she was to the ocean. She stayed as low as she dared until the ice melted, then she quickly rose away from the waves—but almost immediately ice coated her windshield again. She continued her nerve-wracking seesawing flight until dawn's light. Then she noticed her exhaust manifold was vibrating and at the same time discovered her reserve gas tank was leaking. She had to land. Luckily, just then she caught her first sight of land. She flew along the coast until she spotted a safe place—a cow pasture near Londonderry, Ireland. It was not much of a landing but she got down, and to an audience—albeit a very different one than she had hoped for: "I succeeded," she said, "in frightening all the cattle in the country." But Amelia had become the first woman to fly solo west to east across the stormy Atlantic.

It was not just Earhart's flying that made her famous. She was attractive, with a warm smile and an engaging personality. Her lecture tours to promote her books and flights were always packed. Thousands of people thronged to greet her wherever she landed. So inspiring was she that Perdue University hired her as a career counselor. Perdue also enabled Amelia to realize her dream to fly around the world along the equator. The university paid for the plane she would use on the flight, the most advanced plane of its time, a Lockheed Electra 10E.

On March 17, 1937, Earhart began this historic flight. Along with her navigator, Fred Noonan, she flew from California to Honolulu, where, due to engine trouble, she crashed. The plane, which was not badly damaged, was soon

Women must try to do things as men have tried. When they fail, their failure must be but a challenge to others.

fixed and refitted. This incident became the basis of a mystery. Was it really just a simple repair job or, as the conspiracy theorists have alleged, was the crash staged to give the U.S. government an opportunity to fit the plane with experimental new engines and spy cameras so that she could report on Japanese activities in remote areas of the Pacific?

In any case, she took off into the dawn on May 21, 1937, reversing her planned route, flying east rather than west. Earhart and Noonan flew to Brazil, then across the Atlantic to North Africa, across Saudi Arabia to India, then down to Indonesia. By the time she reached her last recorded stop, on June 29, in Lae, New Guinea, she had flown twenty-two thousand miles. But the most dangerous part of the trip lay before them. From Lae they had to navigate to tiny Howland Island, a dot in the vast Pacific Ocean.

She never made it. A U.S. Navy ship stationed near Howland received her last transmission. She said cryptically that she was "running north and south," but her position was never convincingly recorded. She had vanished forever, despite a massive search to find her covering some twenty-five thousand square miles, which was commissioned by President Franklin Roosevelt.

Speculation as to what happened to Amelia Earhart has run rife and is bolstered by rumor. Sightings of her plane were said to have been made in Saipan during World War II. Some observers said they saw a woman fitting her description in Saipan, as a prisoner who was later shot. Perhaps the most bizarre story is that she was rescued from a prison camp at the end of the war, and to hide the U.S. government's role in her adventure, she lived out the rest of her life in obscurity in America. A number of expeditions have searched for her plane and her remains. Tantalizing clues have been found—a shoe, bones, bits of metal, a sextant—but nothing definitive. The final fate of this most remarkable woman remains a mystery.

Reading Between the Lines

MARIE THARP

AMERICAN OCEANOGRAPHIC CARTOGRAPHER

B. 1920

W HEN MARIE THARP first studied the world's ocean floors, very little was known about the earth's structure. Her announcement in 1952 that there was a rift in the ridge of underwater mountains, running thousands of miles down the middle of the Atlantic, was therefore greeted by geologists with both astonishment and derision.

Tharp had studied geology at the University of Michigan; during World War II, when men were called away for war-related jobs, she had managed to get a job as a geologist for an oil company. Later, she was hired by Columbia University's Lamont Geological Observatory, which specialized in studies of the ocean floor, but for fifteen years she was excluded from fieldwork on the boats that took oceanographic soundings, collecting the raw data that was the basis for her scientific work. Marie had to be content with creating her maps of the world's oceans in the backrooms of the lab; indeed, she eventually had to move her lab into her own home.

Luckily for her and for modern geology, mapmaking was in her blood and she would not, perhaps could not, give up. Her father was a soil surveyor for the U.S. Bureau of Chemistry and Soils, and as a child she had moved from county to county, traveling north to south, following the seasons. Her weekend treat was to trail behind him as he surveyed farmlands.

When Tharp arrived at Columbia University in 1948, she met a fellow researcher, Bruce Heezen, who was to become her collaborator for the next thirty years. In 1950 Marie and Bruce began their ambitious project to map the ocean floors.

Mapping the bottom of the ocean, particularly in the days before deepwater techniques had been worked out, was accomplished by ships equipped with sonar and radar. The data that resulted, Tharp saw, was badly flawed. Huge stretches of the earth's submarine surface lay between the paths followed by the survey ships: sometimes as much as five hundred miles separated the bands of numbers. Using her knowledge of geology, Marie was able to guess what lay between the bands. She then drew her maps in what is called physiographic diagrams, which allowed her greater artistic and interpretive freedom. Her "sketching" of the ocean floor produced the first map in 1959, detailing the mountains and valleys under the sea. She utilized known information about earthquakes to fill in many of the blank spots

RIGHT: THARP AT HER DRAWING TABLE AT LAMONT GEOLOGICAL OBSERVATORY IN THE 1950S, WHERE SHE WORKED FOR DECADES WITH BRUCE HEEZEN, CREATING DETAILED MAPS OF THE WORLD'S OCEAN FLOOR.

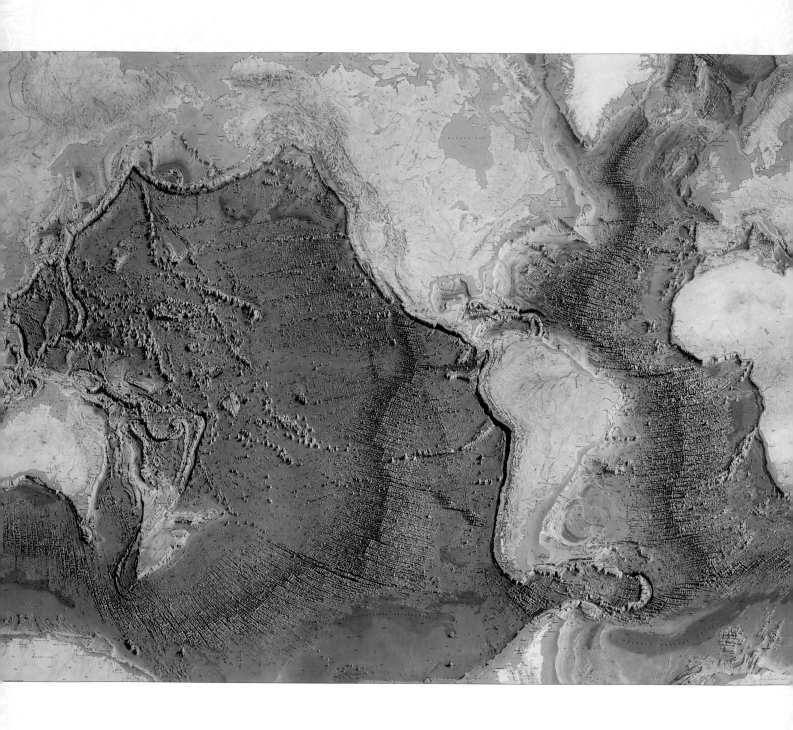

WORLD OCEAN FLOOR
BY BRUCE C. HEEZEN AND MARIE THARP

on her maps. Tharp's vision was later proved correct when the first satellite images of the ocean floor aligned almost perfectly with her hand-drawn maps.

But her truly revolutionary work lay in the proof she could offer of the theory of plate tectonics. This set of hypotheses attempts to explain the way the plates of the earth's surface move and conflict with one another, causing earthquakes and other geological phenomena. As she began to put together her maps of the Atlantic seabed, Marie found what appeared to be the process known above water as "continental drift."

It took her more than a year to convince Bruce Heezen that the deep depressions plotted at the crest of the Mid-Atlantic Ridge represented the edges of surface plates in the act of separating from each other. Together, it took them years more to convince the scientific community. But Tharp stuck by her discovery and eventually she was proved to be correct.

Marie also championed the concept that the world's oceans were one entity, not isolated bodies of water. Her map of the World Ocean remains the standard map used today. In recognition of her contributions, the Phillip Lee Phillips Society of the Library of Congress named her one of the four leading cartographers of the twentieth century.

LEFT: MARIE THARP'S 1977 MAP, "WORLD OCEAN FLOOR," IS IMPORTANT BECAUSE IT EXPOUNDS HER BELIEF THAT THE EARTH IS ENCIRCLED BY ONE CONTINUOUS OCEAN. THARP SPOKE OF HER WORK, SAYING, "IN 1952, EARLY IN MY CAREER I HAD JUST FINISHED THE COMPILATION OF THE SIX TRANSATLANTIC PROFILES OF THE SEA FLOOR IN THE NORTH ATLANTIC. THESE SOUNDINGS HAD BEEN LARGELY OBTAINED BY BRUCE HEEZEN WORKING ON THE *ATLANTIS 1*, OUT OF WOODS HOLE OCEANOGRAPHIC INSTITUTE. . . . A DEEP V-SHAPED CLEFT AT THE CREST OF THE MID-ATLANTIC RIDGE HAD PARTICULARLY INTRIGUED ME, THE POSITION OF WHICH I PLOTTED ON A MAP. THERE IT WAS, A LINE BASED ON SIX POINTS CRASHING DOWN THE CENTER OF THE NORTH ATLANTIC PARALLEL TO THE BORDERING CONTINENTS. WHEN I SHOWED THIS TO BRUCE, HE JUST GROANED AND SAID, 'IT CAN'T BE. IT LOOKS TOO MUCH LIKE CONTINENTAL DRIFT.' IN THE EARLY 1950S THIS WAS TANTAMOUNT TO SCIENTIFIC HERESY, SOMETHING LIKE BEING A COMMUNIST DURING THE McCARTHY ERA."

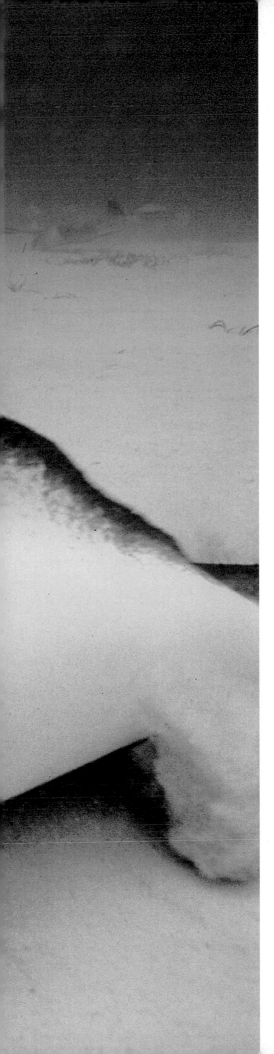

Onward and Downward

SYLVIA ALICE EARLE

AMERICAN

MARINE BIOLOGIST • B. 1935

SYLVIA EARLE was fifteen when she put on a copper diving helmet to make her first dive in Florida's Weekiwachee River. "For twenty blissful minutes," she said, "I became one with the river and its residents." Since that first dive she has spent more than six thousand hours underwater, on more than fifty expeditions. In addition to setting diving records, she has designed and tested submersibles, become an authority on reef ecology, and studied the habits of whales.

Earle came to prominence in 1970, when she joined the Tektite Project, an experiment in prolonged underwater living based off the shore of the Virgin Islands. NASA, the U.S. Navy, and the Department of the Interior wanted to study the effects of long-term isolation and relate it to the space program. Because there was resistance to having men and women live together underwater, an all-woman team, led by Sylvia, was formed. Its unqualified success helped pave the way for the later acceptance of women as astronauts.

ABOVE: SYLVIA EARLE EMERGING FROM A SUCCESSFUL DIVE IN BONAIRE.

OPPOSITE: EARLE FEEDING A STINGRAY IN THE CLEAR WATERS OF THE CAYMANS.

While the project was initiated as a scientific venture, it quickly became a media event. "Suddenly there were microphones in front of me," Earle recalled, "and millions of people were listening to what I had to say." Sylvia and her four fellow "aquababes" became instant heroines.

The media attention gave Earle a platform on which to campaign for the conservation of the oceans. She called for a halt to overfishing and pollution and worked to create marine parks analogous to national parks. She also continued her pioneering underwater exploration.

Together with noted biologists Roger and Katy Payne, and filmmaker Al Giddings, with whom she made the documentary *Gentle Giants of the Pacific,* she focused on the behavior and "songs" of the humpback whales, following them from Alaska to Hawaii. Not content with just dangling a microphone off a boat, she dived among

them. Once, within fifty feet of a humpback, she felt as though she were at a rock concert: "My whole body vibrated with its call. It is so powerful, it almost hurts."

Sylvia would go on to earn the affectionate title "Her Deepness" when in 1979 she volunteered to wear a specially designed one-thousand-pound pressurized underwater diving suit in which she set a record for the deepest untethered dive. She was carried by a submersible to the ocean floor off Hawaii, where she spent two and a half hours exploring the ocean bottom. Pressure at that depth is six hundred pounds per square inch. If any part of her suit had sprung a leak, she could have been instantly crushed.

Alone in the gloomy depths she saw a shark with glowing green eyes, red crabs clinging to pink coral, and huge sea rays hovering above her. Most of the creatures of the deep are bioluminescent, and even the bamboo coral emitted light. "When I reached out to touch them, they flashed blue," she recalled. "Pulses of light raced up and down the stalks."

Earle joined engineer Graham Hawkes—who also became her second husband—to found Deep Ocean Engineering in 1982. Their goal was to create, build, and test deep-venturing submersibles. Their first craft was *Deep Rover,* launched in 1984, which featured a plastic bubble offering an unimpeded view of the sea. In this craft she dived three thousand feet off the California coast to an area never before visited by human beings.

Having engaged in virtually every sea-related activity, Sylvia has come to focus on education. She wants the average person to view the ocean as more than just water and fish as more than a meal. "Ignorance," she says, "is the single most frightening and dangerous threat to the health of the oceans. There is much to learn before it is possible to intelligently create a harmonious, viable place for ourselves on the planet. The best place to begin is by recognizing the magnitude of our ignorance, and not destroy species and natural systems we cannot re-create. Right now we are at a crossroads and we have a chance to make it right."

Earle is an explorer extraordinaire. In 1990 she was appointed chief scientist for the National Oceanic and Atmospheric Administration (NOAA)—the first woman to ever hold that post. Among her achievements and honors are the Explorers Club Gold Medal, awarded to her in 1996; in 1998 *Time* magazine named her a "Hero for the Planet," and that same year she became the explorer-in-residence at the National Geographic Society. Wedded to her life's passion, she has fought tirelessly to protect the part of the world she so loves. Her message, while cautionary, is filled with hope.

ABOVE: DIVING IN THE CAYMAN ISLANDS, EARLE ENCOUNTERS A MORAY EEL.

TOP LEFT: IN OCTOBER 1979, WEARING A JIM SUIT AND STRAPPED TO THE FRONT OF THE SUBMERSIBLE *STAR II*, EARLE DESCENDED 1,250 FEET TO THE SEAFLOOR OFF OAHU, HAWAII. SHE WALKED SOLO FOR TWO AND A HALF HOURS THROUGH A FOREST OF BAMBOO CORAL.

RIGHT: SYLVIA AT THE CONTROLS OF THE *DEEP ROVER.*

My experience underwater made me realize the swiftness with which humans can dramatically alter an environment tens of thousands of years in the making.

Standing in the Midnight Sun

VALENTINA MIHAILOVNA KUZNETSOVA • B. 1937

IRINA MIHAILOVNA KUZNETSOVA • B. 1961

RUSSIAN POLAR EXPLORERS

L IKE MANY RUSSIAN women, Valentina Mihailovna followed a difficult path to adulthood. And like millions of her fellow countrymen and -women, she almost died on the way. As a young girl she was caught with her family behind German lines during World War II, suffered hunger and privation, and was nearly executed with her mother, a partisan fighter. The two were miraculously reprieved, but Valentina was so traumatized by the horror of the moment that she was unable to speak for several years.

After the war, her father became a driver for the Soviet airline, Aeroflot, allowing her to attend school with the children of the elite. But diagnosed with a heart ailment and told she must avoid all strenuous activity, Valentina was ostracized, not only as the poorest and least important girl in her class but also as a nonathlete in a society that valued sports.

Valentina refused to accept her exclusion and made skiing her sport. She took up racing and then long-range endurance skiing. In 1966 she organized a seven-day race averaging one hundred kilometers a day. The success of this venture led her three years later to organize a thirty-three-day, twenty-six-hundred-kilometer race from Moscow to Finland. From this race came her idea for the Metelitsa Expedition.

Metelitsa was the first Russian women's expedition aimed at crossing Antarctica on skis. Valentina had learned that she could cover long distances on skis, even while pulling a sled, and she was sure that other women were equally capable of undertaking this type of grueling physical challenge. However, she had a difficult

TOP: IRINA AND VALENTINA KUZNETSOVA.

ABOVE: VALENTINA KUZNETSOVA.

OPPOSITE: THE METELITSA TEAM ON THE COMPLETION OF THEIR TRANS-ANTARCTIC JOURNEY IN JANUARY 1996, AT THE AMUNDSEN-SCOTT POLAR STATION.

time convincing the Russian authorities, who had always banned women from their polar stations, especially in Antarctica. When they finally relented, she began to plan, select, and train a team. In 1988 the Metelitsa team landed at the Russian Myrny station and skied for thirty days to Vostok in the center of the continent. That trip to Antarctica marked the apex of efforts that had consumed Kuznetsova for fourteen years.

The biomedical research the Metelitsa team conducted provided data used by Russian scientists at innumerable organizations, including the Russian Medical Academy and the Institute of Arctic Geophysics, in planning future explorations of forbidding environments like the moon and other planets. Even more gratifying to Valentina than the public recognition she has received for her work is the fact that her daughter, Irina, joined the team in 1985.

Irina was born in Moscow in 1961 when her mother was still competing in international ski races. She was raised in an apartment in Moscow, which she remembers being always full of women explorers. She recalled:

> *Of course I always wanted to go on one of my mother's expeditions. In 1979, I got a camera and that changed things for me. I saw where I could contribute to her expeditions: I could be the photographer. My first trip with my mother was in 1985 when I was 24. Even though I could ski well, the trip was extremely difficult physically. The ground was very uneven. We had to climb up steep inclines and then down into deep ravines, all on skis and pulling our equipment.*

Irina continues to work with her mother on the program they have created to enable more Russian women to explore the polar regions. To do this, they have had to surmount new problems, as funding for scientific exploration has almost completely vanished since the breakup of the Soviet Union. But the Kuznetsovas' plan is to circumnavigate the Arctic, passing through all the countries that ring the North Pole. This, they hope, will help heighten awareness of the dangers threatening the fragile polar environment and encourage the establishment of monitoring stations along the route to measure pollutants, temperature, radioactivity, and other climatic and environmental conditions.

TOP: THE RUSSIAN WOMEN'S TEAM IN FRANZ JOSEPH LAND IN 1990 PREPARING FOR THE INTERNATIONAL TRANS-ANTARCTIC EXPEDITION.

ABOVE: A SPECIAL POSTAL ISSUE COMMEMORATING THE ACHIEVEMENT OF THE METELITSA TEAM.

BELOW: A CONGRATULATORY TELEGRAM FROM THEN-PRESIDENT MIKHAIL GORBACHEV, ON SUCCESSFUL COMPLETION OF THE EXPEDITION.

A MIDWINTER NIGHT'S DREAM
AMERICAN TRANS-ANTARCTIC TEAM
ANN BANCROFT, EXPEDITION LEADER • B. 1955
SUNNIVA SORBY • B. 1960   ANNE DAL VERA • B. 1953
SUE GILLER • B. 1946

Antarctica, the mysterious frozen continent at the bottom of the world, has inspired some of the most heroic and ill-fated expeditions in the annals of exploration. The adventures of Robert Scott, Sir Ernest Henry Shackleton, and Roald Amundsen on the continent have inspired others—some to their deaths—in this intensely inhospitable environment. The Antarctic is a unique landmass, for it has no human history and no indigenous peoples; no individual has stayed there longer than a few years. Today, most of the people working on the ice are either military personnel or scientists. And until recently, most, if not all, of those individuals have been men.

Recent Russian and American women's expeditions have proved that women are up to the challenge of living under the most extreme conditions the continent has to offer. Coming soon after the Soviet Metelitsa expedition of 1988, an American team of skiers was led to the Antarctic by Ann Bancroft. This experienced mountaineer and skier conceived the idea of an all-women ski expedition crossing Antarctica to the South Pole without being resupplied. It was an ambitious plan, not only because it was physically daunting, but because it was a financial challenge. Bancroft later commented, "The fact that we had no corporate sponsorship, in my mind, is a direct relationship to being a woman's project, particularly as I watch my peers—my male peers—continue to get funded." Although they had the individual support of hundreds of people and had designed a popular educational program about their journey that reached 450,000 schoolchildren, the women were unsuccessful in getting corporate sponsorship; they ended the expedition with a half-million-dollar debt. Comparable male expeditions received substantial corporate sponsorship and were even covered by television crews.

Despite the obstacles and debt, four women—Ann Bancroft, Anne Dal Vera, Sunniva Sorby, and Sue Giller—flew from Chile to Hercules Inlet on the edge of the Antarctic ice shelf. For the next sixty-seven days, they skied and pulled sleds, each loaded with about two hundred pounds of supplies, seven hundred miles across the frozen wasteland toward the South Pole.

Midway into the crossing, one member of the group got hurt. The only way to get medical attention for her injured ankle was to abort the trip, and everyone, including the injured woman, refused to contemplate that. They all agreed that they would find a way to get her to the Pole. But they were only as fast as their slowest member. On they trudged, slowly and at great cost. They made it safely to the South Pole, but they could not continue their journey. They had to put on hold their goal of crossing the continent. Both Sunniva Sorby and Ann Bancroft have expedition plans now under way to fulfill that dream.

ABOVE: THE AMERICAN WOMEN'S EXPEDITION REACH THEIR GOAL. SAYS BANCROFT OF THIS TRIP: "WE DECIDED TO GET TO THE POLE AS A GROUP OF FOUR, AND THE POLE WAS ACTUALLY ANTICLIMACTIC. . . . IT'S REALLY THE JOURNEY."

When it's blowing great guns, there is great opportunity to lose a tent or sleeping bag or have something major go wrong. It was a little bit tense.

ANN BANCROFT

Life in the Dark

LOUISE HOSE

AMERICAN GEOLOGIST • B. 1952

IN THE CHIAPAS highlands of Mexico long ago, the Zoque Indians discovered a dark, sulfurous cave which, they believed, was a passageway to the gods. In the entrance they performed their springtime rituals that ensured a good growing season. For the Zoque, the cave was the source of all life, a sacred place where they could be close to their deities. Later, the Spaniards learned of the cave, naming it Cueva de Villa Luz (Cave of the Lighted House) because of the beams of light shining in from its several entrances.

But for many years little attention was paid to the cave. Then in 1989 caver Jim Pisarowicz called his colleague Louise Hose, a professor of geology and an experienced cave explorer, to tell her about it. Pisarowicz told Hose he had waded up a milky stream filled with peculiar pale pink fish and entered a cave unlike any he had ever seen before. The walls were covered with strange slimy formations and the air was noxious.

When Louise finally came to the cave in 1996, she realized that the seemingly inhospitable cavern was teeming with life. It was, she later wrote, "a world class natural laboratory." The pale fish filled the streams in unbelievable abundance. The viscous formations that clung to the ceiling and walls were, in fact, microbial veils, ingloriously dubbed "snot-tites," that continued for over a mile down the passageways of this lethal corridor. Later analysis of samples showed that these were, in fact, colonies of microbial life never seen before. While most life is dependent on the sun, these tiny organisms obtain their energy from the oxidation process that results from the chemical reaction of hydrogen sulfide venting from deep within the earth, combined with the oxygen in the air. The snot-tites are the first link in a food chain within the cave that includes spiders, bats, and fish, a unique ecosystem based not on sunlight but on chemistry. Hose had discovered new life-forms.

The dream of discovery came early to Louise. Her love of the outdoors and exploration began with the two weeks each summer she and her sisters spent with their parents camping in the Sierra Nevada. "I loved going into the forest and seeing a rock that maybe nobody had ever seen before. I didn't want to go down life's main paths, I wanted to poke down the side passage." Her passion for caves began

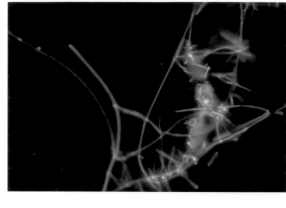

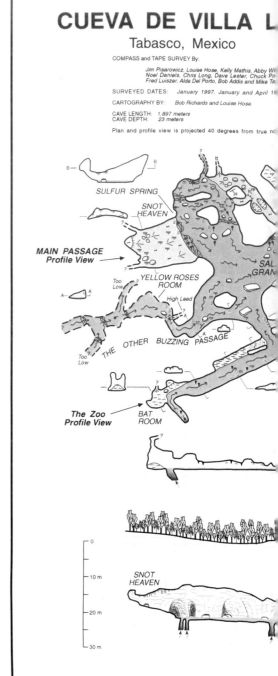

CUEVA DE VILLA L

Tabasco, Mexico

COMPASS and TAPE SURVEY By:

Jim Pisarowicz, Louise Hose, Kelly Mathis, Abby Wil
Noel Daniels, Chris Long, Dave Lester, Chuck Po
Fred Luiszer, Alda Del Porto, Bob Addis and Mike Ta

SURVEYED DATES: January 1997, January and April 19

CARTOGRAPHY BY: Bob Richards and Louise Hose.

CAVE LENGTH: 1,897 meters
CAVE DEPTH: 23 meters

Plan and profile view is projected 40 degrees from true no

in earnest in 1970, when she rappelled into Church Cave in California.

In college in the early 1970s geology was certainly a side passage. Louise was quickly informed that for her, it was also a dead end, since geology was virtually closed to women. She switched her degree to education, but she could not shake her love of geology. Hose turned back to science and got her doctorate in geology, spending her free time exploring and mapping caves in the American southwest.

Since that momentous first trip to Cueva de Villa Luz in 1996, she has returned time after time to map the interior of the cave. Each trip is like a venture into the deep ocean or to the surface of a distant planet, since she has to carry a full array of life-support equipment. The very air is lethal to human beings, yet despite its toxic mix of sulfur, carbon dioxide, and sulfur dioxide, the bacteria and pink fish thrive.

Louise's discoveries have wide-ranging implications. In her own field of geology, it has long been held that limestone caves were formed by nonbiological processes, being the result of the chemistry of rainwater and carbon dioxide, which slowly wore away the underground passages. With the discovery of the microbial veils, earth scientists can explore the possibility that living entities had a hand in creating the vast chambers.

Astronomers are intrigued by the possibilities that this unique environment offers a potential scenario not only for how life might have begun on Earth but also for how it may exist on other planets that are known to have both sulfur and water. In addition, the sulfuric bacteria may become a critical asset for cleaning up toxic sites, such as sulfur mine dumps. Finally, there have been preliminary studies that suggest these exotic bacteria may be useful in the fight against cancer. As Hose says, "Cueva de Villa Luz is the most disgusting cave in the world for recreational cavers. For scientist cavers, it is the most exciting."

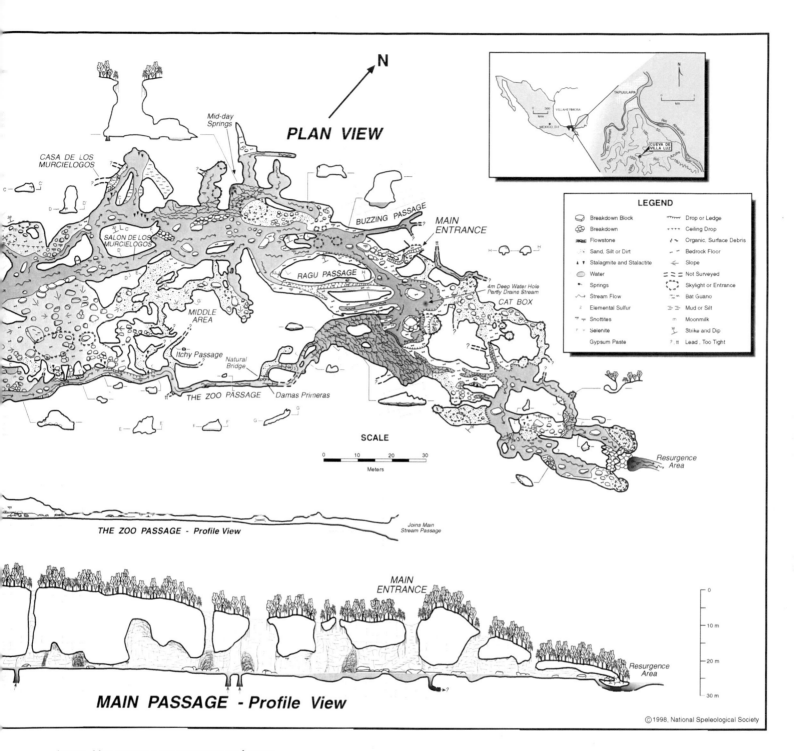

PLAN VIEW

N

Mid-day Springs

CASA DE LOS MURCIELOGOS

BUZZING PASSAGE

MAIN ENTRANCE

SALON DE LOS MURCIELOGOS

RAGU PASSAGE

4m Deep Water Hole Partly Drains Stream

CAT BOX

MIDDLE AREA

Itchy Passage   Natural Bridge

THE ZOO PASSAGE   Damas Primeras

Resurgence Area

SCALE

0   10   20   30
Meters

LEGEND

Breakdown Block		Drop or Ledge	
Breakdown		Ceiling Drop	
Flowstone		Organic, Surface Debris	
Sand, Silt or Dirt		Bedrock Floor	
Stalagmite and Stalactite		Slope	
Water		Not Surveyed	
Springs		Skylight or Entrance	
Stream Flow		Bat Guano	
Elemental Sulfur		Mud or Silt	
Snottites		Moonmilk	
Selenite		Strike and Dip	
Gypsum Paste		Lead, Too Tight	

THE ZOO PASSAGE - Profile View

Joins Main Stream Passage

MAIN ENTRANCE

MAIN PASSAGE - Profile View

Resurgence Area

0
10 m
20 m
30 m

© 1998, National Speleological Society

ABOVE: MAP OF THE CAVE EXPLORED BY LOUISE HOSE. IN ADDITION TO INVENTING THE TERM "SNOT-TITES," THE TEAM LABELED LOCATIONS IN THE CAVE SUCH AS "ITCHY PASSAGE," "BUZZING PASSAGE," AND "SNOT HEAVEN."

OPPOSITE, TOP: A MAGNIFIED VIEW OF SNOT-TITES, STRANGE LIFE FORMS FOUND DEEP WITHIN THE VILLA LUZ CAVE, WHICH HOSE DISCOVERED WITH JIM PISAROWICZ. HOSE WRITES: "MOST CAVES ARE DRY AND DEVOID OF LIFE. THIS CAVE WAS FULL OF LIFE. IT OFFERS A DIFFERENT SCENARIO OF HOW LIFE AND ECOSYSTEMS CAN WORK IN A CAVE SYSTEM."

FAR LEFT: HOSE WITH MASK INSIDE CUEVA DE VILLA LUZ, MEXICO.

I am really attracted to the earth. Caving gave me the confidence to be different. When I was young the message was that only men can do the outdoor things. When I began caving I saw women going down into the Black Hole in Mexico, so I knew I could do it too.

Searching the Heavens

JILL CORNELL TARTER

AMERICAN ASTROPHYSICIST • B. 1944

Beginning early in the twentieth century, signals from Earth—including every television program, radio broadcast, and cellular telephone call—have been streaming into space, creating a babble of noise that would probably deafen any listening aliens. But just as we have been bombarding the universe with signals of our presence, there are a handful of space explorers who are betting that aliens have been doing the same. In an attempt to discover whether or not we share the universe with other intelligent life, NASA has sponsored a project called Search for Extraterrestrial Intelligence, or SETI.

In 1974 scientists led by Frank Drake beamed a powerful three-minute message about our earth and solar system into the universe. The message they sent was aimed at MI3, a cluster of hundreds of thousands of stars within the Milky Way Galaxy. There is, of course, no hope of real communication, because it will take twenty-three thousand Earth years for the message to reach the cluster and presumably a similar amount of time for any intelligent civilization to reply. But the SETI team hopes that sometime in the distant past, a civilization evolved on a planet somewhat like ours and sent a similar message into the void.

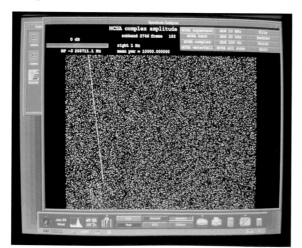

Leading a small band of space explorers dedicated to the task of receiving messages from space is astronomer Jill Tarter. She has spent the past twenty-five years scanning the heavens. To date, her computer screens at SETI's headquarters in Mountain View, California, have been filled with streams of blinking spikes of phosphor representing noise radiating from the one thousand stars in

Top: Portrait of Jill Tarter.

Above: radio signals from *Pioneer 10* in deep space.

Right: Parkes Radio telescope, Australia, one of the largest collecting telescopes, where Tarter and her team search space for signs of alien life.

the Milky Way judged to be the most likely sources. But they have as yet given no hint of true communications. In fact, much of it actually proves to have originated here on Earth. Tarter says wistfully, "So far all we have received is white noise, which looks like snow on the screen. What we hope to find is a straight line within the static or a pulsing light."

In 1985 Jill helped to found the nonprofit SETI Institute, which collaborated with NASA to keep the cost of doing the research as low as possible. When Congress terminated support of the project, it was the SETI Institute that permitted Tarter and her team to keep the search going with private funds.

When the current project ends, Jill hopes that the progress she has made and the enthusiasm she has generated will convince private and public funders to build dedicated telescopes for SETI, perhaps placing a collecting dish on the far side of the moon, where it will be free from earthly noise. Then, picking up again where she began, she hopes to be there herself, listening.

Asked what her quest means to her personally, Tarter notes that any discovery of alien life will profoundly affect us all. "Ever since the beginning of humanity we have been asking, are we alone? It's possible we may be alone, but it seems unlikely to me," she says. "I am willing to devote my life to the search for an answer. Either answer has enormous consequences. If we are alone it may help us to realize that we must be a little more reasonable with other humans and our fragile environment. If not it will help us define our humanity."

LEFT: ARECIBO RADIO TELESCOPE IN PUERTO RICO. CORNELL UNIVERSITY RUNS THE ARECIBO TELESCOPE IN COOPERATION WITH THE NATIONAL SCIENCE FOUNDATION. IT IS AN IMPORTANT LOCATION FOR SETI'S COLLECTION OF DATA.

Notes and Selected Bibliography

BOOKS ON WOMEN EXPLORERS

Adams, H. Davenport. *Celebrated Women Travellers of the Nineteenth Century.* London: W. Swan Sonnenschein & Co., 1883.

Aitken, Maria. *A Girdle Round the Earth.* London: Constable and Co., 1987.

Alic, Margaret. *Hypatia's Heritage.* Boston: Beacon Press, 1986.

Allen, Alexandra. *Travelling Ladies.* London: Jupiter, 1980.

Barstow, Anne. *Witchcraze.* San Fransisco: Pandora, 1994.

Bonta, Marcia. *Women in the Field.* College Station: Texas A & M, 1991.

Casson, Lionel. *Travel in the Ancient World.* Baltimore, Md.: Johns Hopkins University Press, 1994.

D'Auvergne, Edmund. *Adventuresses and Adventurous Ladies.* New York: J. H. Sears and Co. N.d.

Dowie. *Women Adventurers.* London: Fisher Unwin, 1893.

Hamalian, Leo. *Ladies on the Loose.* New York: Dodd, Mead and Company, 1981.

Jansz, Natania and Miranda Davies. *Women Travel.* New York: Prentice-Hall, 1990.

Middleton, Dorothy. *Victorian Lady Travellers.* Chicago: Academy Chicago Publishers, 1982.

Ogilvie, Marilyn Bailey. *Women in Science.* Cambridge, Mass.: MIT Press, 1986.

Olds, Elizabeth Fagg. *Women of the Four Winds.* Boston: Houghton Mifflin, 1985.

Robinson, Jane. *Wayward Women.* Oxford: Oxford University Press, 1990.

————. *Unsuitable for Ladies.* Oxford: Oxford University Press, 1994.

Schiebinger, Londa. *Nature's Body.* Boston: Beacon Press, 1993.

Shteir, Ann. *Cultivating Women, Cultivating Science.* Baltimore: Johns Hopkins University Press, 1996.

Stanley, Jo. *Bold in Her Breeches.* London: Pandora 1995.

Stark, Suzanne. *Female Tars.* Baltimore: US Naval Press, 1996.

Tiltman, Marjorie Hessell. *Women in Modern Adventure.* London: George G. Harrap & Co. Ltd., 1935.

Tinling, Marion. *Women into the Unknown.* Westport, Conn.: Greenwood Press, 1989.

REFLECTIONS IN A DISTANT MIRROR: THE STORIES OF EARLY VOYAGERS

JEANNE BARET

"She will be": Ross, 130; "Jeanne Baret, my": Oliver, 85; "We had seen him": Ross, 129.

de Bougainville, Louis. *A Voyage Around the World in the Years 1766, 1767, 1768 and 1769.* London, 1772.

Oliver, Captain Pasfield. *The Life of Philibert Commerson.* London: John Murray,1909.

"Philibert Commerson, Naturalist." *Edinburgh Review,* vol. 177, no. 2 (April 1893).

Ross, Michael. *Bougainville.* London: Gordon & Cremonesi, 1978.

EARLY CHRISTIAN PILGRIMS

"turn the sea": Webb, 21.

Hallam, Elizabeth. *Saints.* New York: Simon and Schuster, 1994.

Paula and Eustochium to Marcella. "Letter XLVI." Christian Classics Ethereal Library server, at Wheaton College.

Turner, Victor, and Edith Turner. *Image and Pilgrimage in Christian Culture.* New York: Columbia University Press, 1978.

Ward, Benedicta. *Harlots of the Desert.* Kalamazoo, Michigan: Cistercian Publications, 1987.

Webb, Diana. "Women Pilgrims of the Middle Ages." *History Today,* July 1998, 20–27.

EGERIA

"Early on a Sunday morning": Gingras, 51; "We were also shown the place": Ibid., 69; "There is no road": Ibid., 59; "On the next day": translation in Duchesme.

Duchesme, Louis. *Christian Worship.* London, 1923. Found at Web site www.ocf.org.

Gingras, George. *Egeria: Diary of a Pilgrimage.* NY: Paulist Press, 1970.

CATALINA DE ERAUSO

"On July 5th": D'Auvergne, 16; "I went out onto the highway": D'Auvergne, 19; "I had a mind to travel": Steptoe, 17.

D'Auvergne, Edmund. *Adventuresses and Adventurous Ladies.* New York: J. H. Sears and Co. N.d.

Steptoe, Michele, and Gabriel Steptoe. *Lieutenant Nun.* Boston: Beacon Press, 1966.

ISABEL GRANDMAISON Y BRUNO GODIN

The following quote is from the letter to Condamine, found in Pinkerton. "The rememberence of": 269.

Goodman, Edward T. *The Explorers of South America.* Norman: University of Oklahoma Press, 1972.

Pinkerton, John. *A General Collection of the Best and Most Interesting Voyages and Travels in all Parts of the World.* vol. 14. 1813.

Smith, Anthony. *Explorers of the Amazon.* Chicago: University of Chicago Press, 1990.

Von Hagen, Victor. *South America Called Them.* New York: Knopf, 1945.

Wakefield, Celia. *Searching for Isabel Godin*. Chicago: Chicago Review Press, 1995.

MALINCHE
Karttunen, Frances. *Between Worlds*. New Brunswick: Rutgers University Press, 1994.

Schroeder, Susan, Stephanie Wood, and Robert Haskett. *Indian Women of Early Mexico*. Norman: University of Oklahoma, 1997.

LADY SARASHINA
The following quotes are from Morris. "Even as I wander": 99; "I was brought up": 31; "That evening we stayed": 39; "thick cover of unmelting": 69; "I was whiling": 69; "On our first night": 104; "Now that I was able": 99; "wildly the sagebrush": 110; "Even as I wander": 99.

Duchesme, Louis. *Christian Worship*. London, 1923. Found at Web site www.ocf.org.

Omori, Annie Shepley, and Kochi Doi. *Diaries of Court Ladies of Old Japan*. Boston: Houghton, 1920.

Morris, Ivan. *As I Crossed a Bridge of Dreams*. London: Penguin, 1975.

Murasaki, Shikibu. *The World of the Shining Prince*. New York: Knopf, 1978.

VIKING VOYAGERS
Magnusson, Magnus, and Hermann Palsson. *Laxdaela Saga*. London: The Folio Society, 1975.

Sawyer, Peter, ed. *Vikings*. Oxford: Oxford University Press, 1997.

Wernick, Robert. *The Vikings*. Alexandria, Virginia: Time Life Books, 1979.

Wolf, Kirsten. "Amazons in Vinland." *The Journal of English and Germanic Philology*, vol. 95, no. 4 (October 1996).

LADY WEN-CHI
"Now I must abandon": Rorex and Fong, chapter 13.

Frankel, Hans. "Cai Yan and the Poems Attributed to Her." *Chinese Literature Essays, Articles, Reviews*, vol. 5, no. 2 (July 1983).

Rorex, Robert, and Wen Fong, translators and commentators. *Eighteen Songs of the Nomad Flute*. New York: Metropolitan Museum of Art, 1974.

Tomita, Kojiro. "Wen-chi's Captivity in Mongolia and Her Return to China." *Bulletin of the Museum of Fine Arts* XXVI. Boston: Museum of Fine Arts, 40–45.

ELIZABETH VAN DER WOUDE
The following quotes are from Hotz. "We started from Colhorn": 612; "This day, Friday, my dear Father": 614; "Certain Indians": 615; "There was an abundance": 615; "About two o'clock": 616; "I did return alone": 617.

Hotz, Lucy. "A Young Lady's Diary of Adventure in 1677: Journal of Elizabeth van der Woude." *The Blue Peter*, vol. 9 (Dec. 1929): 611–618.

FOREVER NEW HORIZONS: INTREPID EXPLORERS
"I was held spell bound": Harris and Sartor, 145.

Harris, Alex, and Margaret Sartor, eds. *Gertrude Blom: Bearing Witness*. Chapel Hill: University of North Carolina Press, 1984.

DELIA JULIA DENNING AKELEY
"As a woman": Akeley, *Jungle Portraits*, 8; "Finally in the summer": Ibid., 160; "The first part": Ibid., 163; "I'm always frightened": Olds, 153.

Akeley, Delia. *J.T., Jr: The Biography of an African Monkey*. New York: MacMillan, 1928.
———. *Jungle Portraits*. New York: MacMillan, 1928.
———. "On Wings of Fire." *St. Nicholas* vol. LVII, no. 3 (Jan. 1930).
———. Unpublished manuscripts. Lincoln, Mass. Page Collection.

Henderson, Rose. "Delia Akeley Explores Africa." *Independent Woman* vol. XI, no. 3 (March 1932).

Olds, Elizabeth Fagg. *Women of the Four Winds*. Boston: Houghton Mifflin, 1985.

MARY LENORE JOBE AKELEY
"They told me": Forrester, 5; "Here was a chance": Akeley, "My Quest in the Canadian Rockies," 813; "gave immeasurable": Ibid., 814; "A huge ice peak": Ibid., 824; "As a little girl": radio interview, 1935, Mystic Historical Society, Mary Jobe Akeley archive.

Akeley, Mary Jobe. *Adventures in the African Jungle*. New York: Junior Literary Guild, 1931.
———. *Carl Akeley's Africa*. New York: Dodd Mead, 1929.
———. *Congo Eden*. New York: Dodd Mead, 1950.
———. "My Quest in the Canadian Rockies: Locating a New Ice Peak." *Harpers Magazine*, May 1915.
———. *Restless Jungle*. New York: McBride, 1936.
———. *Rumble of a Distant Drum*. New York: Dodd Mead, 1945.
———. *The Wilderness Lives Again*. New York: Dodd Mead, 1940.
———. *Lions, Gorillas and Their Neighbors*. New York: Dodd Mead, 1932.
———. Unpublished manuscripts. Archives of the Mystic, Connecticut Historical Society.

Forrester, Izola. "Plucky New York Girl's Dash Alone into the Wilds." *World Magazine*, Oct. 5, 1913.

ANNIE MONTAGUE ALEXANDER
"As you may know": Stein, "Annie M. Alexander: Extraordinary Patron," 248; "I have not missed": Ibid., 246; "The fever": Stein, "Women in Mammology," 637; "We sat in the dust": *www.Berkeley.edu*; "We sleep again": Grinnell, 25; "My object": Stein, "Annie M. Alexander: Extraordinary Patron," 249; "I'm just a born": Stein, "Women in Mammology," 640; "The sea shall": Zullo, 185-87.

Bonta, Marcia. *Women in the Field*. College Station: Texas A & M, 1991.

Grinnell, Hilda, W. *Annie Montague Alexander*. Berkeley: Grinnell Naturalists Society, 1958.

Stein, Barbara R., "Annie M. Alexander: Extraordinary Patron." *Journal of the History of Biology*, vol. 30 (1997): 243–266. *www.Berkeley.edu*

————. "Women in Mammalogy: The Early Years." *Journal of Mammalogy,* vol. 77, no. 3: (1996): 629–641.

Zullo, Janet Lewis. "Annie Montague Alexander." *Journal of the West* (April 1969): 183–199.

GERTRUDE MARGARET LOWTHIAN BELL

Bell, Gertrude. *The Desert and the Sown.* London: Heinemann, 1907.

————. *The Letters of Gertrude Bell.* London: E. Benn, 1927.

————. *The Persian Pictures.* London: Jonathan Cape, 1940.

Wallach, Janet. *Desert Queen.* New York: Doubleday, 1996.

LADY ANNE BLUNT

"tiring of too": Wilfrid Scawen Blunt (vol. 1), ix; "We are starting": Blunt, *Bedouin Tribes of the Euphrates,* 157; "the Bedouins, when": ibid., 44; "The fact is": Ibid., 44; "Our first thought": Ibid., 149; "toward an unknown": Ibid., 157; "We have left Deyr": Ibid., 261; "Full of gloomy": Ibid., 269; "We were not prepared": Ibid., 359–60; "low, but covers": Ibid., 44; "one advantage": ibid., 73;

Archer, Rosemary, and James Fleming, eds. *Lady Anne Blunt: Journals and Correspondence.* Cheltenham, England: Alexander Heriot & Co. Ltd. 1986.

Blunt, Lady Anne. *Bedouin Tribes of the Euphrates.* New York: Harper and Brothers, 1879.

————. *A Pilgrimage to Nejd.* London: Murray, 1881.

————, trans. *The Celebrated Romance of the Stealing of the Mare.* Translated from the original Arabic by Lady Anne Blunt. Done into verse by Wilfrid Scawen Blunt. London: Reeves and Turner, 1892.

Blunt, Wilfrid Scawen. *My Diaries: Part One.* New York: Knopf, 1921.

ALEXANDRA DAVID-NÉEL

"craved to go": David-Néel, *My Journey to Lhasa,* xxxi; "The pageant": David-Néel, Ibid., xxxi.

David-Néel, Alexandra. *Initiations and Initiates in Tibet.* London: J. Rider, 1931.

————. *Magic and Mystery in Tibet.* New York: Dover, 1971.

————. *My Journey to Lhasa.* New York: Harper, 1927.

Foster, Barbara, and Michael Foster. *The Secret Lives of Alexandra David-Néel,* New York: Overlook, 1998.

SUE HENDRICKSON

All quotes from telephone conversation with authors, spring 1999.

Fiffer, Steve. "Indiana Bones." *Chicago Tribune Magazine,* April 4, 1999.

Hendrickson, Sue. Personal interview with Milbry C. Polk.

McAndrew, Tara. "The Story Of Sue." *The [Springfield, Ill.] State Journal-Registrar,* July 3, 1998.

Webster, Donovan. "A Dinosaur Named Sue." *National Geographic Magazine,* June 1999.

MINA BENSON HUBBARD

"My expedition demonstrated": Hubbard, "My Explorations in Unknown Labrador."

Davidson, James West, and John Rugge. *Great Heart: The History of a Labrador Adventure.* New York: Kodansha, 1997.

Hubbard, Mina. "My Explorations in Unknown Labrador." *Harpers Monthly Magazine,* May 1906.

————. *A Woman's Way Through Unknown Labrador.* New York: McClure, 1908.

OSA LEIGHTY JOHNSON

"For days we marched": Johnson, *I Married Adventure,* 262; "We worked with lions": Ibid., 307; "Hair feeling": Johnson, *Four Years in Paradise,* 326–28.

Imperato, Pascal James, and Eleanor Imperato. *They Married Adventure.* New Brunswick, N.J.: Rutgers University Press, 1992.

Johnson, Osa. *Bride in the Solomans.* New York: Houghton Mifflin, 1944.

————. *Four Years in Paradise.* Philadelphia: Lippincott, 1941.

————. *I Married Adventure.* Philadelphia: Lippincott, 1940.

————. *Last Adventure.* New York: Morrow, 1966.

MARY HENRIETTA KINGSLEY

"The explorer herself": Tooley, 290; "had a perfect horror": Ibid., 291; "I cried": Tinling, 150; "dead tired": Stefoff, 72; "I would much": Tooley, 294; "My aim in": Kingsley, "Travels on the Western Coast of Equatorial Africa," 113; "you have no right": Kingsley, *Travels in West Africa,* 19; "Several times": "Travels on the Western Coast of Equatorial Africa," 120; "you cannot get out": Huxley, 31; "While I was in the Islands": Tooley, 292; "I must say that never": Huxley, 105–106; "One by one": Ibid., 21; "full of fire": Kingsley, "Travels on the Western Coast of Equatorial Africa," 121; "I shall never forget": Huxley, 34; "every hole": Ibid., 120–21; "[I] curled up": Ibid.; "It is impossible": Kingsley, "Black Ghosts," 89.

Frank, Katherine. *A Voyager Out.* Boston: Houghton Mifflin, 1986.

Huxley, Elspeth, ed. *Travels in West Africa.* London: Folio Society, 1976.

Kingsley, Mary. "Black Ghosts." *The Cornhill Magazine* (July 1896): 79–92.

————. "The Story of a Day's March in West Africa." *The Young Woman,* no. 48 (September 1896).

————. *Travels in West Africa.* London: Macmillan, 1897.

————. "Travels on the Western Coast of Equatorial Africa." *The Scottish Geographical Magazine* 12 (Mar. 1896): 113-124.

————. *West African Studies.* London: Macmillan, 1899.

"A Lady Traveller in West Africa," *Illustrated London News,* Jan. 4, 1896.

Oliver, Caroline. *Western Women in Colonial Africa.* Westport, Conn.: Greenwood Press, 1982.

Stefoff, Rebecca. *Women of the World.* Oxford: Oxford University Press, 1992.

Tinling, Marion. *Women into the Unknown.* New York: Greenwood Press, 1989.

Tooley, Mrs. "Adventures of a Lady Explorer." *The Young Woman,* no. 45 (June 1896).

GERALDINE FITZGIBBON MOODIE

"I put in": White, 107.

Eber, Dorothy Harley. *When the Whalers Were Up North.* Norman: University of Oklahoma Press, 1989.

White, Donnie. *In Search of Geraldine Moodie.* Regina: Canadian Plains Research Center, 1998.

STEPHANIE SCHWABE
All quotes from telephone conversations with authors, spring 1999.

Schwabe, Stephanie. *The Black Hole: Caves and Caving.* (BCRA)80: 17–22.

——. *The Petrology of Bahamian Pleistocene Eolianites and Phreatic Dissolution Caves.* Mississippi State University, 1992.

——, and Wheeler, F. "Sterile and General Sampling Techniques for Submerged Cave Environments," in Mylroie, J. E., and White, B., eds. *Proceedings of the Ninth Symposium on the Geology of the Bahamas.* Fort Lauderdale, Florida: CCFL Bahamian Field Station, 1999.

——. *Biogeochemical Investigation of Caves within Bahamian Carbonate Platforms.* England: University of Bristol, 1999.

MAY FRENCH SHELDON
"unnecessary, atrocious": French Sheldon, *Sultan to Sultan,* foreword; "meet the men of": Eagle, 132; "very much thought"; French Sheldon, *Sultan to Sultan,* 270.

Boisseau, Tracey Jean. *The African Adventures of May French-Sheldon.* Ann Arbor: University of Michigan Press, 1996.

Eagle, Mary Kavannaugh Oldham. *The Congress of Women.* New York: Arno Press, 1974.

French Sheldon, May. *Sultan to Sultan.* Boston: Arena Publishing Company, 1892.

——. "What She Saw in Africa." *New York Times,* March 22, 1892.

——. "A White Lady Visits the Masai." *New York Times,* December 11, 1892.

FREYA MADELINE STARK
"The most interesting things": Stark, *The Freya Stark Story,* 155; "to go out": Ibid., 179; "The life I left": Ibid., 190; "Camels appeared": Moorehead, 38–39; "the whole of my future": Stark, *The Freya Stark Story,* 191; "It is, I believe": Stark, *The Journey's Echo,* 106; "the unmapped hills": Stark, *Valley of the Assassins*; "that tightening of the heart": Stark, *The Freya Stark Story,* 214; "I used to walk ahead": Moorehead, 52; "The lure of exploration": Stark, *The Zodiac Arch,* 46.

Geniesse, Jane Fletcher. *Passionate Nomad.* New York: Random House 1999.

Moorehead, Caroline. *Freya Stark.* New York: Viking Penguin, 1985.

Ruthven, Malise. *Traveller Through Time.* New York, Viking, 1986.

Stark, Freya. *The Freya Stark Story.* New York: Coward-McCann, 1950.

——. *The Journey's Echo.* London: John Murray, 1963.

——. *The Southern Gates of Arabia.* London: John Murray, 1936.

——. *Valley of the Assassins.* N.p., n.d.

——. *A Winter in Arabia.* London: John Murray, 1940.

——. *The Zodiac Arch.* London: Murray, 1968.

Stefoff, Rebecca. *Women of the World.* Oxford: Oxford University Press, 1992.

ALEXANDRINE PETRONELLA FRANCINA TINNÉ
"There are Dutch Ladies": Gladstone, 106; "This is our last night": Ibid., 80; "this part of the voyage": Proceedings Royal Geographical Society, Nov. 23, 1863; "I write at present": Ibid., Nov. 23,

1863; "Once more en route": Ibid., Nov. 23, 1863; "The ladies were really": Ibid., Nov. 23, 1863; "I was so sick with sorrow": Gladstone, 164; "Visitors to Algiers": Edwards, 81; "A queer little place": Gladstone, 205; "I cannot tell you": Ibid., 215.

Adams, William. *Celebrated Women Travellers of the Nineteenth Century.* London: Sonnenschein, 1883.

Edwards, Betham. "Alexandrine Tinné, African Explorer." *Leslie Monthly,* vol. XL, no. 1–6 (1881).

"Fraulein Tinné, Her Reported Murder by Camel-Drivers." *New York Times,* August 30, 1869.

Gladstone, Penelope. *Travels of Alexine.* London: Murray, 1970.

Kotschy, Theodore. *Plantae Tinneanae.* Vindobonae, Vienna, 1867.

Oliver, Caroline. *Western Women in Colonial Africa.* Westport, Conn.: Greenwood Press, 1981.

Proceedings Royal Geographical Society 8. 1863–64.

Wells, William. *Heroine of the White Nile.* New York: Carlton & Lanahan, 1871.

TO CATCH A FALLING STAR: IN THE FIELD WITH SCIENTIFIC EXPLORERS
"We contest in toto": *Times [London],* 11; "Females in particular": Norwood, 21; "The first long-term field": Bonta, 222.

Birkett, Dea. *Spinsters Abroad.* Oxford, U.K.: Basil Blackwell, 1989.

Bonta, Marcia. *Women in the Field.* Texas A & M, 1991.

Norwood, Vera. *Made from This Earth.* Chapel Hill: University of North Carolina Press, 1993.

The Times [London], 31 May 1893, 11.

ROSITA ARVIGO
"For every ailment": conversation with authors, spring 1999; "I had never seen": Ibid.; "The old man": Ibid.; "Taking an apprentice": Arvigo, *Sastun,* 63; "After about a year": conversation with authors, spring 1999.

Arvigo, Rosita. *Sastun.* San Francisco: Harper SanFrancisco, 1994.

——, and Michael Balick. *Rainforest Remedies.* Twin Lakes, Wisc: Lotus Press, 1993.

CRISTINA SHELLEY BIAGGI
All quotes from conversation with authors, Palisades, New York, April 1999.

Biaggi, Cristina Shelley. *Habitations of the Goddess.* Glenrock, N.J.: K.I.T., Inc., 1994.

LOUISE ARNER BOYD
"In August": Boyd, *The Fiord Regions of East Greenland,* 1; "Far north": Ibid., 1; "Ice does such eerie": Stefoff, 116; "I may have worn": Olds, 234–35; "These expeditions familiarized me": Boyd, *The Fiord Regions of East Greenland,* 1; "[A] sea dotted": Olds, 234; "obtain before it": Boyd, *Polish Countrysides,* 3; "I spared no effort": Olds, 250.

Boyd, Louise Arner. *The Coast of Northeast Greenland.* New York: American Geographical Society, 1948.

——. *The Fiord Regions of East Greenland.* New York: American Geographical Society, 1935.

——. *Polish Countrysides.* New York: American Geographical Society, 1937.

Olds, Elizabeth Fagg. *Women of the Four Winds.* Boston: Houghton Mifflin, 1985.

Rittenhouse, Mignon. *Seven Women Explorers.* New York: J. B. Lippincott Company, 1964.

Stefoff, Rebecca. *Women of the World.* Oxford: Oxford University Press, 1992.

LUCY EVELYN CHEESMAN

"settle a few": Cheesman, *The Two Roads of Papua,* 60; "for the last ten years": Cheesman, "The Cyclops Mountains of Dutch New Guinea," 21; "those carefree": Cheesman, *Things Worth While,* 25; "sheds and outhouses": Ibid., 12; "There is always so much": Ibid., 314; "It seems to be taken": Ibid., 231; "clung to me": Ibid., 91-92; "it was they who": Cheesman, *Time Well Spent,* 12; "The air was": Ibid., 154; "nothing that Hides": Cheesman, *Things Worth While,* 223; "On my return": Cheesman, *Time Well Spent,* 9; "Working there presented": Cheesman, *Things Worth While,* 153.

Cheesman, Lucy Evelyn. *Camping Adventures in New Guinea.* London: Harrap, 1948.

————. "The Cyclops Mountains of Dutch New Guinea," *The Geographical Journal,* vol. 91 (January—June 1938).

————. *Hunting Insects in the South Seas.* London: P. Allen, 1932.

————. *Insects and Their Secret World.* New York: William Sloan Associates, 1952.

————. *Six Legged Snakes in New Guinea.* London: Harrap, 1949.

————. *Things Worth While.* London: Readers Union 1958.

————. *Time Well Spent.* London: The Travel Book Club, 1960.

————. *The Two Roads of Papua.* London: Jarrolds, 1935.

————. "Two Unexplored Islands Off Dutch New Guinea: Waigeu and Japen." *The Geographical Journal* vol. 95 (Jan.—June 1940).

EUGENIE CLARK

"I'm a simple ichthyologist": Balon, 124; "I never tired": Clark, *Lady with a Spear,* 4; "As the months passed": Ibid., 8; "I wasn't afraid of them": Trupp, 174; "It's hard to decide": telephone conversation with authors, spring 1999; "I was crazy": Stein; "In the sub": telephone conversation with authors, July 1999; "I have a good": Trupp, 180.

Balon, Eugene. "The Life and Work of Eugenie Clark in Women in Ichthyology." *Environmental Biology of Fishes* vol. 41 (1994); 7–8, 89–127.

Clark, E. "Dispatches from a Distant World." *National Geographic,* vol. 178, no. 4 (1990): 12–19.

————. "Gentle Monsters of the Deep: Whale Sharks." *National Geographic.* vol. 182, no. 6 (1992). 120–139.

————. *The Lady and the Sharks.* Sarasota, Fl.: Mote Marine Laboratory, 1969.

————. *Lady with a Spear.* New York: Harper and Brothers, 1953.

————, with Ann McGovern. *Desert Beneath the Sea.* New York: Scholastic, 1991.

LaBastille, Ann. *Women and Wilderness.* Sierra Club, 1980.

McGovern, Ann. *Adventures of the Shark Lady: Eugenie Clark Around the World.* New York: Scholastic, 1998.

————. *Shark Lady: True Adventures of Eugenie Clark.* New York: Scholastic, 1978.

Stein, J. "Eugenie Clark: Sweet Sharks." *Omni* vol. 4, no. 9: 94—98, 115—117.

Trupp, Phill. *Sea of Dreamers: Travels with Famous Ocean Explorers.* Golden, Colorado: Fulcrum, 1998.

JOAN BRETON CONNELLY

All quotes from telephone conversation with authors and conversation at National Arts Club, New York City, spring 1999.

Connelly, Joan. *Votive Sculpture of Hellenistic Cyprus.* New York and Nicosia: NYU Press and Dept. of Antiquities, Cyprus, 1988. *www.nyu.edu/projects/yeronisos*

KONCORDIE AMALIE NELLE DIETRICH

The following quotes are from Sumner. "When I think back": 117; "an unusual talent": 70; "The discomforts which the heat": 117; "I really have arrived": 110; "I have to learn to look": 113; "her coarse grey": 71.

Moyal, Ann. *A Bright and Savage Land.* Sydney: Collins, 1986.

Sumner, Ray. *A Woman in the Wilderness.* New South Wales: University Press, 1993.

ALICE EASTWOOD

"What grand times I had": Bonta, 94; "The only woman": Robertson, 107-108; "I do not feel": Bonta, 98.

Bonta, Marcia. *Women in the Field.* Texas A & M, 1991.

Dakin, Susanna Bryant. *The Perennial Adventure: A Tribute to Alice Eastwood, 1859–1953.* San Francisco: California Academy of Science, 1954.

Eastwood, Alice. *A Collection of Popular Articles on the Flora of Mount Tamalpais.* Published by the author. N.d.

Moore, Patricia Ann. *Cultivating Science in the Field: Alice Eastwood, Ynés Mexía and California Botany, 1890–1940.* Ph.D. thesis. Los Angeles: University of California, 1966.

Robertson, Janet. *The Magnificent Mountain Women.* Lincoln: University of Nebraska Press, 1990.

Wilson, Carol Green. *Alice Eastwood's Wonderland.* San Francisco: 1953 California Academy of Sciences, 1955.

DIAN FOSSEY

"A bright-eyed": Fossey, 167; "Sound preceded sight": Fossey, 13–14; "there are times when": Mowat, 161.

The Dian Fossey Gorilla Fund International
800 Cherokee Avenue, SE
Atlanta, Georgia 30315
1-800-851-0203
www.gorillafund.org

Fossey, Dian. *Gorillas in the Mist.* Boston: Houghton Mifflin, 1983.

Montgomery, Sy. *Walking with the Great Apes.* Boston: Houghton Mifflin, 1991.

Mowat, Farley. *Woman in the Mists.* New York: Warner, 1987.

MARGARET FOUNTAINE

Fountaine, Margaret. *Butterflies & Late Loves.* Topsfield, Massachusetts: Salem House Publishers, 1987.

————. *Love Among the Butterflies.* Boston: Little Brown and Company, 1980.

KATHARINE STEVENS FOWLER-BILLINGS

"It was in the depths": Fowler-Billings, *Stepping Stones,* preface; "I worked alone": Fowler-Lunn, *Gold Missus,* 14; "I loved the mountain": Fowler-Billings, *Stepping Stones,* 45; "On my trips": Ibid., 45; "I did the geology": Fowler-Billings, unpublished manuscript; "contract forbade him": "Alumnae Authors"; "the hinterland of": Fowler-Lunn, *Gold Missus,* 11; "I was to prospect": Fowler-Billings, *Stepping Stones,* 128; "My workers spread": Ibid., 137.

"Alumnae Authors." *Windsor Bulletin,* Spring 1994.
Bryn Mawr Alumnae Bulletin XXIII, no. 3 (April 1943).
Fowler-Billings, Katharine. *Stepping Stones.* New Haven, Conn: Academy of Arts and Sciences, 1996.
———. Unpublished manuscript. Fowler-Billings private archives, New Hampshire.
Fowler-Lunn, Katharine. *Gold Missus.* New York: Norton, 1938.

MARIJA BIRUTE ALSEIKAITE GIMBUTAS

"In our house": Marler, 9; "I fell in love": Ibid., 9; "secular and sacred": Gimbutas, *The Civilization of the Goddess,* x; "This is the only thing": Marler, 20; "that we as a civilization": Gimbutas, *The World of the Goddess* (video); "It is a gross misunderstanding": Gimbutas, *The Civilization of the Goddess,* vii.

Gimbutas, Marija. *The Civilization of the Goddess.* San Francisco: Harper San Francisco, 1991.
———. *The Goddesses and Gods of Old Europe.* London: Thames and Hudson, 1982.
———. *The Language of the Goddess.* London: Thames and Hudson, 1989.
———. *The World of the Goddess.* Mystic Fire Video, 1990.
Marler, Joan. *From the Realm of the Ancestors.* Manchester, Conn.: Knowledge, Trends and Ideas, 1997.

JANE GOODALL

Goodall, Jane. *In the Shadow of Man.* Boston: Houghton Mifflin, 1971.
———. *My Friends the Wild Chimpanzees.* Washington, D.C.: National Geographic Society, 1967.
———. *Through a Window.* London: Weidenfeld and Nicholson, 1990.
———, and Dale Peterson. *Visions of Caliban.* Boston: Houghton Mifflin, 1993.
———, and Mike Nichols. *Brutal Kinship.* New York: Aperture, 1999.
Montgomery, Sy. *Walking with the Great Apes.* Boston: Houghton Mifflin, 1991.

ELPIDA HADJIDAKI-MARDER

All quotes from telephone conversation with authors, January 1999.

Hadjidaki, Elpida. "The Classical Shipwreck at Alonnesos." in *Res Maritimae,* ed. Swincy, Hohlfelder and Swiny, American Schools of Oriental Research, 1996: 125–134.
———. "Et Klassisk Problem—Alonnesosvraget." *Hvad Middelhavet gemer,* 3–61 (Arhus).
———. "The Hellenistic Harbor of Phalasarna in Western Crete." In Raban, Avner, and Kenneth Holum, eds., *Caesarea Maritima.* Leiden; E.J. Brill, 1996.

———. "Underwater Archaeology." *ENA IA* 1992. vol. IV. Athens: Hellenistic Institute of Marine Archaeology, 1996.
———. "Underwater Excavations of a Late Fifth-Century Merchant Ship at Alonnesos, Greece." *BCH* 120, 561–591.
P. Pirazzoli, J. Ausseil-Badie, P. Giresse, E. Hadjidaki, M. Arnold. "Historical and Environmental Changes at Phalasarna Harbor, West Crete." *Geoarchaeology,* (vol. 7 (1992): 371–392.

MARY DOUGLAS NICOL LEAKEY

"It was a place": Leakey, 55; "There is so much": Holloway.

Holloway, Marguerite. "Unearthing History," *Scientific American,* October 1994, 37.
Leakey, Mary. *Disclosing the Past.* Garden City, New York: Doubleday & Company, 1984.
Morell, Virginia. *Ancestral Passions.* New York: Simon & Schuster, 1995.

NICOLE HUGHES MAXWELL

"The most frightening": Maxwell, *Witchdoctor's Apprentice,* 3; "I could make some of those plant": Ibid., 6; "I made a habit": Maxwell, "Medical Secrets of the Amazon"; "Primitive peoples are generally": Halsell, 58; "One was used": Ibid., 59; "big pharmaceutical": Ibid., 59; "The scientific attitude": Ibid., 57; "I was suffering": Ibid., 69.

Halsell, Grace. "Nicole Maxwell, Herb Lady of the Rain Forest." *Prevention* vol. 28, no. 2 (Feb. 1976): 56–61.
Maxwell, Nicole. "Medical Secrets of the Amazon." *Americas* vol. 29, no. 6–7 (June–July 1977).
———. *Witchdoctor's Apprentice.* Cambridge, Mass.: Riverside Press, 1961.
———. Unpublished manuscripts. Private archives.

MARGARET MEAD

"All the courage": Mead, *Letters from the Field,* 19; "Then came the calm": Ibid., 43; "Have I not three": Ibid., 47; "I think that field work": Ibid., 15; "Six times in the last sevent0een": Mead, *And Keep Your Powder Dry,* 3; "the general fear": Mead, *Letters from the Field,* 85; "Knowledge about what man": Mead, *Blackberry Winter,* 296; "Women wanted sons": Ibid., 206.

Bateson, Mary. *With a Daughter's Eye.* New York: William Morrow, 1984.
Howard, Jane. *Margaret Mead: A Life.* New York: Simon and Schuster, 1984.
Mack, Joan. *Margaret Mead.* New York: Oxford University Press, 1999.
Mead, Margaret. *And Keep Your Powder Dry.* New York: William Morrow, 1942.
———. *Blackberry Winter.* New York: William Morrow, 1972.
———. *Coming of Age in Samoa.* New York: William Morrow, 1928.
———. *Growing Up in New Guinea.* New York: William Morrow, 1930.
———. *Letters from the Field, 1925–1965.* New York: Harper and Row, 1977.

YNES MEXIA

"ready to pack": Moore, 229; "to this place": Bonta, 107; "a nature lover": Bonta, 103; "In the two and a half years": Bonta, 110.

Bonta, Marcia. *Women in the Field*. College Station: Texas A & M, 1991.

Mexia, Ynes. "Camping on the Equator." *Sierra Club Bulletin* 22 (Feb. 1937).

———. "Three Thousand Miles Up the Amazon." *Sierra Club Bulletin* 18 (Feb. 1933).

Moore, Patricia Ann. *Cultivating Science in the Field: Alice Eastwood, Ynés Mexía and California Botany, 1890–1940*. Ph.D. thesis. Los Angeles: University of California, 1966. UMT Dissertation Services, Ann Arbor, Michigan, 1998.

Unpublished manuscripts. Bancroft Library, University of California, Berkeley.

Spencer, Jarjorie. "The Botanical Quests of a Woman in Latin America," *Pan American* magazine, April 1930.

CYNTHIA MOSS

"I had this overwhelming": conversation with authors, New York City, May 12, 1999; "compared to most other": Moss, *Elephant Memories*, 125; "it was Teresia's": conversation with authors, May 12, 1999; "After years of": Moss, *Elephant Memories*, 125; "My priority, my love": Ibid., 317; "I have realized": Ibid., 317.

Moss, Cynthia. *Elephant Memories*. New York: William Morrow, 1988.

———. *Portraits in the Wild*. Boston: Houghton Mifflin, 1975.

Pringle, Lawrence. *Elephant Woman*. New York: Atheneum, 1997.

KATY PAYNE

All quotes from telephone conversations with authors and conversations at Explorers Club, New York City, spring 1999.

Payne, Katy. *Silent Thunder*. New York: Simon & Schuster, 1998.

NAOMI PIERCE

All quotes from conversation with authors, Cambridge, Mass., spring 1999.

Kitching, R. L., E. Sheermeyer, R. E. Jones., and N. E. Pierce (eds.) *Biology of Australian Butterflies*. Melbourne: CSIRO Publishing, 1999.

ANNA CURTENIUS ROOSEVELT

"I wanted to be": conversation with authors, National Arts Club, New York City, May 12, 1999; "The Marajoara": Roosevelt, *Moundbuilders of the Amazon*, 1–3; "I must have gotten": from conversation with authors, National Arts Club, New York City, May 12, 1999; "when we exposed": Ibid.; "critical for the survival": Ibid.; "began thinking": Ibid.; "I wanted to go to the": Ibid.; "I look for areas": Ibid.; "Specialized big game": Ibid.; "I like the messiness": Ibid.

Menon, Shanti. "The New Americans." *Discover*, vol. 8 (Jan 1997).

Roosevelt, Anna Curtenius. "Eighth-Millennium Pottery from a Prehistoric Shell Midden in the Brazilian Amazon." *Science*, vol. 254, no. 5038 (13 December 1991).

———. "The Excavations at Corozal, Venezuela: Stratigraphy and Ceramic Seriation." New Haven, Conn.: Department of Anthropology and the Peabody Museum, Yale University, 1997.

———. *Moundbuilders of the Amazon*. San Diego: Academic Press, 1991.

———. "Secrets of the Forest." *The Sciences*, vol. 32, no. 6 (November/December 1992): 22–28.

MEENAKSHI WADHWA

All quotes from telephone conversation with authors, spring 1999.

Wadhwa, Meenakshi, and Mark Robinson. "Messengers from Mars." *Astronomy*, vol. 23, no. 8 (August 1995): 44.

TRANSCENDING TIME AND PLACE: THE VISIONS OF ARTIST EXPLORERS

ELIZABETH ANN ARTHUR

"so addicted to": telephone conversation with authors, spring 1999; "I was in love": Ibid.; "confronted": Ibid.; "Like joining the army": Ibid.; "a huge amount": Ibid.; "There is another": Arthur, *Antarctic Navigation*, 787; "mystical truth": telephone conversation with authors, spring 1999.

Arthur, Elizabeth. *Antarctic Navigation*. New York: Knopf, 1994.

———. *Beyond the Mountain*. New York: Harper and Row, 1983.

———. *Island Sojurn*. New York: Harper and Row, 1980.

———. *Looking for the Klondike Stone*. New York: Alfred L. Knopf, 1993.

www.earthur.com

APHRA JOHNSON BEHN

"She was a most": Jones, 289; "Unusual with my Sex": Todd, 79; "a long voyage to Sea": Behn, "The Dutch Lover," 184; "attacked colonists and" Behn, *Oroonoko*, 54–56; "Those who are nobly": Ibid., 45; "And these people": Ibid., 3;

Behn, Aphra. "The Dutch Lover." In *Selected Writings of the Ingenious Mrs. Aphra Behn*. New York: Greenwood Press, 1969.

———. *Oroonoko or the Royal Slave*. New York: W. W. Norton and Company, 1973.

Jones, Jane. "New Light on the Background and Early Life of Aphra Behn." *Notes and Queries* (September 1990): 288–293.

Todd, Janet. *The Secret Life of Aphra Behn*. New Brunswick, N.J.: Rutgers University, 1996.

ISABELLA LUCY BIRD BISHOP

"At last I am in love": Barr, 22; "living in a new world": Ibid., 22; "a stew of": Bird, *Unbeaten Tracks in Japan*, volume 2, 90; "barley-meal porridge": Ibid., 90; "in mud up to": Ibid., 90; "It was then": Bird Bishop, *The Yangtze Valley and Beyond*, 190.

Barr, Pat. *A Curious Life for a Lady*. New York: Doubleday, 1970.

Bird, Isabella. *The Golden Cheronese and the Way Thither*. London: Murray, 1883.

———. *A Lady's Life in the Rocky Mountains*. London: Murray, 1879.

———. *Six Months in the Sandwich Islands*. Honolulu: University of Hawaii Press, 1964.

———. *Unbeaten Tracks in Japan*. Vol. 2. London: Murray, 1880.

Bird Bishop, Isabella. *Journeys in Persia and Kurdistan*. London: Murray, 1891.

———. *Korea and Her Neighbors*. New York: Revel, 1898.

———. *The Yangtze Valley and Beyond*. London: Murray, 1900.

GERTRUDE ELIZABETH LOERTSCHER DUBY BLOM

"My decision was made": Cardon, 14; "Traveling by horse": Blom.

Blom, Gertrude. "Na-Bolom." Pamphlet produced by Na-Bolom,

San Cristobel de las Casas, Chaipas, Mexico. Distributed by the Na-Bolom Cultural Center.

Cardon, Charlotte. "Gertrude Duby Blom, 'La Reina' of the Jungle." *El Palacio,* Quarterly Journal of the Museum of New Mexico, vol. 85, no. 1 (Spring 1979).

Harris, Alex, and Margaret Sartor, eds.. *Gertrude Blom: Bearing Witness.* Chapel Hill: University of North Carolina Press, 1984.

Price, Christine, and photographs by Gertrude Duby Blom. *Heirs of the Ancient Maya.* New York: Charles Scribner and Sons, 1972.

Marilyn Bridges

"I knew what": conversation with authors, Warwick, New York, February 10, 1999; "many of the sites": Ibid.; "Seeing from the air": Ibid.; "About 250 miles": Bridges, *Planet Peru,* 107.

Bridges, Marilyn. *Egypt.* Boston: Bulfinch Press, 1996.
———. *Markings.* New York: Aperture, Inc., 1986.
———. *Planet Peru.* New York: Aperture, Inc., 1991.
———. *Sacred and Secular.* New York: ICP, 1990.
———. *Sacred and Secular.* New York: CD-ROM Voyager Company, 1996.
———. *This Land Is Your Land.* New York: Aperture, 1997.

Leila Eliott Burton Hadley

"At dawn when I was": Hadley, *Give Me the World,* 148; "I had wanted": Ibid., 1; "My daughter has been:" Hadley, *Journey with Elsa Cloud,* 3; "not far from the Ladies": Ibid., 379; "I feel free": Ibid., 600; "Inside the temple": Ibid., 4.

Hadley, Leila. *Give Me the World.* New York: St. Martin's Press, 1999.
———. *Journey with Elsa Cloud.* New York: Turtle Point Press, 1999.

Emily Hahn

"I've seen crocodiles before": Hahn, *Congo Solo,* 84; "Africa was an unusual": Hahn, *Times and Places*; "I drifted": Ibid., 3; "I was put at": Ibid., 86; "to be found": Hahn, *Congo Solo,* 86; "We were lost": Hahn, *Congo to Me,* 282; "No member of": Hahn, *Times and Places,* 160; "I was taking": Hahn, "I Say This," 35; "I dreaded the change": Hahn, *Times and Places,* 172; "The March after next": Hahn, *Congo Solo.*

Cuthbertson, Ken. *Nobody Said Not to Go.* Boston: Faber and Faber, 1998.
Hahn, Emily. *Congo Solo.* New York: Bobbs Merrill, 1933.
———. *Congo to Me.* N.p., n.d.
———. *Eve and the Apes.* London: Weidenfeld and Nicholson, 1988.
———. "I Say This." *The New Yorker,* July 31, 1995.
———. *On the Side of the Apes.* New York: Crowell, 1971.
———. *Times and Places.* New York: Crowell, 1970.

Zora Neale Hurston

"No one can stay": Hurston, *Folklore, Memoirs and Other Writings,* 456; "I would find myself": Ibid., 470; "not owning pots": Hurston, *Dust Tracks on a Road,* 13; "I used to take a seat": Hurston, *Folklore, Memoirs and Other Writings,* 589; "My search for knowledge": Hurston, *Dust Tracks on a Road,* 178; "Research is formalized": Ibid., 174; "In New Orleans": Hurston, *Folklore, Memoirs and Other Writings,* 699; "My finger was cut": Hurston, *Dust Tracks on a Road,* 192; "When the duppy": Ibid., 44; "lived mostly in silk": Hurston, *Tell*

My Horse, 25; "from the firm belief": Ibid., 179; "bodies without souls": Hurston, *Folklore, Memoirs and Other Writings,* 456; "sucks out his soul": Hurston, *Tell My Horse,* 196; "Folklore is the boiled": Bordelon, 69; "Of my research": Hurston, *Folklore, Memoirs and Other Writings,* 711.

Bordelon, Pamela. *Go Gator and Muddy the Water.* New York: Norton, 1999.
Hurston, Zora Neale. *Dust Tracks on a Road.* New York: Harper and Row, 1984.
———. *Folklore, Memoirs and Other Writings.* New York: Literary Classics, 1995. Unpublished galleys.
———. *Jonah's Gourd Vine.* New York: HarperCollins, 1990.
———. *Mules and Men.* New York: HarperCollins, 1990.
———. *Tell My Horse.* New York: Lippincott, 1938.
———. *Their Eyes Were Watching God.* New York: J. B. Lippincott, 1937.

Margaret Ursula Brown Mee

Mee, Margaret. *Flowers of the Amazon.* Rio de Janeiro: Distribution Record, 1980.
———. *Margaret Mee, In Search of Flowers of the Amazon Forests.* Woodbridge: Nonesuch Expeditions, 1988.
Stiff, Ruth. *Margaret Mee, Return to the Amazon.* Kew: Royal Botanic Gardens, 1996.

Anna Maria Sibylla Merian

"Anna Maria Merian": Davis, 144; "So I was moved:" Ibid., 167; "In January 1701": Ibid., 180.

Davis, Natalie Zemon. *Women on the Margins.* Boston: Harvard University Press, 1997.
Kramer, Jack. *Women of Flowers.* New York: Stewart Tabori Chang, 1996.
Merian, Maria Sibylla. *Flowers, Butterflies and Insects.* New York: Dover, 1991.
———. *Metamorphosis Insectorum Surinamensium.* The Hague, 1717. Private Collection.
Wettengl, Kurt, ed. *Maria Sibylla Merian.* Verlag Gerd Hatje. N.p., N.d.

Lady Mary Pierrepont Wortley Montagu

"It was an act": Mullen; "People in my way": Ibid.; "stoves, which are": Montagu, 39; "They believ'd": Halsband, 68; "I am pretty far gone": Montagu, 79; "Upon the whole": Ibid., 72; "The small-pox": Ropes, 87; "Posterity perhaps": Halsband, 111; "Out of compassion": Ibid., 121; "I was in my travelling": Ropes, 80.

Barry, Iris. *Portrait of Lady Mary Montagu.* Indianapolis, Ind.: Bobbs Merrill, 1928.
Grundy, Isobel. *Lady Mary Wortley Montagu: Comet of the Enlightenment.* Oxford: Clarendon Press, 1999.
Halsband, Robert. *The Life of Lady Mary Wortley Montagu.* Oxford: Clarendon Press, 1956.
Melville, Lewis. *Lady Mary Wortley Montagu.* Boston: Houghton Mifflin Company, 1925.
Montagu, Mary. *The Turkish Embassy Letters.* London: Virago Press, 1996.
Mullen, John. "Contary Mary" *Manchester Guardian,* May 1, 1999. Review of *Lady Mary Wortley Montagu: Comet of the Enlightenment,* by Isobel Grundy.

Ropes, A.R., ed. *Lady Mary Wortley Montagu*. New York: Charles Scribner's Sons, N.d.

Warncliffe, ed. *Letters and Works of Lady Mary Wortley Montagu*. 2 vols. London: Bickers and Son, 1861.

MARIANNE NORTH

North, Marianne. *Recollections of a Happy Life*. London: Macmillan, 1892.

————. *Some Further Recollections of a Happy Life*. Ed. Mrs. John Addington Symonds. London: Macmillan, 1893.

IDA REYER PFEIFFER

All quotes are from Pfeiffer, *A Woman's Journey Around the World*.

Pfeiffer, Ida. *A Lady's Voyage Around the World*. London: Longman, 1852.

————. *A Lady's Second Journey Around the World*. New York: Harper, 1856.

————. *The Last Travels of Ida Pfeiffer, Inclusive of a Visit to Madagascar, with an Autobiographical Memoir of the Author*. New York: Harper, 1861.

————. *A Woman's Journey Around the World*. London: Ingram, Cooke, and Co., 1852.

————. *Visit to Iceland and the Scandinavian North*. London, Ingram, Cooke, 1852.

MARIA REICHE

"They didn't understand": Lama; "I began to walk": Ibid.

Bridges, Marilyn. *Markings*. New York: Aperture, 1986.

Lama, Abraham. "Science-Peru: Maria Reiche to Rest with the Enigmas She Unraveled." *World News*, Lima, June 12, 1998. www.oneworld.net.

Malatesta, Parisina. "Maria Reiche." *Americas*, vol. 49, no. 2 (April 1997): 14.

LENI RIEFENSTAHL

"At last I was": Riefenstahl, *A Memoir*, 462; "I was magically": Ibid., 462; "I saw black figures": Ibid., 411; "Africa had embraced": Ibid.; "The editing room": Ibid., 89; "In the light": Ibid., 468.

Riefenstahl, Leni. *Coral Gardens*. New York: Harper & Row, 1978.

————. *Last of the Nuba*. New York: Harper & Row, 1973.

————. *A Memoir*. New York: St. Martin's Press, 1987.

————. *People of Kau*. New York: Harper & Row, 1976.

RUTH AGNES McCALL ROBERTSON

The following quotes are from Robertson. "An orange": 305; "set the clock": 233.

Robertson, Ruth. *Cherun Meru—The Tallest Angel*. Ardmore, Penn: Whitmore Publishing Company, 1975.

LINDA SCHELE

"It was": McAuliffe; "I became so fascinated": Ibid.

McAuliffe, Kathleen. "Linda Schele." *Omni*, February 1995.

Schele, Linda, and David Friedel. *A Forest of Kings*. Quill, 1992.

Schele, Linda, and Mary Miller. *Blood of Kings*. New York: George Braziller, 1992.

Schele, Linda, David Friedel, and Joy Parker. *Maya Cosmos*. Quill, 1995.

Schele, Linda, and Peter Mathews. *The Code of Kings*. New York: Scribner, 1998.

THE LURE OF THE UNKNOWN: EXPLORERS ON THE EDGE

AMERICAN TRANS-ANTARCTIC TEAM

All quotes are from Rothblum, Weinstock, and Morris, eds. "When it's blowing": 49; "The fact that we had": 47; "We decided": 56.

Dal Vera, Anne. "Endurance on Ice: The American Women's Antarctic Expedition." In *Another Wilderness*. Ed. Susan Fox Rogers. Seattle: Seal Press, 1994.

Rothblum, Esther, Jacqueline Weinstock, and Jessica Morris. *Women in the Antarctic*. New York: Harrington Park Press, 1998.

BESSIE COLEMAN

"I found a brand": Holden and Griffith, 41; "It was a terrible shock": Rich, 32; "The Negro race": Ibid., 85; "I decided blacks": Holden and Griffith, 43.

Holden, Henry, and Captain Lori Griffith. *Ladybirds*. Mount Freedom, N.J.: Black Hawk, 1991.

Rich, Doris. *Queen Bess*. Washington, D.C.: Smithsonian Press, 1993.

AMELIA MARY EARHART

"as soon as": Earhart, *The Fun of It*, 25; "It was clear": Earhart, *The Fun of It*, 210; "something happened": Earhart, *The Fun of It*, 214; "I succeeded": Ibid., 218; "Women must try": Aitken, 193.

Aitken, Maria. *A Girdle Round the Earth*. London: Constable & Co., 1987.

Backus, Jean. *Letters from Amelia*. Boston: Beacon Press, 1982.

Brink, Randall. *Lost Star*. New York: Norton, 1994.

Butler, Susan. *East to the Dawn*. New York: Addison-Wesley, 1997.

Earhart, Amelia. *The Fun of It*. New York: Brewer, Warren & Putnam, 1932.

————. *20 hours, 40 minutes*. London: Putnam's, 1928.

Lovell, Mary. *The Sound of Wings*. New York: St. Martin's Press, 1989.

Rich, Doris. *Amelia Earhart*. Washington, D. C.: Smithsonian Institution Press, 1989.

SYLVIA ALICE EARLE

All quotes from conversations with Milbry Polk, New York City, March 1999, and subsequent telephone conversations.

Broad, William. "Racing to the Bottom of the Deep, Black Sea." *New York Times*, August 3, 1993.

Earle, Sylvia. *Dive!* Washington, D.C.: National Geographic Society, 1999.

————. "Humpbacks, the Gentle Whales." *National Geographic*, vol. 155, no. 1 (January 1979): 2–17.

————. "Life Springs from Death in Truk Lagoon." *National Geographic*, vol. 149, no. 6 (1976): 578–613.

————. *Sea Change*. New York: G.P. Putnam's Sons, 1995.

————, with Al Giddings. *Exploring the Deep Frontier*. Washington, D.C.: National Geographic, 1980.

Lavendel, Brian. "Her Royal Deepness." *Animals*, vol. 132, no. 2 (March 1999): 36.

Rosenblatt, Roger. "Call of the Sea." (Heroes of the Planet.) *Time*, October 5, 1998.

Stover, Dawn. "Queen of the Deep." *Popular Science*, April 1995, page 67.

Wexler, Mark. "Sylvia Earle's Excellent Adventure." *National Wildlife*, April 1999.

LOUISE HOSE
All quotes from conversations with authors, Newark, New Jersey, fall 1998.

Hose, Louise. "Cave of the Sulfur Eaters." *Natural History*, May 1999.

————. "An Explorer's Guide to the Grand Canyon." Unpublished manuscript.

————. "Exploring One of the World's Strangest Caves." *Explorers Club Journal*, vol. 77, no. 1 (Spring 1999).

———— and J. A. Pisarowicz. "Cueva de Villa Luz, Tabasco, Mexico: Reconnaissance Study of an Active Sulfur Spring Cave." *Journal of Cave and Karst Studies*. vol. 61, no. 1, 1999.

VALENTINA MIHAILOVNA KUZNETSOVA AND IRINA MIHAILOVNA KUZNETSOVA

All quotes from conversations with authors, Palisades, New York, winter 1998.

BERYL CLUTTERBUCK MARKHAM
"momentary escape": Markham, *West with the Night* (1983), 280; "bound for a place": Ibid., 280; "She has written so well": Ibid.

Lovell, Mary S. *Straight on Till Morning*. New York: St. Martin's Press, 1987.

Markham, Beryl. *The Illustrated West with the Night*. New York: Stewart, Tabori and Chang, 1994.

————. *West with the Night*. San Francisco: Northpoint Press, 1983.

————. *West with the Night*. Boston: Houghton Mifflin, 1942.

Trzebinski, Errol. *The Lives of Beryl Markham*. New York: W. W. Norton, 1993.

MARIA MITCHELL
"I swept last night two hours": Gormley, 51.

Gormley, Beatrice. *Maria Mitchell*. Grand Rapids, Michigan: Eerdmans Publishing Company, 1995.

ANNIE SMITH PECK
"I felt that": Peck, *A Search for the Apex of America*, ix; "To conquer a virgin": Olds, 16; "Never before": Peck, *A Search for the Apex of America*, 51; "As I was": Ibid., 151; "After my long": Ibid., 123.

Earheart, Amelia. Comments about *Flying Over South America*. Peck Collection, Library of Congress manuscript division.

Olds, Elizabeth Fagg. *Women of the Four Winds*. Boston: Houghton Mifflin, 1985.

Peavy, Linda, and Ursula Smith. *Women Who Changed Things*. New York: Charles Scribner's Sons, 1983.

Peck, Annie Smith. *Flying over South America*. Boston: Houghton Mifflin, 1932.

————. *Industrial and Commercial South America*. New York: E.P. Dutton, 1922.

————. "Practical Mountain Climbing." *Outing Magazine*, September 1901.

————. *A Search for the Apex of America*. New York: Dodd Mead, 1911.

————. *The South American Tour*. New York: George H. Doran, 1914.

————. "Wings of South America." *Scientific American*, July 1929.
www.AnnieSPeck.com

KATHRYN D. SULLIVAN
www.NASA.org.

JILL CORNELL TARTER
All quotes from conversations with authors, Kennedy Airport, New York, April 1999.

Broad, William. "Astronomers Revive Scan of Heavens for Sign of Life." *New York Times*, September 29, 1998.

Gibbs, W. Wayt. "Field of Dreams." *Scientific American*, May 1999.

Greenwald, Jeff. "Who's Out There?" *Discover*, April 1999.

Tarter, Jill. "Brown Dwarfs and Black Holes." *Astronomy*, April 18, 1978.

————. "Communication with Extraterrestrial Intelligence: Report on 1AA 8th Annual CETI Review in Munich, Germany." *Cosmic Search*, vol. 2 (198): 18.

————. "NASA's First Systematic Search for Extraterrestrial Intelligence (SETI)" in *Interstellar Migration and the Human Experience*. B. R. Finney and E. M. Jones, eds. University of California Press, 1985.

————. "Project Phoenix and Beyond." Pesek Lecture. *Acto Astronautica*. Vol. 14, nos. 4–10: 613–622.

————. "Results from Project Phoenix: Looking Up from Down Under." In *Astronomical and Biochemical Origins and the Search for Life in the Universe*. C. B. Cosmovici, S. Bowyer, and D. Werthimer, eds. Bologna, Italy: Editrice Compositori, 1997.

————. "The Search for Extraterrestrial Intelligence." *Atlas of the Universe*. Washington, D.C.: National Geographic Society, 1986.

————. "Searching for Them: Interstellar Communication." *Astronomy*, October 1982.
www.seti.org

MARIE THARP
All quotes from conversations with authors, Nyack, New York, spring 1998 and 1999.

Heezen, Bruce, Marie Tharp, and Maurice Ewing. "The Floors of the Oceans." Palisades, New York: The Geological Society of America Special Paper 65, April 11, 1959.

Lawrence, David. "Mountains Under the Sea." *Mercator's World*, vol. 4, no. 6 (November/December 1999).

Acknowledgments

So many people contributed to this massive effort that it is impossible to mention everyone, but we did want to especially thank the following:

Leila Hadley Luce for her extraordinary friendship.

Our wonderful agents and friends Nicholas Smith and Andrea Pedolski.

Caroline Schimmel, who shares our passion for women explorers and for whose generosity we are so grateful.

Our excellent team at Clarkson Potter: Annetta Hanna, Jan Derevjanik, Marysarah Quinn, Maggie Hinders, Margot Schupf, Jean Lynch, Vanessa Hughes, Elizabeth Royles, Jane Searle, Merri Ann Morrell, Rebecca Strong, and Elizabeth Herr.

Researcher and fellow explorer Nicola Jenns.

Angela Ramirez and Bill Zimmerman.

Gertrude Dole, who first introduced us to the importance of gathering the oral histories of exploring women.

Jane Robinson, Marion Tinling, and Marcia Bonta, whose wonderful scholarship rescued many women from obscurity.

To colleagues and friends, especially William Polk, Francine Douwes Whitney, Diana Green, Steve Soter, Virginia Dean, Nina Prusinowski, Caroline Sheen, Gayle Fitzpatrick, Jeff Liang, and Lisa Sonne.

And:
Paul Abell, our friends from Fishers Island, Isany P. Alexander, Carmela Del Pino, and Austin McPhail, Christiane Amanpour, Melinda Barber, Stacey Bienhorn, Anita and Carl Bleyleben, Andres Branger, Ellen Brush, Dan Buck, Allen Bukoff, Sheldon Caplan, Lauren Cardillo, Karen Clark, Lincoln Colwell, Gertrude Vanderbilt Whitney Conner, Hope Cooke, Anne Doubilet, Brian Drolet, YT Feng, Jeffrey J. Foxx, Loni Garrison, Dave Green, Bob Griffin, Ginger Head, Missy Houghton, Patricia Hubbard, Barbara Hunter, Tad Hyde, Sian Imber, Scottie Brown Jones, Patty Potter Katz, Gale Barrett Kavanagh, Dr. Steven Keeling, Barbara and Justin Kerr, Lindley Kirksey, Jana Kolpen, Lucille Conetta Kravitz, Myke Lattner, Henry Luce III, Neil MacFarquahar, Penny Mar, Christine Miele, Mary Miller, Cecily Morse, Penny Naylor, Caroline Nicholson, Heather O'Meara, Jesse Page, Danielle Parris, George Polk, Lori Belden and Kevin Pope, Bill Price, Bev Rogerson, Jane Safer, Angela and Carl Schuster, Lucy Scott, Susana Sedgewick, Holly and David Seeger, Cecily Selby, Robin Siegel, Robert Spector, Meredith Steinbach, Judith Stiles, Linda Sunshine, Lena Tabori, Missie Rennie Taylor, Catherine Ursillo, Terry Ward and Idanna Pucci, Ellen Warner, Sally Whittaker, and Ted Yeatman.

Milbry's companions in the desert, Margaret and Douglas Griffes, Ibrahim el Shayeb, Ibrahim Helmi, Meshayt, Mohammad, and Belhaq.

Librarians, archivists, and keepers of the flame, especially:
Marilyn Ward of the Royal Botanical Gardens at Kew
Jean Rainwater of John Hay Library, Brown University
Tony Irwin of the Castle Museum
Natural History Museum, London, Lodvina Mascarenhas
Rachel Rowe and the staff of the Picture Library, Royal Geographical Society
Jovanka Ristic of the AGS Collection
Linda Briscoe of the University of Texas
Erica Kelly and Mary Wolfskill of the Library of Congress
Nick and Reba Nichols
Henry Persaud at the Museum of Mankind
Joan Eldridge
Virginia Murray of John Murray Ltd.
Tony Morrison
Janet Baldwin of the Explorers Club
Beatrice Lo and the staff of the Palisades Free Library
Michele Wellck of the California Academy of Sciences
Janet Godwin of Mystic Historical Society
Jose Welbers of Na Balom
Jokull Saevarsson of the National and University Library of Iceland
Barbara Stein at the University of California at Berkeley

Netzin Steklis, Dian Fossey Gorilla Fund International
Lorett Trease, archivist, Bryn Mawr College
The staff at the African Wildlife Foundation
Carola Vecchio
Ken Cuthbertson
Nancy Farnan
Zivile Gimbutas
Rachel and George Billings
Joan Marler
Heather Colburn
Conrad Froelich and Barbara Hinshell and the staff of
    the Osa and Martin Johnson Safari Museum
Seth Shostak of the SETI Institute
Ann Brownell Sloan of the Mead Institute of
    Intercultural Studies, Inc., New York

To countless Internet archivists who diligently uploaded
information on the Web that helped us locate
important leads.

To our intrepid, voyaging, and inspiring foremothers:
Adelaide Roe Polk, Sara Price Cooledge, Joan Cooledge
Elisabeth von Oppenheimer Polk, Janet O'Meara,
Dr. Marjory Smith Goodman, and Muriel Allen.

And thanks to the support of Wings Trust, under whose
auspices this project began long ago.

Finally, what is last is always first in our hearts: A very
special heartfelt thank you to Milbry's husband, Phillip
Bauman, and to Mary's husband, Hubert Pedroli, for their
support and endless patience. And to Milbry's children,
Mary, Bree, and Elisabeth.

Most of all, thank you to the women who
inspired us to write this book.

About the Authors

Before graduating from Harvard in 1976, MILBRY POLK journeyed through Greece, Turkey, Persia, Pakistan, and Japan, surveyed Arthurian sites in Wales, traveled with Bedouin tribesmen in Jordan and Egypt, and kayaked throughout Alaska's Prince William Sound. In 1979 Milbry led a camel expedition retracing the route of Alexander the Great across Egypt. Her photojournalistic work includes stories on sailing the Mediterranean, ancient rock carvings in the Saudi Arabian desert, rafting above the Arctic Circle, and temple art in Burma. Milbry's work with women explorers was featured on *CBS Sunday Morning*. Her previous book was *Egyptian Mummies*. She is a member of the Explorers Club and is a Fellow of the Royal Geographical Society. She lives in Palisades, New York, with her husband and three daughters.

Designer and writer MARY TIEGREEN has been exploring the art of books and book making for most of her life. Working on a variety of projects, she has had the opportunity to learn about diverse areas of interest, including the history of Hollywood (*MGM: When the Lion Roared*), cooking and magic (*The Secrets of Pistoulet*), fashion (*A Passion for Shoes*), sex (*TarotSutra*), and golf (*Let the Big Dog Eat*). *Women of Discovery* is her first foray into the world of exploration. She lives in the Hudson Valley with her husband, Hubert, and big dog, Daisy.

Index

Photo Credits

Title page: Arrival at monasteries in sandstorm. Photograph by Milbry Polk, © 1980.

5: Portrait of William Polk. Photograph by William Mares.

14: Milbry Polk with mayor of Qara. Photograph by Douglas Griffes.

14-15: Crossing the Qattara. Photograph by Milbry Polk, © 1979.

16. Shadows on the sand. Photograph by Milbry Polk, © 1979.

16-17: Crossing the Quattara. Photograph by Milbry Polk, © 1979.

17: Evening fire in the Qattara, Egypt. Photograph by Milbry Polk, © 1979.

18: Bedouin women in tent. Photograph by Milbry Polk, © 1979.

20-21: Jerusalem from the south. Engraving by David Roberts, 1855, courtesy of the Cooledge Collection.

26-27: Handscroll, Eighteen Songs of the Nomad Flute: The Story of Lady Wen-chi. "The Farewell," The Metropolitan Museum of Art, Gift of the Dillon Fund, 1973. Photograph © 1994, The Metropolitan Museum of Art.

29: "Ascent of Sinai." Etching of pilgrims crossing Holy Land. Engraving by David Roberts, courtesy of the Cooledge Collection.

35: "Islandia" map, 1590, by Ortelius Abraham. Courtesy of the National and University Library of Iceland.

37: Aztec drawing of Malinche. University of Texas Collection, The General Libraries, the University of Texas at Austin. Photograph by George Holmes.

40: Portrait of Jeanne Baret. Museum of New South Wales Image Library, State Library of New South Wales.

44-45: Camel caravan. Photograph by Freya Stark, courtesy of Royal Geographical Society.

46: Johnson on a crocodile. Photograph by Martin Johnson, courtesy of Martin and Osa Johnson Safari Museum.

47: Arctic in Winter Quarters. Photograph by Geraldine Moodie. Copyright © The British Museum.

48: Portrait of Moodie. Courtesy of the Eldridge Collection.

48: Inuit women, 1906. Churchill, Manitoba. Photo by Geraldine Moodie, courtesy of the Eldridge Collection.

49: Portrait of Hubbard. Courtesy of the Schimmel collection.

49: Hubbard in camp. Courtesy of the Schimmel collection.

49: Braving the elements. Courtesy of the Schimmel collection.

54-55: Pyramids of Gizeh from the Nile by David Roberts, courtesy of the Cooledge Collection.

54 and 55: Pages from Tinné's book on Sudanese plants. Courtesy of the LuEsther T. Mertz Library of the New York Botanical Garden, Bronx, New York.

58: Lady Anne Blunt on mare. Courtesy of the Archer Collection.

61: Kingsley portrait. By permission of the Syndics of Cambridge University Library.

65: Sheldon portrait. Courtesy of the Library of Congress.

66: Goatherd in Kum Zum Pass. Photograph by Catherine Ursillo. Courtesy of Catherine Ursillo.

67: Néel at hermitage. Courtesy of the Foundation Alexandra David-Néel.

68: Carts in China. Photograph by Alexandra David-Néel. Courtesy of the Foundation Alexandra David-Néel.

70: Delia Akeley under tusks. Courtesy of Jesse Page Collection.

70: Lecture program cover. Courtesy of Jesse Page Collection.

70: Field notebook. Courtesy of Jesse Page Collection.

71: Akeley in hunting gear. Courtesy of Jesse Page Collection.

72-73: Akeley with porters. Photograph from the Mary Jobe Akeley collection and courtesy of Mystic River Historical Society, Inc., Mystic, Connecticut, and M.J. Akeley Trust.

73: Delia with dead elephant. Photograph from the Mary Jobe Akeley collection and courtesy of Mystic River Historical Society, Inc., Mystic, Connecticut, and M.J. Akeley Trust.

74: Akeley and African natives. Photo from the Mary Jobe Akeley collection and courtesy of Mystic River Historical Society, Inc., Mystic, Connecticut, and M.J. Akeley Trust.

74: Akeley camp in Canadian Rockies. Photograph from the Mary Jobe Akeley collection and courtesy of Mystic River Historical Society, Inc., Mystic, Connecticut, and M.J. Akeley Trust.

74: Newspaper article. Photograph from the Mary Jobe Akeley collection and courtesy of Mystic River Historical Society, Inc., Mystic, Connecticut, and M.J. Akeley Trust.

75: Mary Jobe Akeley contemplating sunset. Photograph from the Mary Jobe Akeley collection and courtesy of Mystic River Historical Society, Inc., Mystic, Connecticut, and M.J. Akeley Trust.

76-77: Crossing the Wahputik ice field. Photograph from the Mary Jobe Akeley collection and courtesy of Mystic River Historical Society, Inc., Mystic, Connecticut, and M.J. Akeley Trust.

77: Mary and Carl by tent. Photograph from the Mary Jobe Akeley collection and courtesy of Mystic River Historical Society, Inc., Mystic, Connecticut, and M.J. Akeley Trust.

77: Mary Jobe Akeley with dead lion. Photograph from the Mary Jobe Akeley collection and courtesy of Mystic River Historical Society, Inc., Mystic, Connecticut, and M.J. Akeley Trust.

78: Freya Stark in Arab dress. Courtesy of John Murray (Publishers) Ltd.

78-79: Camel caravan. Photograph by Freya Stark, courtesy of Royal Geographical Society.

81: Bell portrait. Courtesy of the Robinson Library, University of Newcastle-Upon-Tyne.

81: Bell taking measurements. Courtesy of the Robinson Library, University of Newcastle-Upon-Tyne.

82-83: Osa checks her gun. Photograph by Martin Johnson, courtesy of the Martin and Osa Johnson Safari Museum.

83: Osa with dead leopard and dog. Photograph by Martin Johnson, courtesy of the Martin and Osa Johnson Safari Museum.

83: Osa filming game. Photograph by Martin Johnson, courtesy of the Martin and Osa Johnson Safari Museum.

84: Johnson with pygmies. Photograph by Martin Johnson, courtesy of the Martin and Osa Johnson Safari Museum.

85: Osa with wives of Big Namba. Photograph by Martin Johnson, courtesy of the Martin and Osa Johnson Safari Museum.

86: Sue and dinosaur in rock. Courtesy of Sue Hendrickson, © The Black Hills Institute.

87: Hendrickson and dogs. Courtesy of Sue Hendrickson.

87: Sue waving from inside the dinosaur. Courtesy of Sue Hendrickson.

88: Hendrickson on dig for amber. Courtesy of Sue Hendrickson.

89: Hendrickson over cannon. Courtesy of Sue Hendrickson.

89: Hendrickson diving. Courtesy of Sue Hendrickson.

91: Portrait of Alexander with pick ax. Courtesy of the University of California Museum of Paleontology.

91: Four photographs of Alexander on expedition. Courtesy of the University of California Museum of Paleontology.

92: Portrait. Courtesy of Stephanie Schwabe.

93: Diving in the Lothloren cave system. Courtesy of Stephanie Schwabe.

94: North passage of Stargate cave. Photograph by Bill Stone. Courtesy of Stephanie Schwabe.

95: Schwabe examining sample. Photograph by Lisa Sonne. Courtesy of Stephanie Schwabe.

96-97: Dian heading for camp. Photograph by Alan Root/NGS Image Collection.

98: Goodall and Gregoire. Photograph by Michael Nichols.

99: Mead photograph. Courtesy of the Mead Institute for Intercultural Studies, Inc., New York.

100-101: Fiord with snow-capped mountains of Suess Land, 1933. Courtesy of the American Geographical Society Collection, University of Wisconsin-Milwaukee Library.

102: Dietrich portrait. Courtesy of the John Oxley Library. Neg. no. 60188.

104: Collecting Festuca eastwoodae. Courtesy of Special Collections, California Academy of Sciences.

104-105: Eastwood with Eastwoodia elegans. Photo by John Thomas Howell. Courtesy of Special Collections, California Academy of Sciences.

105: Eastwood in lab. Courtesy of Special Collections, California Academy of Sciences.

106: Eastwood on horseback in Yosemite. Courtesy of Special Collections, California Academy of Sciences.

107: Mexia in the field. Courtesy of Special Collections, California Academy of Sciences.

107: Journal page. Courtesy of Special Collections, California Academy of Sciences.

108: Portrait from diary. Courtesy of the Castle Museum.

108, 110: Swallowtail butterflies. Courtesy of the Castle Museum.

109: With butterfly nets and Khalil. Courtesy of the Castle Museum.

109: Open diary. Courtesy of the Castle Museum.

110: Fountaine seated in park; from diary. Courtesy of the Castle Museum.

110: Fountaine sitting in studio. Courtesy of the Castle Museum.

110: Specimen tray. Courtesy of the Castle Museum.

110: Alone with net. Courtesy of the Castle Museum.

111: Adult butterfly. Courtesy of Naomi Pierce.

111: Portrait. Courtesy of Naomi Pierce.

111: Sonogram. Courtesy of Naomi Pierce.

112: Portrait. Courtesy of the Natural History Museum, London.

114: Under a banana leaf. Courtesy of the Natural History Museum, London.

115: Field notebooks. Courtesy of the Natural History Museum, London.

116: Map of Miss Boyd Land. From the American Geographical Society Collection, University of Wisconsin-Milwaukee Library.

117: Portrait of Boyd. Courtesy of the Library of Congress.

118: Icebergs. Courtesy of the American Geographical Society Collection, University of Wisconsin-Milwaukee Library.

119: Ice Fiord, dirt bands. Courtesy of the American Geographical Society Collection, University of Wisconsin-Milwaukee Library.

120: Mead on a canoe, 1925. Courtesy of the Mead Institute of Intercultural Studies, Inc., New York.

122: Mead on a mat, 1971. Courtesy of the Mead Institute of Intercultural Studies, Inc., New York.

122-123: On expedition with Reo Fortune. Courtesy of the Mead Institute of Intercultural Studies, Inc., New York.

123: Mead carried by natives. Courtesy of the Mead Institute of Intercultural Studies, Inc., New York.

124: Fowler-Billings in Sierra Leone, 1930. Courtesy of the Billings Family Collection.

124: Fowler-Billings in Laramie Mountains. Courtesy of the Billings Family Collection.

125: Katharine with pick ax. Courtesy of the Billings Family Collection.

125: Katharine in White Mountains. Courtesy of the Billings Family Collection.

126: Passport photos. Courtesy of the Billings Family Collection.

126: Passport. Courtesy of the Billings Family Collection.

127: Wadhwa in Antarctica. Courtesy of Meenakshi Wadhwa.

128: Nicole Maxwell on trail. Courtesy of The Maxwell Collection.

128: Notecard for Mucura Macho. Courtesy of The Maxwell Collection.

129: Notecards for Asnac Panga, Cana Negra, and Huito. Courtesy of The Maxwell Collection.

129: Nicole dancing. Courtesy of The Maxwell Collection.

130: Ticuna family. Courtesy of The Maxwell Collection.

130: Newspaper clipping. Courtesy of The Maxwell Collection.

131: Maina boys listening to the radio. Courtesy of The Maxwell Collection.

132: Leakey with skull. Photograph by Paul Abell. Courtesy of Paul Abell.

133: Leakey digging. Robert Campbell/NGS Image Collection.

134: Arvigo and Don Eligio Panti. Courtesy of Rosita Arvigo.

135: Map of Terra Nova. Courtesy of Rosita Arvigo.

136: Arvigo and plant. Courtesy of Rosita Arvigo.

136: Botanical card. Courtesy of Rosita Arvigo and the New York Botanical Garden Institute of Economic Botany.

137: Arvigo with healers. Courtesy of Rosita Arvigo.

138: Portrait. Courtesy of the Gimbutas Collection.

138: Figurine of a goddess. Courtesy of Joan Marler.

139: Cristina Biaggi and double spiral of goddesses installation, Phoenix Gallery, New York City, March 1999. Courtesy of Cristina Biaggi.

140: Clark with bull shark. Photograph by David Doubilet/Courtesy of Doubilet Photography Inc.

141: Clark emerging from submersible. Photograph by Emory Kristoff. Courtesy of Eugenie Clark.

142-143: Clark swimming with nurse shark. Photograph by David Doubilet/Courtesy of Doubilet Photography Inc.

145: Dian with gorillas. Courtesy of The Dian Fossey Gorilla Fund International.

146: Dian's grave marker. Courtesy of The Dian Fossey Gorilla Fund International.

147: Jane Goodall and chimp Joujou. Photograph by Michael Nichols.

149: Dian and baby Digit. Courtesy of The Dian Fossey Gorilla Fund International.

150: Elephants. Courtesy of Cynthia Moss/African Wildlife Foundation.

151: Portrait in Amboseli National Park, Kenya. Photograph by Martyn Colbeck. Courtesy of Cynthia Moss/African Wildlife Foundation.

152: Moss with research assistants. Courtesy of Cynthia Moss/African Wildlife Foundation.

152: Elephants. Courtesy of Cynthia Moss/African Wildlife Foundation.

153: Portrait of Katy Payne. Courtesy of Katy Payne.

153: Payne in car. Photograph by Geri Bauer, courtesy of Katy Payne.

154-155: Archaeologists mapping site. Photograph by Anna C. Roosevelt. Courtesy of Anna Roosevelt.

155: Anna Roosevelt recording data. Photograph by Diego Goldberg, courtesy of Anna Roosevelt.

156: Cross-section of dig site. Courtesy of Anna Roosevelt.

156: Rock paintings. Courtesy of Anna Roosevelt.

157: Painted pot. Photograph by Sal Catalano, courtesy of Anna Roosevelt.

158: Portrait on Dokos, 1990. Courtesy of Elpida Hadjidaki-Marder.

159: Coastline of Crete. Courtesy of Elpida Hadjidaki-Marder.

159: Tower ruins. Courtesy of Elpida Hadjidaki-Marder.

160: Diving on wreck. Courtesy of Elpida Hadjidaki-Marder.

160: Grid map of underwater shipwreck. Courtesy of Elpida Hadjidaki-Marder.

161: Portrait beside truck. Courtesy of Joan Connelly.

161: Yronisos Island. Courtesy of Joan Connelly.

162-163: Margaret Mee in boat. Photograph by Tony Morrison. Courtesy of Tony Morrison.

164: Marianne North at easel. Courtesy of the Trustees, Royal Botanic Gardens, Kew.

165: *Oppossums*. Courtesy of Brown University, John Hay Library.

166: Photograph of Linda Schele, by Justin Kerr. Justin Kerr, photographer. Courtesy of Justin Kerr.

167: Painting of tropical plants. Courtesy of the Trustees, Royal Botanic Gardens, Kew.

167: North's painting of Amatungala, *Carissa macrocarpa*.

Royal Botanic Gardens, Kew. Courtesy of the Trustees, Royal Botanic Gardens, Kew.

168: Portrait of Aphra Behn. National Portrait Gallery and Arthur Schlechter (New York). Courtesy of Arthur Schlechter.

170: Metamorphosis. Courtesy of Brown University, John Hay Library.

171: Merian portrait. Courtesy of the Schimmel Collection.

172: Butterflies and plants. Courtesy of Brown University, John Hay Library.

173: Spiders. Courtesy of Brown University, John Hay Library.

174-175: Lizard. Courtesy of Brown University, John Hay Library.

181: Zora Neale Hurston in a canoe. Photograph by Jane Belo. Library of Congress. Used with the permission of the estate of Zora Neale Hurston.

182: Hurston with drum. Library of Congress. Used with the permission of the estate of Zora Neale Hurston.

183: Book cover of *Voodoo Gods*. From the Schimmel Collection. Used with the permission of the estate of Zora Neale Hurston.

183: Zombie. Photo by Zora Hurston. Courtesy of the Schimmel Collection. Used with the permission of the estate of Zora Neale Hurston.

184: Riefenstahl filming underwater. Courtesy of Leni Riefenstahl Produktion.

184: Riefenstahl filming the Nuba in Sudan. Courtesy of Leni Riefenstahl Produktion.

184: Riefenstahl filming in Germany. Courtesy of Leni Riefenstahl Produktion.

185: Four Nuba portraits. Photographs by Leni Riefenstahl. Courtesy of Leni Riefenstahl Produktion.

186: Riefenstahl with the Nuba. Courtesy of Leni Riefenstahl Produktion.

187: Lacandon child. Gertrude Blom, photographer. Courtesy of the Na-Bolom Collection.

187: Blom with Lacandon Indians. Courtesy of the Na-Bolom Collection.

188: Portrait at Angel Falls. Courtesy of the Photography Collection, Harry Ransom Humanities Research Center, The University of Texas at Austin.

189: Field notebook. Courtesy of the Photography Collection, Harry Ransom Humanities Research Center, The University of Texas at Austin.

190: Ship in a storm. Schimmel Collection. Courtesy of the Schimmel Collection.

190: Portrait of Ida Pfeiffer. Schimmel Collection. Courtesy of the Schimmel Collection.

191: Title Page. Schimmel Collection. Courtesy of the Schimmel Collection.

194: Portrait of Hahn. Courtesy of Ken Cuthbertson.

195: Newspaper clipping. Courtesy of Carola Vecchio.

195: Porters at the river. Courtesy of Carola Vecchio.

196: Leila in the rigging. Hadley Collection. Courtesy of Leila Hadley.

197: Passport. Hadley Collection. Courtesy of Leila Hadley.

198: Photo of Leila Hadley in India. Hadley collection. Courtesy of Leila Hadley.

199: Portrait of Elizabeth Arthur. Photograph by Steven Bauer, courtesy of Elizabeth Arthur.

199: Elizabeth Arthur in front of Scott's hut. Courtesy of Elizabeth Arthur.

200: Portrait of Marilyn Bridges. © Photopia 1995, courtesy of Marilyn Bridges.

200-201: Cherhill Horse. Photograph by Marilyn Bridges, © 1985. Courtesy of Marilyn Bridges.

204: Nazca Lines. Photograph by Marilyn Bridges, © 1979.

202-203: Monument Valley. Photograph by Marilyn Bridges, © by Marilyn Bridges. Courtesy of Marilyn Bridges.

203: Mayan temple (Chichen Itza). Photograph by Marilyn Bridges, © by Marilyn Bridges. Courtesy of Marilyn Bridges.

205: Reiche on a ladder at Nasca. Agent/Reiche Collection. Photographer unknown. Courtesy of Tony Morrison.

205: Reiche measuring the lines. Photograph by Tony Morrison, © 1977. Courtesy of Tony Morrison.

206-207: Sullivan in space. Courtesy of NASA.

208: Earle swimming outside *Deep Rover*. Photograph by David Doubilet/Courtesy of Doubilet Photography, Inc.

209: Kuznetsova photographing penguins. Courtesy of Irina Kuznetsova.

210: Portrait of Mitchell with telescope. Courtesy of the Maria Mitchell Association.

211: Kathryn Sullivan with Sally Ride. Courtesy of NASA.

211: Portrait of Sullivan. Courtesy of NASA.

212: Peck in mountaineering gear. Courtesy of Library of Congress.

213: Portrait of Peck in dress. Courtesy of the Schimmel Collection.

214: Tent on snow. Courtesy of the Schimmel Collection.

214: Mount Huascaran. Courtesy of the Schimmel Collection.

215: Cards with mountain. Courtesy of the Schimmel Collection.

215: Back of cards. Courtesy of the Schimmel Collection.

216: Portrait of Coleman. Courtesy of Air and Space Museum.

217: Portrait of Markham. Courtesy of the Sunshine Collection.

218: Plane in crowd. Courtesy of the Air and Space Museum.

219: Portrait of Earhart. Courtesy of Library of Congress.

220-221: Tharp at drawing table. Courtesy of Marie Tharp.

222-223: Map of World Ocean. Courtesy of Marie Tharp.

224: Earle with stingray. Photograph by David Doubilet/Courtesy of Doubilet Photography Inc.

225: Portrait of Sylvia in wet suit. Photograph by David Doubilet/Courtesy of Doubilet Photography Inc.

226-227: Earle with eel. Photograph by David Doubilet/Courtesy of Doubilet Photography Inc.

226: Diving with flag. Courtesy of Sylvia Earle.

227: Inside the *Deep Rover*. Courtesy of Sylvia Earle.

228-229: Group at South Pole. Courtesy of Irina Kuznetsova.

229: Irina and Valentina Kuznetsova. Courtesy of Irina Kuznetsova.

229: Valentina Kuznetsova. Courtesy of Irina Kuznetsova.

230: Team in Franz Joseph Land. Courtesy of Irina Kuznetsova.

230: Postcard. Courtesy of Irina Kuznetsova.

230: Letter from Gorbachev. Courtesy of Irina Kuznetsova.

231: American women's team group photograph. Courtesy of Sunniva Sorby.

232: Hose rappelling. Photograph by Gary Stiles, courtesy of Louise Hose.

233: Hose descending into cave. Photograph by Thomas R. Strong, courtesy of Louise Hose.

234-235: Cave map. Bob Richards and Louise Hose. © 1998 National Speleological Society, courtesy of Louise Hose.

234: Snot-tites. Photograph by Louise Hose and David Lester. Courtesy of Louise Hose.

234: Hose with mask. Photograph by James Pisarowicz. Courtesy of Louise Hose.

234: Page from log book. Courtesy of Louise Hose.

236: Portrait of Tarter. Seth Shostak, photographer. Courtesy of the SETI Institute.

236: Pioneer 10 signal on computer screen. Seth Shostak, photographer. Courtesy of the SETI Institute.

237: Parkes scope, Australia. Seth Shostak, photographer. Courtesy of the SETI Institute.

238-239: Arecibo scope. Seth Shostak, photographer. Courtesy of the SETI Institute.

North C.

Tungusi

S I B E R I A

Iceland

Lapland

Archangel

R U S S I A N   E M P I R E

Yakutsk

Feroe

Petersburgh

Tobolsk

Irkutsk

L. Baikal

Amur

Ireland

Denmark

Baltic S.

London

Prussia

Moskow

R. Wolga

R. Irtish

A S I A

Sweden

Poland

Germany

Hungary

Azof

Astracan

L. Aral

T A R T A R Y

Pekin

France

Black S.

Caspian S.

Thibet

Hoanho R.

Nankin

Portugal

Spain

Mediterranean Sea

Persia

R. Indus

R. Ganges

Delhi

China

Madeira

Algier Tunis

Tripoli

Egypt

Arabia

Persian G.

Canton

Morocco

Red Sea

Bombay

Hindoostan

Bay of Bengal

Philip. Isles

Barbary

Great Desert

Arabian

Madras

Senegambia

Nubia

Nile R.

Sea

China Sea

Senegal R.

A F R I C A

Ceylon

Malacca

Guinea

Benin

Adal

I N D I A N

Ethiopia

G. of Guinea

Sumatra

Moluc

Zanguebar

O C E A N

Ascention

Congo

Benguela

Caffraria

Str. of Mozambique

Madagascar

NEW HO

St. Helena

Amsterdam I.

Hottentots

St. Paul

Saxemburg I.

C. of Good Hope

Goughs

P. Edwards Is.

Desert Is.

Kerguelens Land

S O U T H E R N   O C E A N

Sandwick Land

Circle